2009

Dear Landon,

Congratulations! always praise God for all the abilities and blessings He has already given you and all that He has promised for you now and in the future as you walk with Him, in Christ and by the Holy Spirit.

This book has (is) been (being) a blessing and a challenge to me as I read it most every day. (Get caught up if you get behind! :)) looking forward to running again with you and hearing about your love for the Lord!

Love in Christ,
Mr. Erwin
(Fred)
Rom. 5:1

GRACE FOR TODAY

VOLUME 1

DAILY READINGS

from the Life of

CHRIST

GRACE FOR TODAY

VOLUME 1

DAILY READINGS

from the Life of

CHRIST

JOHN

MACARTHUR

MOODY PUBLISHERS

CHICAGO

© 2008 by
JOHN MACARTHUR

All Scripture quotations, unless otherwise indicated, are taken from the *New American Standard Bible®*, Copyright © 1960, 1962, 1963, 1968, 1971, 1972, 1973, 1975, 1977, 1995 by The Lockman Foundation. Used by permission. (www.Lockman.org)

Scripture quotations marked KJV are taken from the King James Version.

Cover Design: Kirk DouPonce, DogEared Design, www.DogEaredDesign.com
Interior Design: Ragont Design
Editor: Garry Knussman

Published in association with the literary agency of Wolgemuth & Associates, Inc.

Library of Congress Cataloging-in-Publication Data

MacArthur, John, 1939-
 Daily readings from the life of Christ / John MacArthur.
    p. cm.
 Includes bibliographical references.
 ISBN 978-0-8024-5600-7
 1. Jesus Christ–Biography–Meditations. 2. Devotional calendars. I. Title.
 BT301.3.M33 2008
 232.9'5–dc22
                       2008025053

We hope you enjoy this book from Moody Publishers. Our goal is to provide high-quality, thought-provoking books and products that connect truth to your real needs and challenges. For more information on other books and products written and produced from a biblical perspective, go to www.moodypublishers.com or write to:

Moody Publishers
820 N. LaSalle Boulevard
Chicago, IL 60610

1 3 5 7 9 10 8 6 4 2

Printed in the United States of America

To Henry Tolopilo, a true partner in ministry
whose effective Bible preaching on
"Gracia a Vosotros" is reaching effectively
into the Spanish-speaking world and
bearing much fruit for the Kingdom.

INTRODUCTION

*T*HE RAPID PACE of twenty-first-century living is not very conducive to setting aside time to slow down, read the Bible, and pray and meditate on God's Word. Yet such activity ought to be the daily priority of every Christian—it is the primary way God leads us in our sanctification. Just as physical nourishment is essential to physical life, so spiritual nourishment is essential to spiritual life—your growth in Christ depends on it.

The frustration comes for many Christians when they're unable to find the time to study God's Word as they would like. I certainly understand that frustration. While I think you should be striving to carve out as much time as possible to spend with the Lord, which you can do by letting go of less important priorities, I do realize that's not easy to do.

That's why I offer you this book of daily readings from God's Word. The goal of this book is to help you develop a consistency in reading and meditating on the truths of the Bible—yet this does not mean a large time commitment on your part.

However, that doesn't mean this is like other devotional books that merely offer inspirational thoughts and meditations to help you feel good about your life. This book contains substantial, thought-provoking selections that come from my commentaries on the gospels, which are products of my lifetime of study in God's Word.

The focus of this volume and two more to follow is the life of our Lord and Savior, Jesus Christ. My greatest joy in the pulpit has been teaching from the gospels and seeing how our Lord lived and interacted with all sorts of people, from the disciples who truly loved Him, yet were weak in their faith, to the masses of people who were mesmerized by His miraculous acts, yet many of whom never believed in Him, and to the religious hypocrites who pretended to want to know Him, yet always wanted to kill Him. In short, by observing how Christ interacted with people you'll gain great insight into how you can live as He did.

In each of the selections that follow, you'll draw daily nourishment from a nugget of God's Word. In this volume I focus on the first year or so of Jesus' life and ministry. Each entry will challenge you to meditate and act on significant truth. My desire for you as you conclude this first year of reading and meditating is a growing commitment to deeper subsequent study, meditation, and prayer with our great heavenly Father.

JESUS' PUBLIC BAPTISM

Then Jesus arrived from Galilee at the Jordan.

MATT. 3:13A

*T*HERE IS SOMETHING majestic about Jesus' baptism that brought all the previous events of His earthly life into focus. Here He came fully onto the stage of the gospel story and His work and ministry truly began.

Following an eternity past in heaven and thirty years of obscurity in Nazareth, God presented the Savior publicly to the world. John the Baptist, as "the voice of one crying in the wilderness," had heralded the coming of the Messiah (3:3; cf. Isa. 40:3), and now He was fully and publicly prepared to begin the fulfillment of His earthly mission.

A parallel passage in Luke tells us that this was no private or secluded ceremony: "Now when all the people were baptized, Jesus was also baptized" (Luke 3:21). The word translated "arrived" in Matthew 3:13 often indicated an official arrival or public appearance by a dignitary. From now on Jesus would be in the public eye and call no place His permanent earthly home (8:20).

This important episode from the beginning of Christ's ministry clearly shows us that Jesus, though knowing what a high degree of visibility would ultimately cost Him, obediently stepped from the comfort of obscurity into the high-risk position of a public figure. His work would invite strong opinion, but in order to accomplish the Father's will, it must take place in full view of the world. It must come at the cost of being widely observed.

Ask YOURSELF

We are called to be salt and light, not merely to enjoy God's seasoning and illumination in our own lives but to be His conveyors of grace to others. How does this public calling alter the way you express and live your Christianity? Pray that you will live not in fear but in faith.

JESUS' PURPOSEFUL BAPTISM

Then Jesus arrived . . . coming to John, to be baptized by him.

MATT. 3:13 A, B

*I*N THE ORIGINAL TEXT of this passage, the wording "to be baptized" emphasizes purpose in this momentous appearance by the Lord Jesus. But it was extremely difficult for John the Baptist to understand why the God-Man would need to be baptized.

John's baptism was for the confession of sin and repentance (3:2, 6, 11), but Jesus as the Lamb of God (John 1:29) had no need for such a baptism. It is hard to see why One who would take away sin would need to submit Himself to a ceremony that symbolizes death to sin and rising to spiritual life.

Because John knew so well that Jesus was the sinless Messiah, come to fulfill God's redemptive purpose, he "tried to prevent Him" (Matt. 3:14). The Greek pronouns in John's statement "I have need to be baptized by *You*, and do *You* come to *me*?" are all in the emphatic position, underscoring his strong bewilderment over the situation. This was not a direct refusal, as Peter might have given (cf. Matt. 16:22), but the Baptist no doubt misunderstood Jesus' request, thinking He could not possibly intend to undergo baptism.

All sinners need the repentance that baptism symbolizes, but many, such as the Jewish teachers and leaders of Jesus' day, do not seek true repentance. Jesus, on the other hand, purposed to receive John's baptism to show His complete obedience to God's will.

Ask YOURSELF

The same Jesus who walked with such resolve and determination throughout His own earthly life has a distinct and daily purpose for yours. What pieces of this plan are becoming clearer to you? Pray that He will continue to reveal . . . and that you will continue to follow.

TESTIMONY TO JESUS' SINLESSNESS

John tried to prevent Him, saying, "I have need to be baptized by You, and do You come to me?"

MATT. 3:14

JOHN THE BAPTIST'S INITIAL reluctance to baptize Jesus is a testimony to Jesus' sinlessness—and John's awareness of his own sinfulness.

In effect, John said to Jesus, "I'm a sinner, just like everyone else I baptize, so why should You, the sinless Son of God, want me to baptize You?" In an indirect yet definite fashion, John agreed with the later description of Christ by the writer of Hebrews, "One who has been tempted in all things as we are, yet without sin" (4:15).

Jesus Himself testified to His perfect righteousness and His reason for wanting to be baptized, "Permit it at this time; for in this way it is fitting for us to fulfill all righteousness" (Matt. 3:15). Jesus' words did not deny His superiority to John the Baptist or His sinlessness. "Permit it at this time" is an idiomatic expression meaning that Christ's baptism, though seemingly not appropriate or necessary, was actually appropriate for this special time.

The Lord understood John's strong hesitation, and knew it came from deep spiritual commitment and sincerity. Thus He gave John divine permission to do what he was otherwise reluctant to do, so he could perfectly fulfill the Father's plan.

Ask YOURSELF

How do you think you would have reacted to Jesus' request for baptism? How do you react today when you're in His presence, in awe of His holiness and purity? Pray for the spiritual understanding to know that by His grace, He has washed this same righteousness over you.

SYMBOLS FROM JESUS' BAPTISM

Jesus answering said to him, "Permit it at this time; for in this way
it is fitting for us to fulfill all righteousness."

MATT. 3:15A

*T*HE MOST IMPORTANT SYMBOL Jesus' baptism gives us is a perfect example of obedience to God the Father. Our Lord always modeled obedience in all things (e.g., Phil. 2:6–8; cf. Matt. 17:25–27). In submitting to baptism, Jesus affirmed the validity of John's standard of righteousness and demonstrated that baptism was God's will to which every believer should be obedient.

Furthermore, Jesus' baptism is a profound, symbolic identification with sinful humanity. Hundreds of years earlier the prophet Isaiah stated that the Messiah "was numbered with the transgressors; yet He himself bore the sin of many, and interceded for the transgressors" (Isa. 53:12). The sinless One took His place among sinners, and that in part entailed submitting Himself to a sinner's baptism.

Finally, Jesus' baptism is a symbol of His death and resurrection, and therefore a prefigurement of our Christian baptism. Concerning His death, Jesus later said, "I have a baptism to undergo, and how distressed I am until it is accomplished!" (Luke 12:50). In pointing to His obedient identification with sinners (cf. Isa. 53:11; 2 Cor. 5:21) and His subsequent atoning death and bodily resurrection, the key symbols stemming from Jesus' baptism remind believers of their need to faithfully obey and be baptized.

*Ask*YOURSELF

He became one of us, identifying with our sin. Marvel again at the amazement and immensity of this truth. What grace! What humility! What kind of worship should flow from this reality? Worship Him today as the One who was not ashamed to take your place, who stooped down so that you could stand.

TRUE BAPTISM—CHRIST IMMERSED

After being baptized, Jesus came up immediately from the water.

MATT. 3:16A

*C*HRISTIANS, ESPECIALLY NEW BELIEVERS, sometimes wonder what mode of baptism Jesus underwent, and therefore wonder which is correct for them to experience. Since genuine baptism represents cleansing from sin and symbolizes the believer's identification with Christ's death and resurrection, the ordinance must involve immersion, not merely sprinkling or pouring.

The Greek word (*baptizo*) literally means to dip or submerge an object into water or another liquid. Confusion regarding the word's meaning resulted largely because Latin and more modern-language translations of Scripture simply transliterated many occurrences of the Greek word.

Until the Middle Ages, the Christian church knew and officially practiced no form of baptism but immersion. Then the Roman Catholic Church formally introduced and sanctioned baptism by sprinkling or pouring. Prior to that, even the great Catholic theologian Thomas Aquinas wrote, "In immersion the setting forth of the burial of Christ is more plainly expressed, in which this manner of baptizing is more commendable."

That Jesus "came up immediately from the water" indicates He had been completely *in* the water—in other words, almost surely immersed. John baptized people in the Jordan River (Matt. 3:6) and at other places where "there was much water" (John 3:23). That would not make sense if he had baptized only by pouring or sprinkling (cf. Acts 8:38–39). Unlike immersion, those other modes just do not fully symbolize dying to sin and being raised to new life.

*Ask*YOURSELF

Baptism is a one-time exercise in obedience, but the reality of being crucified with Christ and raised to "walk in newness of life" (Rom. 6:4) is an ongoing experience. How do you remind yourself of this on your average day? Pray that the gift of God's grace never loses its wonder.

THE HOLY SPIRIT VALIDATES JESUS

The heavens were opened, and he [John] saw the
Spirit of God descending as a dove and lighting on Him.
MATT. 3:16B

*A*BOUT THE SUPERNATURAL SIGN that occurred at the conclusion of Jesus' baptism, one commentator has suggested, "Just as the veil of the Temple was rent in twain to symbolize the perfect access of all men to God, so here the heavens are rent asunder to show how near God is to Jesus, and Jesus to God."

But did Jesus really need an anointing from the Holy Spirit? When He came to earth, Jesus retained His full deity. In His complete humanity, however, He needed divine strengthening for ministry. Like any human being, Jesus experienced fatigue, hunger, sleepiness, and the like. Only the Holy Spirit could strengthen such humanness (cf. Matt. 4:1; Luke 4:14).

That the Spirit came upon Him at His baptism was a fulfillment of the prophet's words, "The Spirit of the Lord God is upon me, because the Lord has anointed me to bring good news to the afflicted; He has sent me to bind up the brokenhearted, to proclaim liberty to captives and freedom to prisoners" (Isa. 61:1). It was also the sign God had given to John the Baptist so that he would know Jesus when he saw Him (John 1:33).

This anointing by the Holy Spirit was unique in several ways, including being the only New Testament instance in which the Holy Spirit appeared as a dove. Most important, however, this act not only empowered Jesus as the Son of Man for redemptive service, but it was a confirming sign to everyone present—and to us as well—that Jesus is indeed the Messiah.

Ask YOURSELF

If Jesus was dependent on the Spirit's empowering for effective service, how much more do we need His help and strengthening? In what ways are you making yourself fully open to the Holy Spirit's power and direction? Pray that He will make you ever aware of your need for Him.

BELOVED JESUS—SUPERIOR TO ALL SACRIFICES

A voice out of the heavens said, "This is My beloved Son, in whom I am well-pleased."

MATT. 3:17

*N*O OLD TESTAMENT SACRIFICE, no matter how carefully selected, was genuinely and completely pleasing to God. The people could not possibly find an animal without some imperfection. Furthermore, the blood of the sacrificial animals was at best only symbolic, "for it is impossible for the blood of bulls and goats to take away sins" (Heb. 10:4; cf. 9:12). But the Cross would effect a sacrifice that would be "with precious blood, as of a lamb unblemished and spotless, the blood of Christ" (1 Peter 1:19).

It was this reality that rang out in the Father's declaration of blessing at the Jordan that day—the day of Jesus' baptism. His use of the word "beloved" connotes a rich, profound, ultimately satisfying relationship between the Father and the Son. Forms of this word occur elsewhere in the New Testament to denote God's love for believers (Rom. 1:7) and to describe the ideal love they should have for one another (1 Cor. 4:14). But in God's eyes the Lord Jesus ever remains the most beloved among any living being—past, present, or future.

This means that Christians, too, are a delight to their heavenly Father, because they are now "in Christ" and adopted into God's eternal, spiritual family. If God can find no imperfection in His Son, He likewise by His grace finds no defect in His saints (cf. Rom. 3:26; Eph. 1:3–6).

Ask YOURSELF

Is the Son "beloved" in your eyes as well? How does your love for Him express itself in your conversation, your interactions, your behavior, your worship? If you couldn't say that He is your "first love" (Rev. 2:4), ask God to help you return Him to His rightful place of adoration.

JESUS' DEITY—CENTRAL TO THE GOSPEL

A voice out of the heavens said, "This is My beloved Son, in whom I am well-pleased."

MATT. 3:17

HE TRUTH THAT JESUS CHRIST is God's perfect Son is a key feature of the gospel message. The author of the letter to the Hebrews makes this clear at the outset of his writing:

> God, after He spoke long ago to the fathers in the prophets in many portions and in many ways, in these last days has spoken to us in His Son, whom He appointed heir of all things, through whom also He made the world. And He is the radiance of His glory and the exact representation of His nature, and upholds all things by the word of His power. When He had made purification of sins, He sat down at the right hand of the Majesty on high, having become as much better than the angels, as He has inherited a more excellent name than they. For to which of the angels did He ever say, "You are My Son, today I have begotten You"? And again, "I will be a Father to Him and He shall be a Son to Me"? And when He again brings the firstborn into the world, He says, "And let all the angels of God worship Him." And of the angels He says, "Who makes His angels winds, and His ministers a flame of fire." But of the Son He says, "Your throne, O God, is forever and ever, and the righteous scepter is the scepter of His kingdom." (1:1–8; cf. Col. 1:15–19; 2:9)

The New Testament presents God more as the Father of Jesus (John 14:6–11; Phil. 2:9–11) than as the Father of believers (Matt. 6:9). We cannot worship God unless we also worship Christ as one with Him (cf. John 5:23).

Ask YOURSELF

Are you as "well-pleased" with the Son—your Savior—as the Father is? And are you willing to declare it, as if boomed from the heavens? Pray that God would renew your love for Him today and fill you with boldness to pronounce your devotion at every opportunity.

PREPARATION FOR TESTING

Then Jesus was led up by the Spirit into the wilderness to be tempted by the devil.

MATT. 4:1

ONE OF LIFE'S IMPORTANT TRUISMS is that strong temptation tends to follow every major personal triumph. The apostle Paul warns, "Let him who thinks he stands take heed that he does not fall" (1 Cor. 10:12). In the aftermath of significant successes, we are often tempted to think the accomplishment came solely by our own strength and ingenuity. But just when we think success is here to stay, we become vulnerable to pride—and failure. Even Christ in His incarnation was not exempt from testing, such as what came on the heels of His God-affirming baptism.

In a parallel passage, Mark says, "Immediately the Spirit impelled Him to go out into the wilderness" (Mark 1:12). Mark's use of "impelled" denotes the necessity of the Lord's temptation, or testing. Although the testings would come from Satan, it was God's will that Jesus undergo them in advance of His earthly ministry and redemptive work.

So after His ministry and Person had been validated by the Father and the Spirit at the scene of His baptism, Jesus confronted the first great challenge to His mission. Our Savior was not intimidated by the prospect of temptation but fully conscious of His divine mission and strengthened in His humanity by the abiding presence and power of God. That is what Satan sought to forever undermine and destroy.

Ask YOURSELF

What specific temptations often awaken in your own heart following times of encouragement or accomplishment? How do you deal with them and defeat them? May God be seen as your continual supply, even at times when you're tempted to think you can manage on your own.

GOD'S PLAN FOR TEMPTATION

Then Jesus was led up by the Spirit into the wilderness to be tempted by the devil.

MATT. 4:1

*J*ESUS' TEMPTATION IN THE WILDERNESS did not catch His Father by surprise. The Son was specifically "led up by the Spirit into the wilderness to be tempted by the devil." The word translated "tempted" is from a morally neutral term that means "to test." But sometimes, as here, the context clearly indicates that the testing was aimed at enticing one to do evil. That the devil was going to present certain temptations to Jesus thus justifies rendering the word "tempted"—it gives us the negative connotation of Satan's sinister intentions.

God sometimes uses Satan's temptations toward evil as part of His larger plan to test believers for good (cf. Job). Whereas the devil wanted to lead Christ into sin and disobedience in the wilderness, God used the circumstances to reconfirm Christ's holiness and worthiness. This is God's plan for all His saints (cf. James 1:2–4, 12–13)—that Christ's righteousness be revealed in us.

Joseph's severe mistreatment at the hands of his brothers in the Old Testament and his subsequent "misfortunes" in Egypt could have driven him to despair and sinful bitterness, but by faith he recognized God's sovereign hand in it all (Gen. 50:20). Whether God tests us directly or uses Satan to challenge us, He will always use the situation to eventually produce good fruit in us.

Ask YOURSELF

What positive benefits does temptation serve in your own life? As unwanted and unwelcome as it is, what does its mere presence keep before you, thereby thwarting the aspirations of the enemy? Pray that God would gain His desired objectives in you, even through times of testing.

FASTING AS PART OF PREPARATION FOR TESTING

After He had fasted forty days and forty nights, He then became hungry.

MATT. 4:2

*F*OR A QUITE LENGTHY PERIOD PRIOR to the three diabolical temptations directed at Jesus, He fasted. We don't know exactly what He did during the forty-day period, but He likely spent most of the time communing with His heavenly Father.

Even in His perfect humanity, Jesus needed solitary preparation time in meditation and prayer, as we all do in anticipating a major testing. Consider how Moses spent forty years in Midian in preparation for his leadership of Israel out of Egypt to the Promised Land, or that the apostle Paul lived three years in the desert of Arabia before launching his extensive ministries.

Matthew reports, with much simplicity and directness, that at the end of the period of fasting, Jesus "became hungry." Hunger weakens us physically and somehow leaves us more vulnerable to spiritual attack, which is precisely why Satan often assails us at such times. But temptations that we have anticipated and prayed about have little power to harm us, if we constantly rely on the Lord.

Jesus, though spending more than a month in fasting, is a tremendous example to us of remaining alert to spiritual danger, which He did as Satan approached. During the temptations, He did not yield on the slightest point.

*Ask*YOURSELF

What other feelings and conditions—like hunger—serve as ready-made points of entry for spiritual temptation? Knowing this, how can you better "keep watching and praying" that you not fall into sin (Mark 14:38)? Pray for the courage to live with such keen awareness.

THE TEMPTER IS REAL

And the tempter came and said to Him . . .

MATT. 4:3A

*I*T IS NOT POPULAR TODAY TO BELIEVE in a literal, personal devil, even among professing Christians. The devil is increasingly seen as being somewhere between a figment of our imagination and a useful device to coerce obedience.

Yet in addition to the name used here ("tempter"), the New Testament gives Satan many other names: "ruler of this world" (John 12:31; 14:30; 16:11); "the prince of the power of the air" (Eph. 2:2); "the god of this world" (2 Cor. 4:4); "Abaddon" and "Apollyon," both of which mean "destroyer" (Rev. 9:11); and "the serpent of old" (Rev. 12:9).

With these and many other references to the devil in God's infallible Scripture—all of which assume a real, supernatural person—it's clear that Satan does exist. And he never made himself more personally manifest than when he confronted Jesus in the wilderness. The Lord's opponent was an actual, personal foe in every sense of that expression.

Since the Fall, Satan has directed his full attention and fury against God and His kingdom work. While Christ was on earth, that opposition was particularly intense against the Son and His redemptive mission, beginning at the very outset of His ministry. Yet all the forces of hell continue to present us with real challenges as we endeavor to advance God's kingdom. Thus all believers must remain ever vigilant and prayerful against a genuine spiritual foe.

Ask YOURSELF

Have you grown lax in guarding yourself from the "roaring lion" (1 Peter 5:8) who actively seeks to devour you? He is not to be feared, for your God is triumphant, but he is definitely in need of accounting for. Ask the Lord to make you wise and wary of the enemy's presence.

TESTING JESUS' DIVINE RIGHTS

"If You are the Son of God, command that these stones become bread."

MATT. 4:3B

*B*EFORE SATAN TEMPTED JESUS more directly, he threw out a cynical challenge to test Christ's deity. The devil's conditional statement, "If You are the Son of God," assumed that Jesus was indeed God's beloved Son (3:17). But he hoped to persuade Him into a demonstration of divine power that would violate God's plan, which called for Jesus to set aside His divine power while on earth and use it only when the Father commanded. If Satan could make Jesus presume upon His divine rights and act independently of His Father, this would amount to disobedience.

Obviously, then, the purpose of the first temptation went far beyond getting Jesus to satisfy His physical hunger by wrongly using miraculous power. The devil wanted Him to doubt the Father's word, love, and provision—to disobediently declare that being hungry was simply not fit for God's only Son.

Satan's argument was, "Hadn't He endured enough humiliating circumstances already (the stable, the flight to Egypt, obscurity in Nazareth, this time in the wilderness) in an effort to identify with unworthy humanity?" But unlike Eve in the Garden of Eden (cf. Gen. 3:1f.), Jesus stayed true to God's will and did not cast doubt on the Father's word or His already secured position as God's Son.

Ask YOURSELF

Yes, there is more at stake in temptation than the mere subject of the enticement. There are significant matters of trust and freedom and identity involved. How seriously are you taking these threats to your Christian calling? Pray that God would help you see the battle for what it is.

JESUS' REAL FOOD—OBEYING THE FATHER

He answered and said, "It is written, 'Man shall not live on bread alone,
but on every word that proceeds out of the mouth of God.'"

MATT. 4:4

*A*BOVE ALL, SATAN'S TEMPTATIONS OF Jesus Christ solicited His rebellion against the Father. But Jesus had come to earth to do the Father's will and nothing else. In fact, His will and the Father's were precisely the same (John 5:30; cf. 10:30; Heb. 10:9).

Case in point: In the ultimate test of obedience, just prior to His arrest and betrayal, Jesus prayed in the Garden of Gethsemane, "My Father, if it is possible, let this cup pass from Me; yet not as I will, but as You will.". . . "My Father, if this cannot pass away unless I drink it, Your will be done" (Matt. 26:39, 42). This supreme example of absolute trust and submission by Jesus to His Father is what Satan tried to smash. In his proudest and wickedest manner, the enemy attempted to fracture the Trinitarian nature of the Godhead.

But Christ, in His immeasurable humility and righteousness, replied to Satan's first words, "It is written, 'Man shall not live on bread alone, but on every word that proceeds out of the mouth of God.'" All three of our Lord's responses to Satan would begin with the simple but straightforward appeal to the Word of God—"It is written" (cf. Ps. 119:11). In quoting Deuteronomy 8:3, Jesus affirmed that believers are far better off depending on God and waiting on His provision than they are in grabbing for their own satisfaction—something we all are tempted to do.

Ask YOURSELF

You may feel unsure of what God's will is for you, but much of it is spelled out clearly in Scripture. How well are you obeying the aspects of His will that have already been revealed to you? In seeking to know His plan, a good place to start is always obedience to His Word.

TRUSTING SELF IS NEVER JUSTIFIED

He answered and said, "It is written, 'Man shall not live on bread alone,
but on every word that proceeds out of the mouth of God.'"

MATT. 4:4

*C*HRISTIANS ARE NEVER JUSTIFIED IN trusting solely in themselves to meet their basic needs. No matter how worried we might become, if we turn to God in faith and obedience, He will meet all our essential needs in His own way, according to His sovereign schedule. Implicit in this understanding is that God will meet every need, both physical and spiritual, as Paul promises us, "My God will supply all your needs according to His riches in glory in Christ Jesus" (Phil. 4:19; cf. Matt. 6:8, 33).

It is always best to follow Jesus' example, obeying God and trusting wholeheartedly in His gracious provision, than to impulsively and selfishly attempt to meet our own needs in ways that could disobey or compromise God's Word.

To trust first of all in ourselves to meet our needs—circumventing or modifying God's will in the process—not only demonstrates a lack of faith but rests on the false assumption that our earthly well-being is our most crucial need. Jesus contradicts such thinking, which is so natural to fallen humanity, both to unbelievers as well as believers who slip into carnal mind-sets. Therefore our Lord quoted Deuteronomy 8:3, "'Man shall not live on bread alone, but on every word that proceeds out of the mouth of God.'" The all-sufficient and sustaining power of God is the only true source that meets our every need.

Ask YOURSELF

Where does your dependence lie? Are you trusting in your paycheck? Your insurance policies? Your physical strength and smarts? Or have you finally realized that everything hinges on God, His Word, and His sovereign plan for your life? Find your sense of security in Him alone.

TRUST IN GOD TRANSCENDS THE TEMPORAL

He answered and said, "It is written, 'Man shall not live on
bread alone, but on every word that proceeds out of the mouth of God.'"

MATT. 4:4

JAMES, THE LORD'S EARTHLY HALF-BROTHER, reminds us that this life is very temporary and uncertain—it is not even guaranteed that we will have an earthly future. James's practical letter teaches us: "Yet you do not know what your life will be like tomorrow. You are just a vapor that appears for a little while and then vanishes away. Instead, you ought to say, 'If the Lord wills, we will live and also do this or that'" (James 4:14–15).

Like Jesus, what we are all about and the ultimate goals of our lives should focus on the eternal, not the temporary. The guiding principle and central motive of our lives must be to please God and trust Him for absolutely everything (cf. Matt. 6:33). Jesus posed some searching questions in the Sermon on the Mount:

Why are you worried about clothing? Observe how the lilies of the field grow; they do not toil nor do they spin, yet I say to you that not even Solomon in all his glory clothed himself like one of these. But if God so clothes the grass of the field, which is alive today and tomorrow is thrown into the furnace, will He not much more clothe you? You of little faith!" (Matt. 6:28–30)

We always suffer and miss out to some extent on spiritual blessings when we shortsightedly worry about the temporal instead of focusing on the eternal. Jesus' response to the devil's temptations is again our model.

Ask YOURSELF

How much time do you spend listening to the nagging complaints of worry? How much is fretting a part of your thought process? When are you most susceptible to letting anxiety rise up within you, stealing your joy and perspective? Pray for freedom from anxiety—and the faith to replace it.

JANUARY 17

JESUS REFUSES TO TEST GOD

Then the devil took Him into the holy city and had Him stand on the pinnacle of the temple.

MATT. 4:5

*I*N CONFRONTING OUR LORD JESUS CHRIST, Satan persisted in trying to undermine or destroy the Son's relationship to His Father. This time he goaded Jesus with this statement: "If You are the Son of God, throw yourself down." To fortify his challenge and make it more plausible, the adversary— with a subtle and clever twist—quoted Scripture: "For it is written, 'He will command His angels concerning You'; and 'On their hands they will bear You up, so that You will not strike Your foot against a stone'" (from Ps. 91:11–12).

Now Satan surely had Christ backed into a corner, he likely reasoned, using his misguided and evil sense of logic. "If the Messiah lives only according to the Word of God, then I should confront Him with something *from* that Word." If Jesus wouldn't use His own power to help Himself and meet His immediate needs, maybe He would let God work on His behalf—after all, this was a "scriptural test," according to Satan. Jesus could thus let God fulfill a promise from Psalms and prove to others that He was indeed God's Son and Messiah.

But no matter how persuasive Satan's argument—undergirded with a proof text—may have sounded, Jesus did not agree to it, not wanting to presumptuously test God or jump ahead of the divine timetable for the Savior's redemptive ministry.

Ask YOURSELF

Yes, Scripture can be turned and twisted to suit anyone's ends. What safeguards do you have in place against misusing the Word of God, while still maintaining a bold, believing faith in its sense of direction? Ask the Spirit to guide you into its truth. That's His job (John 16:13).

DON'T COUNT ON SENSATIONALISM

"If You are the Son of God, throw yourself down; for it is written,
'He will command His angels concerning You.'"

MATT. 4:6A

THROUGHOUT HISTORY, sensationalism has often appealed to average people who are looking for dramatic events that titillate the senses and pander to fleshly curiosity. Toward the end of His ministry Jesus warned, "False Christs and false prophets will arise and will show great signs and wonders, so as to mislead, if possible, even the elect" (Matt. 24:24).

Even when signs are from God, they usually do not bring unbelievers to faith, but only confirm the faith of those who already believe. God's many miracles on behalf of the wandering Israelites just made many of them more presumptuous and unbelieving, as did Jesus' signs to the Jews who opposed Him. The apostle John writes, "But though He had performed so many signs before them, yet they were not believing in Him" (John 12:37). Jesus Himself, as the Messiah and Son of God, was the greatest sign God ever gave to humanity, yet "He was despised and forsaken of men" (Isa. 53:3).

Demanding sensational signs, as Satan did from Jesus, does not manifest faith but rather skepticism and unbelief (cf. Matt. 12:39; 16:4). Because a fascination with the sensational is far removed from true faith, Jesus would take no part in it. For those who, apart from special signs, believe in God the Father and trust in His Son— our Savior—it is well evident that Christ has already proved Himself.

Ask YOURSELF

The best Christian witness in the world remains the power of a changed life. People will respond to your testimony of God's love and mercy much more often than to a high-energy worship service. How are you making Christ known through your own life? Look for the simplest of ways.

WHY JESUS REJECTED SENSATIONALISM

"On the other hand, it is written, 'You shall not put the Lord your God to the test.'"

MATT. 4:7

*T*HE LORD JESUS HAD TWO good reasons for not participating in a worldly spectacle such as jumping from the temple roof. *First*, such sensationalism is captive to the laws of diminishing returns. To generate and hold people's allegiance to Him merely by stunning signs, Jesus would have needed to produce greater and greater signs. People would never have been satisfied and would always have demanded just one more miracle, one additional showy event. Real faith would not have been certain; they would have been lovers of sensation more than God, which similarly could happen to any of us who don't trust God's already revealed will.

Second, and more important, for Jesus to participate in sensational signs would have demonstrated a profound mistrust in His heavenly Father and a presumptuous, faithless testing of God. But that's what the devil wanted so that Jesus' sin would shatter His claim to divinity and ruin humanity's hope of salvation. Such an action would have questioned the Father's providence and love—and the wisdom of His redemptive plan.

If our sinless Savior and Lord shunned sensationalism, we as imperfect men and women ought never to live recklessly or carelessly, expecting God to rescue us when we get into earthly trouble or spiritual peril.

*Ask*YOURSELF

Perhaps you don't consider yourself a risk-taker. But looking honestly at your own life, do you spot some behaviors that are spiritually risky, actions that presume on the grace of God? In humble repentance today, surrender these things to the Lord. Receive, but don't force, His great mercy.

JANUARY 20

SATAN TESTS JESUS' ULTIMATE ALLEGIANCE

Again, the devil took Him to a very high mountain.

MATT. 4:8A

*S*ATAN'S FINAL TEMPTATION was a last-ditch effort to corrupt and derail Christ and His saving mission. The greatest of all adversaries sought to complete a sinister bargain in which extremely attractive and enticing possessions were offered to Jesus in exchange for His subservience to Satan.

The location ("a very high mountain") where Satan took Jesus no doubt allowed them to have a comprehensive view of the earth for hundreds of miles in every direction. But their vantage point was clearly spiritual and supernatural as well. They would have seen the power and dominance of Rome, the glories of Egypt, and the splendor of various Greek city-states. All the wonders of the ancient world, including the magnificence of Jerusalem, would have been included.

As the King of kings, Jesus already had the rights to own and govern all the world's kingdoms, but Satan tried to twist that reality for his own purposes. He wanted Jesus to leap ahead of God's promised plan and reign as a king before it was fully time to do so—and at the unthinkable cost of worshiping him. If our enemy can tempt Jesus to be impatient and impulsive and grasp things prematurely, that is all the more reason for us to be on guard against such attacks.

Ask YOURSELF

Timing is everything. And Jesus displayed an infallible sense of what to do—and when—in every situation. Is there anything in your own life that you're trying to speed ahead with, whether God wants you slowing down or not? Find peace in His timing. It's always perfect—more perfect than we think.

SATAN'S PROMISES—CORRUPT STRINGS ATTACHED

The devil took Him to a very high mountain and showed
Him all the kingdoms of the world and their glory.

MATT. 4:8

*S*ATAN OFFERED THE WORLD'S kingdoms to Jesus on his own corrupt terms. God allowed this test to prove that Christ was and is a worthy Son, fit to one day inherit the world and rule from His throne. The devil, on the other hand, wanted to prove the Son's unworthiness by getting Him to prematurely grab the kingdoms God had already promised Him.

The enemy approaches Christians also with corrupt bargaining chips. Whatever they might want in the realm of business, politics, fame, or anything else, he claims it can be theirs for a "reasonable" price or trade-off. He says we can be or have whatever we want, just so long as we pursue it according to the world's way—which is also Satan's way. In effect, it's like saying to ourselves, "Why wait for a heavenly reward when you can cut corners, shade the truth, run ahead of God's schedule, and have what you want now?"

But when we grab hold of Satan's corrupt strings, we put self first and God last. Instead of seeking God's kingdom first (Matt. 6:33), we act more like Abraham, who sought God's promise of an heir through his own impatient, selfish act with Hagar (Gen. 16:1–6). The result of that sin was tragic and heart-breaking, and has been to this day.

Ask YOURSELF

"The world" doesn't really know what "glory" is. And if we had a keener, more realistic sense of God's awesome splendor, we'd see the world's flimsy reflections for what they really are. What seems glorious and glamorous about the world to you? Ask God to help you see it truthfully.

SATAN REVEALED AS A LIAR

[The devil] said to Him, "All these things I will give
You, if You fall down and worship me."

MATT. 4:9

*S*ATAN'S PROMISES FOR BETTER THINGS, obtained more quickly and in a "preferred" manner to God's plan, are actually counterfeit offers. He always wraps them in claims that seem easier, less expensive, and far less burdensome. After all, that's the savvy way to success, he reasons. Our adversary's argument is essentially just a form of the old "end justifies the means" concept.

But Satan has been a liar from the beginning of redemptive history. With his third temptation of Jesus he was actually just seeking to buy Christ's soul and His permanent allegiance. The cost for the Lord, had He accepted the offer of the world's kingdoms, would have been devastating beyond measure.

Similarly for us, Satan's price is always far more than we are led to believe— and the goods always unfathomably fall short of what we had expected. Thankfully, Jesus in His omniscience and infinite wisdom recognized these truths and did not succumb to the final temptation in the wilderness. Had He accepted Satan's sinister offer, Christ would have disqualified Himself as both Savior and King. Instead of redeeming the world, He would have joined it; instead of inheriting it, He would have lost both it and us.

Ask YOURSELF

If coming in the front door doesn't work, our enemy has no qualms about executing the sneak attack, catching us off guard and by surprise. How seriously are you taking the call to be on the alert at all times, resisting Satan's temptations and boldly obeying God's will? Trust Christ for both radar and resistance.

JANUARY 23

CHRIST SOVEREIGNLY MASTERS SATAN

Jesus said to him, "Go, Satan! For it is written, 'You shall worship the Lord your God, and serve Him only.'"

MATT. 4:10

*T*HE DEVIL'S FINAL PROPOSAL WAS so outlandish and beyond the boundaries of God's will that Jesus dismissed him with the terse, firm command, "Go, Satan!" Satan can wield his present power only by God's permission; therefore he had no choice but to leave Christ's presence. This last interaction is a prime example of our Lord's sovereign mastery over the enemy.

If the Savior would not compromise on a mundane matter such as turning stones to bread, He certainly would not compromise on the major issue of worshiping and serving anyone besides the Father and the Father alone.

Christ will finally inherit God's kingdom in God's perfect time, and we will inherit it with Him (Matt. 5:5; 25:34; Rom. 8:17). This glorious truth doesn't mean God will not give us many good things in this life, because no one desires our happiness more than our heavenly Father. Jesus Himself later taught, "If you then, being evil, know how to give good gifts to your children, how much more will your Father who is in heaven give what is good to those who ask Him!" (Matt. 7:11). Knowing this, why should any of us want to settle for any of the cheap, fleeting substitutes of instant gratification that Satan offers?

Ask YOURSELF

What inspires you the most about Jesus' reactions to Satan's three temptations? What are the most convicting or compelling aspects of His testimony that would look good on you as well? Thank Him for His sturdy, steady faithfulness—and ask Him to grow the same in you.

ANGELS MINISTER TO JESUS

Then the devil left Him; and behold, angels came and began to minister to Him.
MATT. 4:11

*A*FTER JESUS' GREATEST FOE LEFT, "angels came and began to minister to Him." It is quite fitting that holy angels should come to care for and comfort Him after the prince of the fallen angels had harassed Him with three major temptations. To provide the benefits of angelic ministry was just another way for the Father to register His approval of the Son and signify the Son's worthiness.

At the first sign of confrontation with Satan, Christ could easily have summoned help from "more than twelve legions of angels" (Matt. 26:53). But He obediently waited for the Father to send assistance according to the divine schedule. We are not told what kind of ministry the angels performed, but they undoubtedly brought Jesus food to relieve His hunger. And spiritually they would have worshiped the Son and delivered to Him many words of assurance and comfort from His Father.

The devil's temptations of Jesus failed, whereas God's testings of His Son succeeded. Time after time, Jesus had answered with the ideal response to each test. The Lord also provides His saints with the power to resist the adversary's schemes (James 4:7), knowing that Satan will certainly persist in challenging believers, just as he challenged Jesus. But for every new or repeated temptation, God always gives us a way of escape (1 Cor. 10:13).

*Ask*YOURSELF

Perhaps you're the giving, ministry type. You freely give and share and do and give comfort. But how well do you *receive* God's comfort and His ministry to you? How welcome are you to the caring compassions of others? To meet needs is noble, but to admit our own is still necessary.

BELIEVERS' TEMPTATIONS SIMILAR TO JESUS'

The tempter came and said to Him . . . Then the devil . . . Again, the devil . . .

MATT. 4:3A, 5A, 8A

*O*UR TEMPTATIONS ARE SIMILAR IN kind to what Jesus faced. First, Satan tries to get us to distrust God's providential care and solve our own difficulties by our own strength and cleverness. Second, the devil will tempt us to presume on the Lord's protection by having us willingly place ourselves in danger's pathway, where we can meet all kinds of physical and spiritual harm. Third, he appeals to our selfish ambitions in hopes we might grasp after God's promises in our own strength. The apostle John mentions these same temptations: "All that is in the world, the lust of the flesh and the lust of the eyes and the boastful pride of life, is not from the Father, but is from the world" (1 John 2:16).

Those three major sources of temptation are all around us, so how do we resist? Consider the man who trained his dog by placing a piece of meat in the center of the floor. Whenever the dog tried to take the meat, its owner swatted it and said, "No." Before long the dog learned to associate the swat with "No" and simply left the meat alone when it heard the word. Finally, whenever the meat was placed on the floor, the dog would not even look at the meat, but instead at its master, waiting for his word of approval or denial. In a way, this illustrates how we must deal with temptation—keep our eyes on the Master rather than the temptation, and wait for His command.

Ask YOURSELF

One of the grandest things about heaven will be the freedom of living without the burden of temptation or the inclination to obey it. Till then, what can you do to keep your "eyes on the Master," resisting Satan's attempts at deception and destruction? Pray for sharper, surer spiritual eyesight.

CHRIST OUR EXAMPLE IN OVERCOMING TEMPTATION

But He answered and said, "It is written . . . it is written . . . it is written . . ."
MATT. 4:4A, 7B, 10B

*T*HE LORD JESUS CHRIST IS INDEED our supreme example for how to resist temptation. Hebrews 4:15 reminds us, "We do not have a high priest who cannot sympathize with our weaknesses, but One who has been tempted in all things as we are, yet without sin" (cf. 2:18). Our responsibility is to consider the many ways He was tempted, look to Him, and follow His example in turning away from sin.

Jesus met the worst temptations Satan could hurl at Him, and He emerged victorious. Now He is ready to share the joy of victory with all His saints: "No temptation has overtaken you but such as is common to man; and God is faithful, who will not allow you to be tempted beyond what you are able, but with the temptation will provide the way of escape also, so that you will be able to endure it" (1 Cor. 10:13).

The key to our triumph over temptation is to resist it the way Jesus did, by completely obeying God and His Word. Just as in every aspect of the Christian life, we will have success in resisting temptation by "fixing our eyes on Jesus, the author and perfecter of faith" (Heb. 12:2). Like the hurdler who learns to keep his eyes on the finish line as he runs, thereby not tripping over any individual hurdle, so we must keep our eyes on the ultimate goal—being with our glorious Lord and Savior forever in heaven.

Ask YOURSELF

God's Word is such that the more time we spend in it, the more it sinks into us—into our hearts, into our thoughts, into our impulses, reactions, and conversations. Are you mining daily from this treasure? Make sure Satan has to climb over a lot of Scripture to get to you.

THE LORD'S MINISTRY ALL ACCORDING TO PLAN

*He withdrew into Galilee; and leaving Nazareth, He came
and settled in Capernaum, which is by the sea.*

MATT. 4:12B–13A

*N*OTHING WAS ACCIDENTAL OR happenstance about Jesus' earthly ministry. He did not go from Judea to Galilee because Herod or the Jewish leaders forced Him to or because He had nowhere else to go. He left Judea because His work there was finished for the time being. And He came to Galilee because that was the next place, according to the Father's plan, for Him to minister.

Humanly speaking, Jesus left the lower Jordan region for Galilee because of the Jewish leaders (cf. John 4:1, 3). His close association with John the Baptist as well as His growing number of followers had caused the scribes and Pharisees to hate Jesus as much or more than they hated John. Jesus was not afraid of their hatred but removed Himself from the leaders' immediate influence because it was not yet time for them to fully turn their wrath on Him.

The Lord by no means avoided the Jewish leaders permanently, for at the appropriate, foreordained time, He faced them without flinching and denounced them far more harshly than John the Baptist ever did (cf. Matt. 23:1–36). Jesus was simply forever safe from wicked human schemes and devices. He knew He would die, but it would be according to the will of His Father, not that of His earthly enemies (cf. John 10:17–18). He also knew He would rise from the dead, all according to the divine plan.

Ask YOURSELF

Can Christians live with the same kind of bold assurance that Jesus did, fearlessly walking through life at the Spirit's direction? If the worst that could happen would only put us that much closer to Jesus, what reason do we have for fear? Why not resolve to follow Jesus' example?

CHRIST'S GALILEAN MINISTRY FULFILLS PROPHECY

This was to fulfill what was spoken through Isaiah the prophet.

MATT. 4:14

*C*ENTURIES BEFORE THE INCARNATION, the prophet Isaiah foretold this great truth: "'The land of Zebulun and the land of Naphtali, by the way of the sea, beyond the Jordan, Galilee of the Gentiles—the people who were sitting in darkness saw a great Light, and those who were sitting in the land and shadow of death, upon them a Light dawned'" (from Isa. 9:1–2).

And eight hundred years later—just as prophesied—the despised, unbelieving Galileans glimpsed the Messiah and, ahead of many of the Jews in Jerusalem, saw the dawning of God's new covenant.

The Jews in Galilee were less sophisticated and traditional than those in Judea. The Jewish historian Josephus noted that the Galileans "were fond of innovations and by nature disposed to change, and they delighted in seditions." They even had a regional accent distinct from the Judeans (cf. Matt. 26:73). Jesus likely chose His apostles from Galilee because they too would have been less bound to Jewish tradition and more open to the gospel.

Jesus' going to Galilee to really begin His ministry shows that salvation was for sinners everywhere, with no distinctions or restrictions. It fulfilled Old Testament truth, which God revealed through the Jews (cf. Rom. 3:1–2). However, it was not an accommodation to the proud, exclusive Judaism prevalent in Jesus' day. It was no accident that "the Light of the world" (John 8:12) first proclaimed Himself and His message in Galilee.

Ask YOURSELF

As we'll continue to see, Jesus often went to the least expected, the least admired, the least in the pecking order to administer His grace and reveal His identity. What is your level of concern and compassion for those in the greatest need of the gospel? Pray for a heart that beats like Jesus' heart did—and does.

JANUARY 29

JESUS' AUTHORITATIVE PREACHING

From that time Jesus began to preach.

MATT. 4:17A

*O*UR LORD HERALDED THE GOSPEL message with certainty. His mission was not to dispute or argue with His opponents but to preach the truth of salvation. He did not merely proclaim certainties, but He did so with the utmost authority (cf. Matt. 7:29).

The scribes could not teach with authority because they had mingled so many man-made opinions and interpretations in with biblical truths that any sense of authority for them had long since disappeared. It was thus quite astounding when the people again heard one like Jesus preach with real authority, as the prophets had (cf. Matt. 7:28–29).

Jesus also preached precisely and only what His Father commissioned Him to proclaim, which no doubt gave added weight to His authority. He testified to this fact quite directly, "I did not speak on My own initiative, but the Father Himself who sent Me has given Me a commandment as to what to say and what to speak" (John 12:49; cf. 3:34; 8:38).

Based on this divine authority, Christ sends us out into the world as His ambassadors by saying, "All authority has been given to Me in heaven and on earth. Go therefore and make disciples of all the nations" (Matt. 28:18b–19a). All believers who are faithful witnesses for the gospel will proclaim God's certain truth by His authority—and with His power.

Ask YOURSELF

The authority of Jesus that registered with the people of His day also had something to do with His authenticity. If people don't show much respect for God and His Word today, how much of it is due to a lack of authenticity in His people? Pray that we would exude His grace-filled reality.

THE GOSPEL'S FIRST DEMAND—REPENTANCE

From that time Jesus began to preach and say, "Repent,
for the kingdom of heaven is at hand."

MATT. 4:17

*T*HE MESSAGE THAT JESUS BROUGHT to the people—the "great light" He revealed to those "sitting in the land of shadow and death"—was always very clear: "Repent, for the kingdom of heaven is at hand." Our Lord thus began with the same basic exhortation that His herald, John the Baptist, had begun with (cf. Matt. 3:2).

Repentance is a crucial but often neglected or omitted element of the gospel. "Repent" means to turn from sin, to change your orientation, and in so turning to seek a new way of life. The person who repents has a radical change of will and heart, and as a result, a change of behavior (cf. Matt. 3:8). The repentant sinner will radically change the way he or she views sin and righteousness.

Repentance was, is, and always will be the foremost demand of the gospel. It is quite simply the first part of the saving work of the Holy Spirit in the sinner's soul. In his Pentecost sermon, Peter also issued a call for repentance: "Repent, and each of you be baptized in the name of Jesus Christ for the forgiveness of your sins" (Acts 2:38). Paul reassured Timothy that repentance leads "to the knowledge of the truth" (2 Tim. 2:25). If repentance was crucial for the people of Jesus' day, it is even more imperative for everyone today, because the kingdom is nearer than ever.

Ask YOURSELF

Like all of us, you've confessed many things, many times before. But today is another good opportunity to take repentance seriously. What sins need its corrective touch in your life? Bring them before the Father. Receive His mercy. Walk away refreshed and in freedom.

JESUS SUMMONS PETER AND ANDREW

Now as Jesus was walking by the Sea of Galilee, He saw two brothers,
Simon who was called Peter, and Andrew his brother.

MATT. 4:18A

*W*HEN JESUS CALLED HIS FIRST DISCIPLES, such as Peter and Andrew, He was gathering together the original group of evangelists to help fulfill His Great Commission. The Lord had the sovereign prerogative to carry out the Great Commission by Himself, but that was not His plan. Instead, He wanted to have partners in ministry. His plan was to use disciples to make other disciples. Jesus would teach them other things and mandate other responsibilities, but His first call to the disciples was for them to be "fishers of men."

Jesus' decision to select twelve apostles follows the pattern God established many centuries earlier. The Father always chose His most significant partners in ministry, such as Noah, Abraham, Moses, David, and all the prophets. He chose Israel as an entire nation of ministry partners—"a kingdom of priests and a holy nation" (Ex. 19:6). So it is no wonder that Christ told the disciples, "You did not choose Me but I chose you, and appointed you that you would go and bear fruit, and that your fruit would remain" (John 15:16; cf. 6:70; 13:18; Rom. 16:5).

Our Lord commands that all His followers be evangelistic fishermen. The command "follow Me" in the Greek literally means "come here." The original text also has the term "after," which indicates the place we must come to: "Your place is following *after* Me!" This is His chosen place and posture for you.

Ask YOURSELF

If we truly knew the gravity of this, we would never get over our amazement that the God of the universe has chosen to live in relationship with us. What goes missing from your life when you forget that you have been personally called by God to your kingdom tasks and priorities?

OBEYING JESUS' CALL

He said to them, "Follow Me, and I will make you fishers of men."
Immediately they left their nets and followed Him.

MATT. 4:19–20

*P*ETER AND ANDREW OBEYED JESUS' call right away—"Immediately they left their nets and followed Him"—an indication of how determined they were to go with the Lord. The word "followed" carries the meaning of being committed to imitating the one he or she follows.

Past surveys have shown that 95 percent of all professing Christians have never led someone to faith in Jesus Christ. Too often they are like the reclusive, frugal man many years ago who accumulated 246 expensive violins in the attic of his house in Italy. Because he selfishly acquired and held on to those instruments, the world never heard the beautiful music the violins were intended to play. Many believers hide their light and store away the great treasure they possess as children of God. As a result, 95 percent of the world's spiritual violins have not been played for others.

Evangelist D. L. Moody especially admired two similar paintings. The first depicted a person in the midst of a storm clinging with both hands to a cross firmly planted in a rock. The other picture also showed a person in a storm firmly grasping a cross. But in this one the man was reaching out with his other hand to rescue someone who was about to drown. Both paintings pictured a Christian valiantly holding on to Christ. But the second one portrayed the believer reaching out for another who was about to be lost. For us, as for D. L. Moody, the second picture should be the favorite.

Ask YOURSELF

Would "immediately" describe the way you travel to Jesus' side when He calls? How quickly does His Word make its way from your conscious mind into conscious action?

JAMES AND JOHN—RAW RECRUITS

Going on from there He saw two other brothers, James the son of Zebedee, and John his brother,
in the boat with Zebedee their father, mending their nets; and He called them.
Immediately they left the boat and their father, and followed Him.

MATT. 4:21–22

*W*HEN JESUS FIRST CALLED JAMES and John, they were unrefined, tough fishermen by trade. The Holy Spirit had already drawn them to faith in the Savior (John 1:35–51; 2:11), but now Jesus summoned them to work as evangelists in spreading His gospel. Like Peter and Andrew, they did not hesitate to leave the fishing business, which for James and John meant leaving the fishing to their father to follow Jesus right away.

These disciples lacked formal education and likely didn't have much religious training either, nor was their spiritual perception noticeably apparent. They showed no more ability to fully understand Jesus' teaching than any of the others, even when He taught in parables. They often demonstrated only slight potential for dependability, much less for greatness.

Jesus' disciples were probably not all such raw recruits as James and John (or Peter and Andrew), but Jesus did not choose any of the Twelve from the Jewish elite religious leaders (cf. 1 Cor. 1:26–29). That omission undoubtedly caused many of those men—the scribes, Pharisees, Sadducees, priests, and rabbis—to reject the Lord and Savior. They could not fathom how someone who was not an official Jewish leader Himself and who chose no leaders to be among His closest associates could possibly be the Messiah.

Paul was the only apostle who had been a Jewish leader, and of course he was not among the original Twelve but considered himself "one untimely born," exceptionally called to be an apostle (cf. 1 Cor. 15:8–10). As with everyone who believes, God's call came by His exceeding grace.

*Ask*YOURSELF

Jesus had purpose for calling the ones He did into His ministry, just as He has purpose for calling you. If you're failing to see the value He has placed on you, let the fishermen's story encourage you today. He has more in mind for you than you can imagine—if you'll just keep following.

QUALITIES OF FISHERMEN/EVANGELISTS

He said to them, "Follow Me, and I will make you fishers of men."
MATT. 4:19

*O*UR LORD DID NOT MERELY COMMAND His new disciples to become "fishers of men," He promised to help them catch people's souls. He would remind them many times that they would never be effective disciplers—or successful disciples at all—if they didn't rely on His power: "I am the vine, you are the branches; he who abides in Me and I in him, he bears much fruit, for apart from Me you can do nothing" (John 15:5).

Certain qualities that make a person a good fisherman also can make Christians good evangelists. Consider the following four fisherman traits and how they can apply to evangelism.

First, a fisherman knows he often must be patient to locate a school of catchable fish. *Second,* a good fisherman must have perseverance in going from place to place, sometimes repeatedly, until he finds the fish. *Third,* effective fishermen have good instincts about being in the right place at the right time for dropping their line or net. Poor timing has lost many catches, both of fish and people. *Finally,* a good fisherman stays out of sight as much as possible. Similarly, the effective evangelist does not get in the way of his or her witnessing, so as not to be a hindrance to sinners coming to Christ.

Following Christ's example and realizing the qualities of good evangelists, our churches must not only call us to evangelism but continually encourage us in that calling (cf. Matt. 28:18–19).

Ask YOURSELF

How much "fishing" have you been doing lately? This is not a job for the trained and educated but for all who have been called by God into His service. You won't always come away with a catch, but you can know you were faithful to drop your line into the water.

JESUS, THE MODEL SOUL-WINNER

Now as Jesus was walking by the Sea of Galilee, He saw two brothers . . .
and He said to them, "Follow Me." . . . Going on from there
He saw two other brothers . . . and He called them.

MATT. 4:18–19, 21

*E*VERY BELIEVER WHO WOULD BE A soul winner must emulate the key principles Jesus exemplified as the model evangelist—not only in this one occasion but throughout His earthly ministry. Think about the following six, and seek to implement them as you witness for Him.

First, Jesus was always available. He never refused a genuine request for help from penitent sinners or the downtrodden.

Second, Jesus showed no favoritism. Neither Jairus nor the Roman centurion had an advantage over the woman of Sychar or the woman caught in adultery.

Third, the Lord was completely sensitive to the needs around Him. He always could discern the open heart of someone ready to come to Him. In spite of the pressing crowd, He noticed and responded to the woman who touched the hem of His garment (Matt. 9:20–22).

Fourth, Christ usually secured a public profession or testimony from the sinner, even including a specific instruction (e.g., the man delivered from demons, Mark 5:19).

Fifth, Jesus showed love and tenderness to those He witnessed to. The Samaritan woman at the well was one such recipient. She was a religious outcast and an adulterer, yet He clearly and gently led her to saving faith.

Sixth, Jesus always had time to speak to others. Even while on the way to heal Jairus's daughter, He stopped long enough to heal the woman who had a hemorrhage for twelve years.

Ask YOURSELF

We still live in a time of gracious evangelism, as so perfectly exemplified by our Lord and Savior. How obedient is your church being to this model? How obedient are you being to it as an individual?

KINGDOM GOOD NEWS AND JESUS' HEALINGS

*Jesus was going throughout all Galilee, teaching in their synagogues and proclaiming the gospel of the
kingdom, and healing every kind of disease and every kind of sickness among the people.*

MATT. 4:23

*G*OSPEL MEANS "GOOD NEWS," and it was the good news of God's kingdom—around which all of Jesus' teaching revolved—that He preached throughout
Galilee. His emphasis never veered off into politics, economics, social activism,
or resolution of personal disputes, which is as it should be for any faithful gospel
messenger.

Jesus' primary teaching was always the divine good news—God's gracious offer
to deliver sinners "from the domain of darkness ... to the kingdom of His beloved
Son" where they are saved and forgiven of their sins (Col. 1:13–14).

Initially, synagogues were the places where Jesus proclaimed the good news, the
places where sincere, God-fearing Jews came to worship and hear God's Word. Essentially, it was in those facilities that Jesus expected to find receptive audiences to
His words, but He did not restrict His outreach to the people of Israel. The basic
message of entering the sphere of God's rule by faith in the saving gospel was and always has been open to anyone who trusts Christ's invitation.

Jesus' powerful, eternal words were unlike the words any other teacher had
ever proclaimed. Even His fellow residents of Nazareth knew this and "were speaking well of Him, and wondering at the gracious words which were falling from His
lips" (Luke 4:22). People at Capernaum also "were amazed at His teaching, for His
message was with authority" (v. 32). Jesus' teaching on the kingdom of God and His
subsequent healings were the surest credentials that the Father had sent Him.

*Ask*YOURSELF

Jesus' priorities were plainly obvious by the way He conducted Himself and
the activities He chose to involve Himself in on a typical day. How would you enu-
merate your own priorities? And what day-to-day actions of yours back this up?

HEALINGS VALIDATE JESUS' EARTHLY MINISTRY

The news about Him spread throughout all Syria; and they brought to Him
all who were ill, those suffering with various diseases and pains,
demoniacs, epileptics, paralytics; and He healed them.

MATT. 4:24

JESUS' MIRACULOUS HEALING ministry powerfully augmented the divine veracity of His teaching and preaching ministry. But any completely honest observer will concede that our Lord's words alone provide sufficient evidence that He was the Messiah. The apostles left everything to follow Him before He did any healing or performed any other miracle. Many who heard and believed when Jesus taught in their villages had no need for healing, and neither did their relatives or friends. In that sense they were like those who believed John the Baptist's message even though "John performed no sign" (John 10:41).

Yet in spite of the overwhelming adequacy of Jesus' verbal teaching, His Father saw fit to provide a healing ministry to supplement it. Alexander Maclaren has written, "It may be doubted whether we have an adequate notion of the immense number of Christ's miracles. Those recorded are but a small portion of those done. Those early ones were illustrations of the nature of His kingdom; they were His first gifts to His kingdom subjects."

Concerning the gospel of the kingdom, Hebrews 2:3–4 says, "After it was at the first spoken through the Lord, it was confirmed to us by those who heard, God also testifying with them, both by signs and wonders and by various miracles and by gifts of the Holy Spirit according to His own will." Like Christ's words, His healings and other miracles provided a preview of His glorious earthly kingdom.

Ask YOURSELF

How dependent are you on the specific, visible, measurable acts of God on your behalf? How often does His Word alone brighten your heart, even when your prayers seem to be waiting on His answer? What does one do to get his or her heart operating this way?

HEALINGS' EXTRAORDINARY CONFIRMATIONS

*Large crowds followed Him from Galilee and the Decapolis
and Jerusalem and Judea and from beyond Jordan.*

MATT. 4:25

*T*HE HEALING MIRACLES OF JESUS accomplished things that surpassed and were far more significant than the obvious, immediate benefit to those healed. *First,* they demonstrated He was the Son of God, since no mere man could do such feats. Jesus later instructed Philip and the other disciples, "Believe Me that I am in the Father and the Father is in Me; otherwise believe because of the works themselves" (John 14:11).

Second, the marvelous healings revealed that God, through Christ, was and is compassionate to all who suffer: "Moved with compassion, Jesus touched their eyes; and immediately they regained their sight and followed Him" (Matt. 20:34).

Third, Jesus' healings proved He was the predicted Messiah of the Old Testament. Jesus directly told John the Baptist's disciples, "Go and report to John what you hear and see: the blind receive sight and the lame walk, the lepers are cleansed and the deaf hear, the dead are raised up, and the poor have the gospel preached to them" (Matt. 11:4–5; cf. Isa. 35:5–10; 61:1–3).

Finally, the healing miracles proved that God's kingdom is a reality (cf. Matt. 9:35; 10:7–8). Perhaps even more marvelous for us is that Jesus' healings were a foretaste of a future kingdom: "The eyes of the blind will be opened and the ears of the deaf will be unstopped. Then the lame will leap like a deer, and the tongue of the mute will shout for joy" (Isa. 35:5–6; cf. Ps. 96:10).

Ask YOURSELF

Certainly, many in the "large crowds" came for what they viewed as a sideshow, an entertaining diversion from the humdrum. But are we often guilty of following while expecting nothing? Are you still willing to believe God for the unexplainable?

SERMON ON THE MOUNT'S SIGNIFICANCE

When Jesus saw the crowds, He went up on the mountain;
and after He sat down, His disciples came to Him.

MATT. 5:1

*T*HE GOSPEL OF THE KINGDOM'S foundational truth (contained in the Sermon on the Mount) has had an impact for two thousand years on all who read and hear it. At least five reasons come to mind as to why Jesus' greatest of sermons is so important.

First, the Sermon demonstrates the necessity of the new birth. In order for us to recognize our sin, Jesus made a fuller, clearer presentation of the law, followed by His offer of salvation. Jesus' message here clarifies the reasons for sin's curse and shows that we have no righteousness of our own to survive God's scrutiny. Only those who have a new nature through Christ can meet the law's demands. By no other way but saving faith can we have righteous attitudes as well as actions and be fully right with God.

Second, the Sermon points all listeners to their dependence on Christ's enabling power to meet God's standards.

Third, Jesus' message gives us the Father's pattern for true happiness and peace (cf. John 14:27; Phil. 4:7). It provides the real pathway to the believer's sanctification.

Next, the principles in the Sermon on the Mount are some of the greatest scriptural resources for evangelism. If you as a Christian personify these truths, your life will attract others to the Lord.

Last, the life that is obedient to the Sermon's teachings is the only one that truly pleases God—and that is the highest, noblest objective of the Christian life.

Ask YOURSELF

Embarking on a devotional study of something as monumental as the Sermon on the Mount, you're always sure to discover truths and insights you've never noticed before. Which one or two of the five statements above do you think you're most ready to hear more about?

THIS SERMON IS FOR TODAY

He opened His mouth and began to teach them.

MATT. 5:2

*B*ECAUSE OF THE SERMON on the Mount's seemingly impossible demands and behavioral standards that are counter to everything the world practices and holds dear, many Christians have taught that the Sermon applies only to the millennial age. If it were not just for a future kingdom era, the argument goes, Jesus would not have commanded believers to be perfect, just as their "heavenly Father is perfect" (Matt. 5:48).

But such an argument is invalid, for a number of reasons. *First*, and most obvious, the body of Jesus' sermon nowhere indicates or even implies that its message should be set aside for a future age. *Second*, Jesus was delivering these instructions to people of the present age—His original hearers and us—not those living in the Millennium. *Furthermore*, many of the teachings become meaningless if we apply them to the Millennium. (For instance, there will be no persecution of Christians at that time; see Matt. 5:10–12, 44.)

The fourth reason these teachings have to apply now is that every principle and command Jesus sets forth is further applied by the writers of the New Testament epistles, directed to believers both then and now. And *fifth*, many other New Testament passages teach us standards that are equally unattainable as those in the Sermon on the Mount. Only with aid of the indwelling Spirit can these be done, even part of the time (cf. Phil. 1:9–10; Col. 3:1–2; 1 Peter 1:15–16).

Jesus' sermon certainly does apply to us, marking out the distinctive lifestyle we should display to all those around us.

*Ask*YOURSELF

Which of the individual teachings from the Sermon on the Mount have you basically dismissed as being unattainable? Why have you classified one or more in this way? What could this deliberate refusal to obey tell you about the condition of your heart?

DISTINCTIVENESS OF THE BEATITUDES

Blessed are the poor in spirit, for theirs is the kingdom of heaven.

MATT. 5:3

*T*HE SERIES OF CONDITIONAL blessings Jesus promises, beginning with this verse and continuing through verse 12, are known as the Beatitudes. This name refers to a state of happiness or bliss. The blessedness promised in each is a divine characteristic, one that men and women can realize only as they share in God's nature (cf. 2 Peter 1:4). When believers are truly blessed, they don't experience merely an external, circumstantial feeling of happiness, but a deep sense of spiritual contentedness and well-being based on the objective spiritual reality that they belong to God.

We must understand that Christ's beatitudes are distinctive and firm pronouncements, not merely ambiguous probabilities. Our Lord does not say that if we have the qualities the Beatitudes set forth, we are only *likely* to be happy; nor is this simply His wish for us. Adherence to these attitudes and practices *will* result in blessedness, just as surely as judgmental woes await those who are the subject of His pronouncements in Matthew 23.

The blessed life is the opposite of the cursed life. Blessedness is possessed by those who truly have the inner characteristics of the Beatitudes. Conversely, cursedness represents those who don't know the Beatitudes, such as the Jewish religionists of Jesus' time.

The Beatitudes are also distinctively progressive, each leading to the next in logical succession. Poverty of spirit demonstrates a right attitude about ourselves. That leads to mourning, gentleness, hungering and thirsting for righteousness, showing mercy, purity of heart, and peacemaking. If we have these traits we will rebuke the world so that it persecutes us and allows us to be lights in its midst.

*Ask*YOURSELF

We have often stated—rightly so—that God is more interested in making us holy than making us happy. So does it surprise you to see that happiness is a gift Jesus offers to those who take His Word to heart? What's wrong with a theology that looks suspiciously at happiness?

WHAT IS POVERTY OF SPIRIT?

Blessed are the poor in spirit, for theirs is the kingdom of heaven.

MATT. 5:3

*P*OVERTY OF SPIRIT MEANS recognizing how truly deficient we are apart from God. It means seeing ourselves as we really are: spiritually lost, hopeless, and helpless. Without the gospel of Jesus Christ, everyone is spiritually impoverished, regardless of his or her material accomplishments, educational achievements, or even religious knowledge and church activities.

The "poor in spirit" are people who have recognized their spiritual destitution and their total inability to save themselves—their complete dependence on God. They know their only hope of salvation is to repent and ask for forgiveness, leaning on the sovereign grace and mercy of God. Such a person knows he has no spiritual merit of his own and that his personal strength or wisdom is insufficient to earn him lasting spiritual reward.

"In spirit" expresses the understanding that poverty of spirit can't be merely a hypocritical, outward act. Being a genuine spiritual beggar reflects true humility, not some phony, pretentious, mild-mannered behavior. Real poverty of spirit is what the prophet said the Lord looks for and affirms: "But to this one I will look, to him who is humble and contrite of spirit, and who trembles at My word" (Isa. 66:2; cf. Pss. 34:18; 51:17).

Augustine in his *Confessions* says pride was his greatest barrier to salvation. Until he realized that his achievements and possessions were nothing, Christ could do nothing for him. It's the same for any who would be poor in spirit.

Ask YOURSELF

What specific items or attitudes threaten your ability to remain "poor in spirit"? How does a person maintain a comfort level in God's presence without losing the perspective of being undeserving of the privilege?

WHY THE PRIORITY OF HUMILITY?

Blessed are the poor in spirit, for theirs is the kingdom of heaven.

MATT. 5:3

THIS BEATITUDE WAS UTTERED first because humility is the foundation of all other graces and a crucial aspect to salvation (cf. Matt. 18:3–4). The door into Christ's kingdom is narrow and low, and no one who sees himself or herself too large or too tall will ever pass through. It makes about as much sense to attempt to grow fruit apart from a tree and its branches as to expect the other graces of the Christian life to grow apart from humility.

Until we humble ourselves to recognize our own spiritual poverty and our need of Christ, we cannot see and experience His gracious, saving riches. Jesus said of the contrite tax collector, "I tell you, this man went to his house justified rather than the other [the Pharisee]; for everyone who exalts himself will be humbled, but he who humbles himself will be exalted" (Luke 18:14).

No person can receive the kingdom of God until he or she realizes they are unworthy of that kingdom. The proud Laodicean church declared collectively, "I am rich, and have become wealthy, and have need of nothing," but in reality the members were "wretched and miserable and poor and blind and naked" (Rev. 3:17). People like the Laodiceans remind us of the story of the Roman slave girl who would not recognize her blindness, insisting that her world was just permanently dark.

Until the proud are willing to be poor in spirit, they can't receive the King or enter His kingdom.

Ask YOURSELF

We see that pride is the chief barrier between people and God, between sinful souls and Christ's glorious salvation. But what else does pride restrict us from experiencing and enjoying? What other residual costs does it incur in our lives?

THE WAY TO HUMILITY

Blessed are the poor in spirit, for theirs is the kingdom of heaven.

MATT. 5:3

*A*CHIEVING HUMILITY DOESN'T mean merely putting yourself down. Because of sin, you are already spiritually down, whether you know it or not; humility just recognizes this truth. Furthermore, this recognition comes only from God, which is why asceticism, self-denial, and other human efforts are so futile in seeking humility.

Yet even though genuine humility results from God's sovereign, saving work, He still commands it of men and women (cf. Matt. 18:4; 23:12; James 4:10; 1 Peter 5:5). Therefore it is always helpful to remember some basic steps to take from our side of the divine equation.

First, we must take our eyes off ourselves and look to God—through study of the Word, time in prayer, and sincerely desiring to be close to Him. *Second,* we must starve our flesh by removing the things on which it feeds. This means removing those things that promote pride. *Third,* and most important, we must simply ask for it. God alone can help us keep our lives in balanced perspective, and He will respond when we seek humility with all our hearts. David prayed, "Create in me a clean heart, O God, and renew a steadfast spirit within me" (Ps. 51:10). He desired to be steadfastly humble, and knew only God could grant such a request. The Father stands ready to answer this prayer long before we even utter it—humility is that important.

Ask YOURSELF

Fashion your own prayer today, deliberately confessing your tendency toward pride, acknowledging your inability to conjure up true humility within yourself, and asking for the Lord's enablement in pursuing a life of genuine, godly perspective. He will love hearing this prayer from you.

RECOGNIZING OUR HUMILITY, PART 1

Blessed are the poor in spirit, for theirs is the kingdom of heaven.

MATT. 5:3

THE PURITAN THOMAS WATSON, in his book *The Beatitudes*, discusses many principles to help the believer recognize his or her humility—those spiritual fruits that enable us to determine whether or not humility is actually growing within us. Here are three.

First, if we are truly humble, we will be weaned from ourselves and have no more constant self-preoccupation. Paul expresses it beautifully this way: "I have been crucified with Christ; and it is no longer I who live, but Christ lives in me; and the life which I now live in the flesh I live by faith in the Son of God, who loved me and gave Himself up for me" (Gal. 2:20).

Second, if we are really humble we will be lost in the wonder of Jesus Christ. We will contemplate "as in a mirror the glory of the Lord ... being transformed into the same image from glory to glory" (2 Cor. 3:18). We'll look forward to the day when we'll be just like our Lord.

And third, no matter how bad life's situations get, we will not complain. We'll understand that we deserve far worse than anything we experience in this life. When tragedy comes, our first response won't be, "Why me, Lord?" Instead, we'll fully appreciate that "the sufferings of this present time are not worthy to be compared with the glory that is to be revealed to us" (Rom. 8:18).

Ask YOURSELF

Could you honestly say you're detecting growth in these three areas? It's not "proud" to recognize it, to give God glory for what He's producing in you by His Spirit. If you're not seeing this kind of spiritual development, ask yourself what needs to change.

RECOGNIZING OUR HUMILITY, PART 2

Blessed are the poor in spirit, for theirs is the kingdom of heaven.

MATT. 5:3

*C*ONTINUING FROM YESTERDAY, a *fourth* principle for determining our humility, which Thomas Watson recognizes, is that we will see the strengths and virtues of others as well as our own weaknesses and sins. As the apostle instructs, we will "regard one another as more important than" ourselves (Phil. 2:3) and will "give preference to one another in honor" (Rom. 12:10).

Fifth, we will spend a lot of time in prayer. As the physical beggar pleads for earthly sustenance, spiritual beggars ask regularly for spiritual food. Just as when Jacob wrestled with an angel (Gen. 32:24–28), we will not quit until we receive the Lord's blessing.

Sixth, we will accept Christ on His terms, not ours or any other terms. We will not try to have Him while maintaining our sinful habits. We will not crowd Him aside by our own preferences or traditions, not even by familiar church standards. The Bible alone will be our guide.

And finally, when we have true humility we will praise and thank God for His grace to us. We will gratefully realize that the Father's grace is "more than abundant, with the faith and love which are found in Christ Jesus" (1 Tim. 1:14). We will know above all else that every mercy God showers on us is solely from His love and kindness.

Ask YOURSELF

Remember these seven signposts that point inward to a growing humility. Write them briefly in an appointment calendar or notebook so you can return to them at a later point in time to see how you're coming along. Humility is worth striving for with that kind of purpose.

What Did Jesus Mean by Mourning?

Blessed are those who mourn, for they shall be comforted.

MATT. 5:4

*I*F YOU HAVE SPIRITUAL POVERTY and true humility, they will lead you to godly sorrow. That's what Jesus meant by "mourn" here in this second beatitude. Paul told the Corinthians about this kind of sorrow: "For the sorrow that is according to the will of God produces a repentance without regret, leading to salvation, but the sorrow of the world produces death. For behold what earnestness this very thing, this godly sorrow, has produced in you" (2 Cor. 7:10–11).

Of the nine different New Testament words that indicate the commonness of human sorrow, the one Matthew used here is the most severe. Usually it was used only to denote the grieving over the death of a loved one (cf. Mark 16:10; Rev. 18:11, 15). It conveys the notion of deep, inner agony that is not necessarily expressed by outward weeping or wailing.

Yet genuine, biblical mourning produces results that are surprisingly wonderful because God does something tangible in response to it—the forgiveness of your sins—a holy infusion of real happiness that breathes into you a sigh of relief.

Therefore, this is not simply a psychological or an emotional experience that makes you feel better. No, this mourning is met by blessedness. Genuine spiritual mourning invites communion with the true God, to which He responds with an objective reality—the reality of forgiveness that David knew: "How blessed is he whose transgression is forgiven, whose sin is covered! How blessed is the man to whom the Lord does not impute iniquity, and in whose spirit there is no deceit!" (Ps. 32:1–2).

Ask YOURSELF

When was the last time the gravity of your sins fell around you, burying you under its full weight? If it's been awhile, you're missing out on the sweet awareness of God's forgiveness.

True Happiness vs. Worldly Happiness

Blessed are those who mourn, for they shall be comforted.

MATT. 5:4

*T*HE WORLD STILL OPERATES ACCORDING to the old popular song lyrics that say, "Pack up your troubles in your old kit bag, and smile, smile, smile." This philosophy basically tells us to hide all our problems and pretend to be happy; and of course people apply this outlook to sin all the time.

Nevertheless Jesus says, "Blessed are those who mourn." Godly mourning and confession of sins bring the only kind of happiness worth having—godly happiness that no amount of human effort, optimistic pretense, or positive thinking can produce.

There is a real need in today's church to cry instead of laugh. The foolishness, frivolity, and embracing of the world's view of happiness in the name of Christianity should make us mourn, because we know the difference between empty happiness and true happiness. God's rebuke to the self-satisfied and indulgent happy is strong: "Draw near to God and He will draw near to you. Cleanse your hands, you sinners; and purify your hearts, you double-minded. Be miserable and mourn and weep; let your laughter be turned into mourning and your joy to gloom. Humble yourselves in the presence of the Lord, and He will exalt you" (James 4:8–10).

True happiness does not ignore sin or make light of it; instead it sorrows over sin, turns from it, and flees to God for genuine forgiveness. And in so doing, it finds lasting joy.

Ask YOURSELF

Does this message sound depressing and cheerless to you? Have you bought the world's line that happiness can be found only by ignoring sin, not by dealing with it? Aren't you tired, though, of constantly coming up empty, never quite satisfied? Run weeping into the welcoming arms of God's forgiveness.

THE RESULT OF GODLY MOURNING

Blessed are those who mourn, for they shall be comforted.

MATT. 5:4

*T*HE POSITIVE RESULT FOR those who mourn is very clear: "they shall be comforted." God reserves the blessing of His comfort exclusively for the contrite of heart. Those of us who mourn over sin will have our tears wiped away by Jesus' loving hand.

The Old Testament similarly speaks of God's comfort for the true spiritual mourners. Isaiah said that Messiah would come "to comfort all who mourn, to grant those who mourn in Zion, giving them a garland instead of ashes, the oil of gladness instead of mourning" (Isa. 61:2–3; cf. Ps. 23:4).

In one sense, this "comfort" will be realized only when we meet our Messiah face-to-face. In heaven the Lord "will wipe away every tear from [our] eyes; and there will no longer be any death; there will no longer be any mourning, or crying, or pain" (Rev. 21:4). Even the most discontented Christian is assured that eternal comfort awaits God's children in glory.

But God is also the God of present comfort. As we continually mourn over sin, He will continually comfort us. The Scripture declares that "God our Father" has already "given us eternal comfort and good hope by grace" (2 Thess. 2:16; cf. Rom. 15:4; 2 Cor. 1:3). May we walk, therefore, in the light and joy of His blessed comfort, even on this side of its heavenly fulfillment.

Ask YOURSELF

Have you given up hope of finding comfort in your here and now? The promise of God's comfort can be yours to claim as you grieve over sin and surrender your heart to holiness. You needn't wait to feel relief. It's as near as your next humble prayer.

HINDRANCES TO TRUE MOURNING: LOVE OF SIN

Blessed are those who mourn, for they shall be comforted.

MATT. 5:4

A GENERAL LOVE OF SIN IS the greatest hindrance to true spiritual mourning, because holding on to sins causes our hearts to harden.

One of the less advertised but more common sins is the sin of *despair*, which is essentially the same as giving up on God and putting ourselves outside His grace— refusing to believe He can save or help us. The prophet Jeremiah wrote this of such people: "But they will say, 'It's hopeless! For we are going to follow our own plans, and each of us will act according to the stubbornness of his evil heart'" (Jer. 18:12). Despair attempts to hide God's mercy behind our self-made cloud of doubt.

Another hindrance to mourning is the sin of *conceit*. It seeks to hide the sin itself and tell us we really have nothing to mourn about. Conceit is analogous to a physician treating cancer as if it were just a common cold. If Christ had to shed His blood on the cross for our sin, then sin must be significant and something over which we must mourn.

To be a true mourner, it's imperative that you remove all basic, sinful hindrances that keep you from mourning. Otherwise you will grieve the Holy Spirit, question the truth of His Word, and restrict His grace from plowing up your hard heart and leading you to obey Him.

Ask YOURSELF

It's time to get honest about your sins today, identifying and confessing anything that stands between you and free-flowing fellowship with your Lord and Savior. Is it despair? Conceit? Whatever it is, you probably know it well. Repent of it all. And walk again in the beauty and freedom of holiness.

HINDRANCES TO TRUE MOURNING: PRESUMPTION AND PROCRASTINATION

Blessed are those who mourn, for they shall be comforted.

MATT. 5:4

*W*E TALKED YESTERDAY ABOUT two specific sins that hinder biblical mourning. Let's consider two others today. The sin of *presumption* is actually a form of pride. Presumption is satisfied with cheap grace and expects God to forgive just a little bit because it sees so little to be forgiven. It leads us to think our sins are not really bad enough for us to confess them, repent of them, and forsake them. But Isaiah exhorts sinners as follows: "Let the wicked forsake his way and the unrighteous man his thoughts; and let him return to the Lord, and He will have compassion on him, and to our God, for He will abundantly pardon" (Isa. 55:7). The kind of gospel (so popular today) that omits any need for repentance and mourning is a false, unscriptural gospel—or as Paul calls it, "a different gospel" (Gal. 1:6).

Procrastination, as the term suggests, hinders true mourning simply by putting it off. We tend to think when things are better and the time is more convenient, we will ask God to cleanse and forgive our sins. But that is foolish and risky because "you do not know what your life will be like tomorrow. You are just a vapor that appears for a little while and then vanishes away" (James 4:14). If we do not deal with sin sooner rather than later, we can't be sure God's comfort will ever come.

The best and surest way to eliminate hindrances to mourning is to look, through prayer and the Word, to the holiness of God and Christ's great atoning sacrifice for sins.

Ask YOURSELF

Unlike some of our sins, these tend to be more subtle and soft-pedaled. But sins of all kinds are capable of blinding us to our utter dependence on God and His forgiveness. Ask Him to reveal to you any hidden sins, wanting to bring to the surface everything that dishonors Him.

ARE YOU MOURNING AS CHRIST COMMANDS?

Blessed are those who mourn, for they shall be comforted.

MATT. 5:4

*T*WO CRUCIAL DETERMINANTS WILL tell you if you are mourning over sin as Jesus commands. First, you will have true sensitivity to and sorrow for your sins. Your primary concern will be how your sin detracts from God's glory, not how its exposure might embarrass you or hurt your reputation.

The mock piety of hypocrites demonstrates no sensitivity to sin, only to their personal prestige and pride (cf. Matt. 6:1–18). Likewise, the mock gratitude of those like the Pharisees who think they are better than others (cf. Luke 18:11) certainly does not show mourning for sin. King Saul twice admitted he had sinned when he did not destroy King Agag and all the Amalekites, and even asked Samuel for pardon, but he was more concerned for his own honor than God's (1 Sam. 15:10–35).

If your mourning is godly, you will lament the sins of other believers and the world, as well as your own. You will agree with the psalmist, "My eyes shed streams of water, because they do not keep Your law" (Ps. 119:136). You will weep over your community, as Jesus did over His (Luke 19:41).

The *second way* to know if you are mourning rightly is to check your sense of God's forgiveness. Have you experienced the sense of spiritual freedom and real release that comes with knowing your sins are forgiven? Can you point to true happiness, peace, and joy in your life that only God gives in response to mourning for sin (cf. Ps. 126:5–6)?

Ask YOURSELF

What is your main problem with sin—only that it gives you that sick feeling of guilt and hypocrisy? Only that it seems to expose you around those who know you best? Take all the personal inconveniences out of the equation, and be more gravely concerned that your sin offends the God you profess to serve.

GENTLENESS AS DEFINED BY JESUS

Blessed are the gentle, for they shall inherit the earth.

MATT. 5:5

*I*N THIS VERSE, "GENTLE" (a word often rendered "meek" in other translations) means mild or soft. Looking ahead to His triumphal entry, the prophet hailed
Christ this way: "Behold your King is coming to you, gentle, and mounted on a don-
key" (Matt. 21:5; cf. Zech. 9:9).

From Old Testament times, gentleness has been God's way for mankind. The
book of Job says God "sets on high those who are lowly, and those who mourn are
lifted to safety" (5:11; cf. Ps. 25:9). "Moses was very humble, more than any man who
was on the face of the earth" (Num. 12:3).

Gentleness does not connote weakness, but rather a way of utilizing all its resources and emotions appropriately (cf. Prov. 16:32; 25:28). The gentle person has
died to self and therefore does not resort to violence to defend himself, knowing his
person has nothing to commend before God. Gentleness is not cowardice, lack of
conviction, or niceness. It is the spirit of Christ, who defended the Father's glory,
not His own, and left us an example: He "committed no sin, nor was any deceit found
in His mouth; and while being reviled, He did not revile in return; while suffering,
He uttered no threats, but kept entrusting Himself to Him who judges righteously"
(1 Peter 2:22–23).

Christ's gentleness, however, did not mean He was passive in defending righteousness. He guarded the temple against the moneychangers (John 2:14–15), denounced the hypocritical religious leaders (Matt. 23:1–33), and warned the
disobedient of judgment (Matt. 25:45–46). His gentleness was power completely surrendered to God's control.

Ask YOURSELF

What's been your interpretation of "meekness" or "gentleness"? Is this a quality
you value and aspire to? If gentleness was more a part of your demeanor, what benefits would you begin to see in your daily life?

THE RESULT OF GENTLENESS

Blessed are the gentle, for they shall inherit the earth.

MATT. 5:5

*G*OD REWARDS THE GENTLE WITH His own joy and gladness. But more specifically, He allows such saints to "inherit the earth." In the future the Father will completely reclaim earth, and believers will rule it with Him. Because only believers are truly gentle, Jesus could confidently proclaim "they shall inherit the earth."

"Inherit" denotes the receiving of one's allotted portion and correlates perfectly with Psalm 37:11—"the humble will inherit the land." We sometimes wonder why the godless seem to prosper while the godly suffer, but God assures us that He will ultimately make things right (cf. Ps. 37:10). We must trust the Lord and obey His will in these matters. He will settle everything in the right way at the right time. Meanwhile, we can trust His promise that we, as those who are gentle, will inherit the earth. This promise also reminds us that our place in Christ's kingdom is forever secure (cf. 1 Cor. 3:21–23).

The promise of a future inheritance also gives us hope and happiness for the present. More than a century ago George MacDonald wrote, "We cannot see the world as God means it in the future, save as our souls are characterized by meekness. In meekness we are its only inheritors. Meekness alone makes the spiritual retina pure to receive God's things as they are, mingling with them neither imperfection nor impurity."

Ask YOURSELF

Yes, it often seems as though *everyone* "inherits the earth" but us mild-mannered believers. But what truly makes life enjoyable on the earth? And why do the curt and the coarsest among us not really get to experience its simple pleasures?

WHY GENTLENESS IS NECESSARY

Blessed are the gentle, for they shall inherit the earth.

MATT. 5:5

*F*OUR BASIC REASONS PROVE the necessity for people to demonstrate Jesus' trait of gentleness. *First,* genuine spiritual gentleness is necessary for salvation. Jesus later instructed His listeners that "unless you are converted and become like children, you will not enter the kingdom of heaven" (Matt. 18:3; cf. Ps. 149:4).

Second, gentleness is necessary because God commands it. James exhorts his readers, "Putting aside all filthiness and all that remains of wickedness, in humility receive the word implanted, which is able to save your souls" (James 1:21). Centuries earlier, the prophets agreed with James's concern (e.g., Zeph. 2:3), knowing that without a gentle, humble spirit we can't even hear God's Word correctly, much less grasp and apply it.

Third, gentleness is a necessity for effective witnessing. Peter tells us, "Sanctify Christ as Lord in your hearts, always being ready to make a defense to everyone who asks you to give an account for the hope that is in you, yet with gentleness and reverence" (1 Peter 3:15). Pride will always be a barrier between us and those we talk to.

Lastly, gentleness is necessary because it always glorifies God. Pride wants its own glory, but gentleness wants God's. Gentleness in relation to fellow believers especially glorifies Him: "Now may the God who gives perseverance and encouragement grant you to be of the same mind with one another according to Christ Jesus, so that with one accord you may with one voice glorify the God and Father of our Lord Jesus Christ" (Rom. 15:5–6).

*Ask*YOURSELF

Oh, what we lose by not choosing a life of gentleness, by not letting the Lord grow in us what (for some) is perhaps the most unnatural of His character traits. What temptations work the hardest against your desire to personify the meekness of Christ?

THE MEANING AND NECESSITY OF SPIRITUAL HUNGER

Blessed are those who hunger and thirst for righteousness, for they shall be satisfied.

MATT. 5:6

THE "HUNGER AND THIRST" Jesus speaks of here are far more intense than even strong physical pangs for food and drink, which come when we miss several meals. All true followers of Christ have a continuing hunger and thirst for righteousness—they will regularly long for holiness. Jesus' analogy shows us that righteousness is necessary for spiritual life just as food and water are necessary for physical life.

But sadly, most people are by nature starved for spiritual life. The tendency of such unbelievers is to turn toward their physical appetites and the world's ways rather than toward spiritual life (cf. Prov. 26:11; 2 Peter 2:22). Apart from divine revelation and the Spirit's promptings, these people don't recognize their spiritual needs or know what will truly satisfy them.

Seeking satisfaction for our spiritual hunger only in God and His gracious provision identifies us as members of His kingdom. Such people sincerely want their sin to be replaced with virtue and their disobedience with obedience.

The first three beatitudes are essentially negative and require costly and painful personal sacrifice to accomplish, even with the help of God's Spirit. This fourth one, however, is more positive, coming about when we possess the other three. When we have put aside self and our enslavement to sin and turned to the Lord, we will have a genuine, growing desire for righteousness. The true Christian desires to obey God, even though he or she still struggles with unredeemed humanness (cf. Rom. 8:23).

Ask YOURSELF

What spiritual hungers are growling the loudest in your heart right now? When you have sought to satisfy them in disobedience or in any way other than God intends, what has always been the result? How do you intend to see them fed now?

SPIRITUAL HUNGER'S FIRST OBJECT—SALVATION

Blessed are those who hunger and thirst for righteousness, for they shall be satisfied.

MATT. 5:6

*T*HE FIRST OBJECTIVE OF spiritual hunger by the lost sinner is salvation. The righteousness the unbeliever begins to hunger for—after he or she sees their sin, mourns over it, and gently submits self to God—is the righteousness that repents of sin and submits to the lordship of Christ.

In the Old Testament, righteousness is often a synonym for salvation. Through Isaiah, God declared, "My righteousness is near, My salvation has gone forth" (Isa. 51:5). Daniel said, "Those who have insight will shine brightly like the brightness of the expanse of heaven, and those who lead the many to righteousness, like the stars forever and ever" (Dan. 12:3).

In Jesus' day, the great obstacle to receiving the gospel for so many members of His Jewish audience was self-righteousness—their confidence in their own works to achieve a self-styled holiness. They believed that as members of God's chosen nation of Israel, they were assured of entrance into heaven. But Christ taught them that they would not find the path to salvation unless they hungered and thirsted for the Father's righteousness instead of their own. And that is the case for everyone today, no matter what race, religion, or economic status.

Ask YOURSELF

It's easy for the wonder and majesty of our salvation to be lost on us as time goes by. Let today be another opportunity to realize how empty you were before and how full He has made you in Christ. Put your worship into prayerful words.

SPIRITUAL HUNGER'S SECOND OBJECT—SANCTIFICATION

Blessed are those who hunger and thirst for righteousness, for they shall be satisfied.

MATT. 5:6

*F*OR THE CHRISTIAN, the object of hungering and thirsting is growth in sanctification, which is a crucial mark of the genuine believer. No one who follows Christ attains complete sanctification until heaven, and to claim otherwise would be the height of presumption. Thus saints in this life always need to strive for more holiness, which will be seen in their lives through obedience to the Word. Paul prayed that the Philippian believers might "abound still more and more in real knowledge and all discernment, so that [they] may approve the things that are excellent, in order to be sincere and blameless until the day of Christ" (Phil. 1:9–10).

The Greek grammar Matthew used in quoting Jesus indicates that righteousness is the unqualified and unlimited object of "hunger and thirst." Our Lord is describing people who earnestly desire all the righteousness there is (cf. Matt. 5:48; 1 Peter 1:15–16).

In the original text the definite article appears before "righteousness," which means that Jesus is not speaking of just *any* general righteousness, but *the* righteousness—the true one that comes from God. In fact, it is the Father's very own righteousness that the Son also possesses.

Because we as believers cannot possibly have our longing for godliness satisfied during our earthly lives, we must continually hunger and thirst until the glorious day when we receive the complete clothing of Jesus Christ's righteousness.

Ask YOURSELF

Not on Sunday morning but on Tuesday afternoon, on Thursday morning, on Friday night in front of the television—are you hungering for "all the righteousness there is"? Does the call of Christ's holiness register at off times of day?

SATISFYING YOUR SPIRITUAL HUNGER

Blessed are those who hunger and thirst for righteousness, for they shall be satisfied.

MATT. 5:6

*T*HE ALL-IMPORTANT RESULT for any believer hungering and thirsting after righteousness is to "be satisfied." The verb translated "satisfied" frequently refers to the feeding of animals until they want no more. In a parallel to this, Jesus declares that people who hunger and thirst for righteousness will gain complete satisfaction. This satisfaction comes from God. Our part is to seek; His is to satisfy us.

Paradoxically, Christians continually seek God's righteousness, always wanting more and never getting their fill in this life. Yet the Lord still satisfies them. Again, we can make the analogy to food. We can eat our fill of our favorite dishes, yet our taste for those foods remains. The satisfaction we derive only makes us want more. Believers who crave God's righteousness will find it so satisfying that they will always want more.

Psalms speaks repeatedly about God's satisfying our spiritual hunger. The most well-known psalm opens, "The Lord is my shepherd, I shall not want," and later says, "You prepare a table before me … my cup overflows" (23:1, 5). A later psalm assures us that God "has satisfied the thirsty soul, and the hungry soul He has filled with what is good" (Ps. 107:9; cf. 34:10).

Jesus on another occasion told the crowds, many of whom were among the five thousand fed, "I am the bread of life; he who comes to Me will not hunger, and he who believes in Me will never thirst" (John 6:35). Our spiritual hunger will always be satisfied (cf. John 4:14).

Ask YOURSELF

It may not happen all at once, but Jesus will always reward your hunger for righteousness with the deep satisfaction reserved for the humbly obedient. How has He satisfied you in the past? Think of a time when you and He celebrated what sanctification was accomplishing in you.

JESUS' DEFINITION OF MERCY

Blessed are the merciful, for they shall receive mercy.
MATT. 5:7

*J*ESUS HERE IS NOT TEACHING that being merciful to others merely results in their being merciful to us, but that showing mercy to people brings mercy to us from God. As with the other beatitudes, God blesses those who obey His commands.

"Merciful" derives from the word meaning beneficial or charitable. Christ is our perfect example of mercy and the supreme dispenser of it as our "merciful and faithful high priest" (Heb. 2:17). In the Old Testament the idea has the meanings of love, lovingkindness, and steadfast love (cf. Pss. 17:7; 51:1; Isa. 63:7; Jer. 9:24), and denotes helping the afflicted and rescuing the helpless. It is compassion in action.

So for Jesus, mercy is not a detached, powerless sentiment that merely sympathizes with but is unable or unwilling to provide tangible help for the needy. Our Lord also is in no way endorsing a pretend mercy that gives help only to ease a guilty conscience or impress others with phony virtue. Mercy is genuine compassion expressed in genuine help—and its motives are completely selfless.

Mercy means giving food to the starving, comfort to the bereaved, love to the unloved, forgiveness to the wrongdoer, and friendship to the friendless. Mercy is thus one of the finest and most decent of all Christian virtues.

Ask YOURSELF

How have you received mercy from another person in your various dealings? What did it cost them? What did it mean to you? What is an example of mercy that *you* could extend to another, perhaps even in the coming day?

MERCY COMPARED TO FORGIVENESS, LOVE, AND GRACE

Blessed are the merciful, for they shall receive mercy.

MATT. 5:7

*T*O UNDERSTAND THE SIGNIFICANCE of mercy, let's compare it to three amazing attributes of God. First, mercy has much in common with forgiveness, although it is distinct from it. God's forgiveness of our sins flows from His mercy. But mercy is greater than forgiveness, because God is merciful to us even when we do not sin, just as we can be merciful to those who have never done anything against us. God's mercy does not just forgive our transgressions but reaches to all our weaknesses and needs.

Just as forgiveness flows out of mercy, mercy flows out of love: "But God, being rich in mercy, because of His great love with which He loved us, even when we were dead in our transgressions, made us alive together with Christ" (Eph. 2:4–5). Love is greater than mercy—it can manifest itself even when there is no wrong to forgive or need to meet.

Finally, mercy is also related to grace, which flows out of love. Grace and mercy have the closest possible relationship, yet they are different. Mercy deals with the consequences of sin, while grace deals with sin itself. Mercy offers relief from punishment; grace offers pardon for the crime.

Just look at what the Good Samaritan did. When he found a Jewish traveler who had been robbed and beaten, he held no animosity toward him. Love motivated him to show the man mercy when he bound up his wounds. And when he took him to an inn and cared for him, he showed grace. Such is the expression of mercy working with forgiveness, love, and grace.

Ask YOURSELF

Is there someone to whom you need to show God's mercy, expressed through your love, your grace, your forgiveness? Think of how you can turn your merciful intentions into practical action.

MERCY AND JUSTICE

Blessed are the merciful, for they shall receive mercy.

MATT. 5:7

*T*HE RELATIONSHIP OF MERCY and justice is a confusing one because on the surface they seem the exact opposite. Justice gives exactly what is deserved; mercy gives less punishment and more help than is deserved. So the great question is: How can God be both just and merciful at the same time? The truth is God does not show mercy without punishing sin. For Him to offer mercy without punishment would negate His justice.

Mercy that ignores sin is false mercy and is all too common today. Some think it is unloving and unkind to hold people responsible for their sins. That is what is known as cheap grace—which is neither merciful *nor* just, nor does it offer punishment or pardon for sin. Because it overlooks sin, it leaves sin untouched and unforgiven. The one who relies on this sort of mercy is left in his sin.

The good news of the gospel, however, is that Christ paid the penalty for all sins so that God might be merciful to all sinners. On the cross Jesus satisfied God's justice. And when a person trusts in His sacrifice, God opens the floodgates of His mercy. God did not gloss over sin and compromise justice. The good news is that in the shedding of Christ's blood, He satisfied His justice, forgave sin, fulfilled righteousness, and made His mercy available. There is never an excuse for sin, but there is always a remedy.

Ask YOURSELF

What is true of God's mercy should be true of ours. Rather than simply letting people get away with abuse, mistreatment, or destructive habits, we must realize that for mercy to truly be merciful, it must lead others toward health and holiness. Mercy is tougher than we think. How then might it look in practice?

GOD THE SOURCE OF MERCY

Blessed are the merciful, for they shall receive mercy.

MATT. 5:7

*P*URE MERCY IS A GIFT of God that comes with the new birth. People can be merciful only when they have experienced God's mercy.

God has both absolute and relative attributes. His absolute attributes—such as love, truth, and holiness—have characterized Him from all eternity. But His relative attributes—like mercy, justice, and grace—were not manifested until man, whom He created in His own image, sinned and became separated from his Creator. Apart from sin and evil, mercy, justice, and grace have no meaning.

When man fell, God extended His love to His fallen creatures in mercy. Only when they receive His mercy can they reflect His mercy. Thus God is the source of mercy. "For as high as the heavens are above the earth, so great is His lovingkindness [mercy] toward those who fear Him" (Psalm 103:11). It is because we have the resource of God's mercy that Jesus commanded, "Be merciful, just as your Father is merciful" (Luke 6:36).

We cannot have the blessing apart from the Blesser. We cannot even meet the condition apart from the One who set the condition. We are blessed by God when we are merciful to others, and we are able to be merciful to others because we have already received salvation's mercy. Furthermore, when we share the mercy we have received, we will receive even more mercy.

Ask YOURSELF

When we talk about Christ's character being formed in us, we understand the concept in theory. But what are some of the telltale signs that He is actually working His will through us in our interactions with others? How do you know when it's Him, not you—when it's the Spirit of God bearing fruit in your life?

PRACTICING MERCY

Blessed are the merciful, for they shall receive mercy.

MATT. 5:7

*T*HE MOST OBVIOUS WAY we can show mercy is through physical acts. Jesus specifically commands us to feed the hungry, clothe the naked, visit the sick and imprisoned, and offer any other practical help to those who need it. When we serve others in need, we demonstrate a heart of mercy.

The way of mercy did not begin in the New Testament. The Old Testament law taught, "You shall not harden your heart, nor close your hand from your poor brother; but you shall freely open your hand to him, and shall generously lend him sufficient for his need in whatever he lacks" (Deut. 15:7–8).

Mercy is also to be shown in our attitudes. Mercy does not hold a grudge, harbor resentment, capitalize on another's failure or weakness, or publicize another's sin.

Mercy is also to be shown spiritually. *First*, it is shown through pity. The sensitive Christian will grieve more for lost souls than for lost bodies. *Second*, we are to show spiritual mercy by confrontation. Paul says that, as Christ's servants, we should gently correct "those who are in opposition, if perhaps God may grant them repentance leading to the knowledge of the truth" (2 Tim. 2:25). *Third*, we are to show spiritual mercy by praying. The sacrifice of prayer for those without God is an act of mercy. *Finally*, we are to show mercy by proclaiming the saving gospel of Jesus Christ. That is the most merciful thing we can do.

Ask YOURSELF

How has your life been transformed by being the blessed recipient of these various acts and expressions of mercy? What might occur in the lives of your children, your spouse, your parents, your friends—anyone to whom you begin to show consistent compassion?

WHAT RESULTS FROM MERCY?

Blessed are the merciful, for they shall receive mercy.

MATT. 5:7

*W*HEN WE ARE MERCIFUL and we receive mercy, we experience God's cycle of mercy. God is merciful to us by saving us through Christ; in obedience we are merciful to others; and God in faithfulness gives us even more mercy, pouring out blessing for our needs and withholding severe chastening for our sin.

But only those who are merciful qualify to receive mercy. David said of the Lord, "With the kind You show Yourself kind" (2 Sam. 22:26). Yet James says, "For judgment will be merciless to one who has shown no mercy" (James 2:13). The emphatic truth is that God will respond with chastening for an unforgiving disciple.

Jesus is not speaking, however, of our mercy gaining us salvation. We cannot earn salvation by being merciful. We must be saved by God's mercy before we can truly be merciful. We cannot work our way into heaven even by a lifetime of merciful deeds, any more than by good works of any sort. God does not give mercy for merit; He gives mercy in grace. He gives mercy because it is needed, not because it is earned.

If we have received from a holy God unlimited mercy that cancels our unpayable debt of sin, it surely follows that we should be merciful to others.

Ask YOURSELF

At several points along the way, we've paused to celebrate the immensity of our salvation. Here at the end of our look at mercy, let's drop to our knees again in awe and thanksgiving, realizing the depths He has pulled us from and imagining the glories that await us—all because of His grace and love through Christ.

SIGNIFICANCE OF THE HEART

Blessed are the pure in heart, for they shall see God.
MATT. 5:8

*T*HROUGHOUT SCRIPTURE the heart is used metaphorically to represent the inner person, the seat of motives and attitudes, the center of personality. But in Scripture it also includes the thinking process, particularly the will. Proverbs 23:7 says, "As [a man] thinketh in his heart, so is he" (KJV). The heart is the control center of the mind and will, as well as emotion.

Jesus said that it is in the inner person, in the core of our very being, that God requires purity. This was not a new truth but an old one long forgotten in ceremony and tradition. "Watch over your heart with all diligence, for from it flow the springs of life," counseled the writer of Proverbs 4:23.

God has always been concerned above all else with the condition of a person's heart. When the Lord called Saul to be Israel's first king, "God changed his heart" (1 Sam. 10:9). Until then Saul had been handsome and athletic, but not much more. Soon the new king began to revert to his old heart patterns. He refused to live by the new heart God had given him.

Consequently, the Lord took the kingdom from Saul and gave it to David because David was "a man after [God's] own heart" (1 Sam. 13:14). David's deepest desire was, "Let the words of my mouth and the meditation of my heart be acceptable in Your sight, O Lord, my rock and my Redeemer" (Ps. 19:14). May that be your desire as well.

Ask YOURSELF

What are some things you've learned about your heart over the years? What motivates it to action? How trustworthy is it? Where does it usually like to lead you? When do its passions most vividly fire into flame? How inclined is it to purity?

PURITY IS MORE THAN SINCERITY

Blessed are the pure in heart, for they shall see God.

MATT. 5:8

*P*URITY OF HEART IS MUCH MORE than sincerity. A motive can be sincere yet can easily lead to worthless and sinful things. The pagan priests who opposed Elijah demonstrated great sincerity when they lacerated their bodies to induce Baal to send fire down to consume their sacrifices (1 Kings 18:28). But their sincerity did not produce the desired results, and it did not enable them to see the error of their paganism because their sincere trust was in that very paganism.

Even genuinely good deeds that do not come from a genuinely good heart are of no spiritual value. A person may be extremely religious and constantly engaged in doing good things, yet he or she cannot please God unless their heart is right with Him.

The ultimate standard for purity of heart is perfection of heart. Later in the Sermon on the Mount, Jesus said, "Therefore you are to be perfect, as your heavenly Father is perfect" (Matt. 5:48). One hundred percent purity is God's standard for the heart, which makes God Himself the standard.

You can't be pleasing to God until you are pure as He is pure—until you are holy as He is holy and perfect as He is perfect. Only purity of heart through Jesus Christ will reconcile people to God. What standard of purity are you following?

Ask YOURSELF

To what extent is your measure of purity defined by culture or others' opinions or anything other than the Word of God and the testimony of Jesus Christ? Check yourself in this, for if staying a few shades cleaner than current society makes you feel pure by comparison, your standards will do nothing but slip over time.

THE WAY TO HOLINESS

Blessed are the pure in heart, for they shall see God.

MATT. 5:8

*T*HROUGHOUT THE HISTORY of the church, many have thought the best way to achieve spiritual purity and holiness is by living apart from the normal cares and distractions of the world and devoting oneself entirely to meditation and prayer. The problem with sin, however, is not primarily the world around us but the worldliness within us, which we cannot escape by living in isolation from other people.

But God always provides for what He demands, and He has provided ways for us to live purely. *First*, we must realize that we are unable to live a single holy moment without the Lord's guidance and power. "Who can say, 'I have cleansed my heart, I am pure from my sin'?" (Prov. 20:9). The obvious answer is, "No one." Cleansing begins with recognition of weakness, which in turn reaches out for the strength of God.

Second, we must stay in God's Word. It is impossible to stay in God's will apart from His Word. Jesus said, "You are already clean because of the word which I have spoken to you" (John 15:3).

Third, it is essential to be controlled by and walking in the will and way of the Holy Spirit. Galatians 5:16 says, "Walk by the Spirit, and you will not carry out the desire of the flesh."

Fourth, we must pray. We cannot stay in God's will or understand and obey His Word unless we stay near Him. With David we cry, "Create in me a clean heart, O God" (Ps. 51:10).

Begin to pursue the right ways to develop holiness in your life.

Ask YOURSELF

How is impurity showing itself most visibly in your heart—or perhaps disguising itself most subtly? Realize afresh that holy living is impossible outside of a living, active relationship with Christ and the ongoing enablement of the Holy Spirit. Commit yourself to surrendering all to follow Him in righteousness.

RESULTS OF OBTAINING HOLINESS

Blessed are the pure in heart, for they shall see God.

MATT. 5:8

*T*HE GREAT BLESSING OF THOSE who are pure in heart is "they shall see God." Notice that it is only "they"—the pure in heart—who shall see God. Intimate knowledge of and fellowship with God is reserved for the pure.

When our hearts are purified at salvation, we begin to live in the presence of God. We begin to see and comprehend Him with our new spiritual eyes. Like Moses, who saw God's glory and asked to see more (Ex. 33:18), the one who is purified by Jesus Christ sees again and again the glory of God.

To see God was the greatest hope of the Old Testament saints. Like Moses, David wanted to see more of God: "As the deer pants for the water brooks, so my soul pants for You, O God. My soul thirsts for God, for the living God; when shall I come and appear before God?" (Ps. 42:1–2).

Purity of heart cleanses the eyes of the soul so that God becomes visible. One sign of an impure heart is ignorance, because sin obscures the truth (John 3:19–20). Other signs of an impure heart are self-centeredness (Rev. 3:17), pleasure in sin (2 Tim. 3:4), unbelief (Heb. 3:12), and hatred for purity (Mic. 3:2). But if you belong to God, you will exchange all of those things for integrity and purity.

*Ask*YOURSELF

How have you "seen" God during long stretches of faithful, obedient living? If this is not your current experience, don't you long to return to this kind of lifestyle— to the daily joys of animated, refreshing, ongoing interaction with your Lord and Savior? Take steps toward a fresh start with Him today.

JESUS' DEFINITION OF PEACE

Blessed are the peacemakers, for they shall be called sons of God.
MATT. 5:9

ONE OF THE MOST OBVIOUS facts of world history is that peace does not characterize man's earthly existence. Yet two thousand years ago Jesus instructed God's people to be peacemakers. He gave us a special mission to help restore the peace lost at the Fall.

The peace of which Christ speaks is unlike anything the world knows or strives for. His peace is not concerned with resolving conflict between governments and nations, with righting the wrongs of human oppression. His peace is the inner, personal peace that only He can give to the soul of man, a peace that only His children can emulate.

What makes Jesus' kind of peace different? Instead of focusing on the absence of conflict and strife, Jesus' peace produces righteousness, for only righteousness can bring two antagonistic parties together. It is what brings the unsaved person to God. It is God who reconciles a person to Himself, imputes Christ's righteousness to him, and makes peace with him or her.

Only righteousness can usher in harmony and true well-being. James confirms the nature of God's peace when he writes, "But the wisdom from above is first pure, then peaceable" (James 3:17). Peace cannot be divorced from holiness. "Righteousness and peace have kissed each other" is the beautiful expression of Psalm 85:10. Where there is true peace, there is righteousness, holiness, and purity. May those things characterize you as you strive to be a peacemaker.

Ask YOURSELF

What situations in your own life are in desperate need of peace and restoration? How do you think God wants to use you as a peacemaker in the midst of it? You've surely tried. You've wanted to see righteousness and justice returned. Pray that the Lord would show you how to exhibit His brand of peace in fresh, new ways.

MARCH 11

The Great Enemy of Peace

Blessed are the peacemakers, for they shall be called sons of God.

MATT. 5:9

THE GREAT ENEMY of peace is sin. Sin separates people from God and causes disharmony and enmity with Him. To talk of peace without establishing the need for repentance from sin is foolish. The corrupt religious leaders of ancient Israel proclaimed, "Peace, peace," but there was no peace, because they and the rest of the people were not "ashamed because of the abomination they had done" (Jer. 8:11–12).

To be an effective peacemaker, you must recognize that any conflict is the result of sin. If you separate conflicting parties from each other but don't confront their sin, at best you will create only a temporary truce. You can't circumvent sin; it is the source of every conflict.

In what appears on the surface to be the antithesis of the seventh beatitude, Jesus says, "Do not think that I came to bring peace on the earth; I did not come to bring peace, but a sword" (Matt. 10:34). His meaning is clear: the peace He brings is not peace at any price. The sword Christ uses is His Word—the sword of truth and righteousness. Like the surgeon's scalpel, it must cut before it heals, because peace cannot exist where sin remains.

To be a peacemaker you must live a holy life and call others to embrace the gospel of holiness.

Ask YOURSELF

How have you seen sin decimate and destroy relationships? How has your own sin contributed to whatever strain exists between you and another person? If you have not yet repented of a sin that has caused distance between you and someone else, choose repentance today. If others need correction, ask for the Lord's grace and supply in seeking it.

PEACE: ITS ULTIMATE SOURCE AND MANIFESTATION

Blessed are the peacemakers, for they shall be called sons of God.

MATT. 5:9

*T*HE APOSTLE PAUL WROTE to the Ephesians, "But now in Christ Jesus you who formerly were far off have been brought near by the blood of Christ. For He Himself is our peace" (2:13-14). He also told the Colossians, "It was the Father's good pleasure for all the fullness to dwell in Him, and through Him to reconcile all things to Himself, having made peace through the blood of His cross" (1:19–20).

How did the cross bring peace? At the cross all of man's hatred and anger was vented against God. On the cross the Son of God was mocked, cursed, spit on, pierced, reviled, and killed. Jesus' disciples fled in fear, the sky flashed lightning, the earth shook violently, and the veil of the temple was torn in two. Yet through that violence God brought peace. God's greatest righteousness confronted man's greatest wickedness, and righteousness won.

The one who does not belong to God through Jesus Christ can neither have peace nor be a peacemaker. God can work peace *through* us only if He has worked peace *in* us.

As a Christian, you might be enduring great turmoil and strife. But in your deepest being you have peace that passes all understanding (Phil. 4:8). Many live in favorable circumstances, but without God they will never find peace, while those who cling to God in the worst of circumstances need never lack peace.

Ask YOURSELF

This peace that "passes all understanding"—when have you experienced that before? Recall a time when God's peace was every bit as real as the circumstance was dire. The next time you find yourself over your head in strife and conflict, call out for His incomprehensible peace, and expect to receive it.

CHARACTERISTICS OF PEACEMAKERS, PART 1

Blessed are the peacemakers, for they shall be called sons of God.
MATT. 5:9

*T*HE APOSTLE TELLS US THAT "God has called us to peace" (1 Cor. 7:15), that He "reconciled us to Himself through Christ and gave us the ministry of reconciliation" (2 Cor. 5:18). The ministry of reconciliation is peacemaking. Those whom God has called to peace He also calls to make peace.

Today and tomorrow we're going to look at four things that characterize a peacemaker. *First*, he is one who has made peace with God. Before we came to Christ, God was at war with us. Whatever we may have thought consciously about God, our hearts were against Him. But "while we were enemies we were reconciled to God through the death of His Son" (Rom. 5:10). God reconciled us to Himself through the work of Christ on the cross. Our battle with God ended and our peace with Him began. And because we have been given God's peace, we are called to share God's peace with others (Eph. 6:15).

Second, a peacemaker leads others to make peace with God. Christians are a body of sinners cleansed by Jesus Christ and commissioned to carry His gospel to the rest of the world. Once freed from the shackles of sin, a Christian doesn't look down on his fellow sinners; he or she realizes they are beggars who have been fed and are now called to help feed others. Our purpose is to preach "peace through Jesus Christ" (Acts 10:36). To lead a sinner to saving knowledge of Jesus Christ is the most peacemaking act a believer can perform. That's your ministry as an ambassador of Christ.

*Ask*YOURSELF

Have you ever thought about this before—that you are "called" to the ministry of peacemaking? How does that change your responsibilities as you go through the day? How does it affect the obligation you feel when others continue in stirring up discord and disharmony?

CHARACTERISTICS OF PEACEMAKERS, PART 2

Blessed are the peacemakers, for they shall be called sons of God.
MATT. 5:9

*C*ONTINUING FROM YESTERDAY, let's look at two more characteristics of peacemakers.

First, a peacemaker helps others make peace with others. Once you see your duty as a peacemaker in the world, you'll be looking for ways to build bridges between people and God and then to build them between persons.

By definition, a bridge can't be one-sided. It must extend between two sides or it can never function. And once built, it continues to need support on both sides or it will collapse. In any relationship our first responsibility is to see that our own side has a solid base. But we also have the responsibility to help the one on the other side build his base. Both must be built on righteousness and truth or the bridge will not stand.

Often the first step in the process is to confront others about their sin, which is the supreme barrier to peace (Matt. 18:15–17). Such confrontation usually causes turmoil, yet the way of righteousness is the only way to peace. Sin that is not dealt with is sin that will disrupt and destroy peace.

Finally, a peacemaker finds a point of agreement. God's truth and righteousness must never be compromised or weakened. But we are to contend without being contentious, to disagree without being disagreeable, and to confront without being abusive. The peacemaker should speak the truth in love (Eph. 4:15).

When you hunger and thirst for holiness in your own life, you'll have a passionate desire to see those virtues in the lives of others. That's a true peacemaker.

Ask YOURSELF

If the desire for peacemaking is missing from your heart, it points to a deeper problem—that your love for others is not what it should be. Would you say this might be true of you? What are the usual symptoms of a heart that's grown at least somewhat cold toward others?

THE PRIZE OF PEACE—ETERNAL SONSHIP

Blessed are the peacemakers, for they shall be called sons of God.

MATT. 5:9

*T*HE RESULT OF PEACEMAKING is eternal blessing as God's children in God's kingdom. Peacemakers "shall be called sons of God."

Most of you are thankful for your heritage, your ancestors, your parents, and your family name. It is especially gratifying to have been influenced by godly grandparents, parents, or both. But even the greatest human heritage cannot match our heritage in Christ (Rom. 8:17). After all, what could compare to being a child of God?

Peacemaking is a hallmark of God's children. Only God determines who His children are, and He has determined that we are to be humble, penitent over sin, gentle, seekers of righteousness, merciful, pure in heart, and ultimately peacemakers.

As the next beatitude makes abundantly clear, we often don't have peace in the world; we have persecution instead. In Christ we have forsaken the false peace of the world, and consequently we won't find much peace with it. But as God's children we can always have peace within, even while we are in the world—the peace of God, which the world can't give and the world can't take away.

Today begin to live as a peacemaking child of God—it is your calling.

Ask YOURSELF

Review the beatitude summaries mentioned in today's reading—those qualities of life that distinguish the sons and daughters of God from others. Is anything worth keeping you from exemplifying these characteristics? Can anything rival being known as a child of God?

THE NATURE OF PERSECUTION

Blessed are those who have been persecuted for the sake of righteousness, for theirs is the kingdom
of heaven. Blessed are you when people insult you and persecute you, and falsely say all kinds
of evil against you because of Me. Rejoice and be glad, for your reward in heaven is great;
for in the same way they persecuted the prophets who were before you.
MATT. 5:10–12

OUR LORD'S TEACHING ON the beatitudes climaxes with this great and sobering truth: those who faithfully live according to the first seven beatitudes are guaranteed at some point to experience the eighth. Godliness generates hostility and antagonism from the world. Holy people are singularly blessed, but they pay a price for it.

However, persecution is one of the surest and most tangible evidences of salvation. If we never experience ridicule, criticism, or rejection because of our faith, we have reason to examine the genuineness of it. "For to you it has been granted for Christ's sake, not only to believe in Him, but also to suffer for His sake, experiencing the same conflict which you saw in me, and now hear to be in me" (Phil. 1:29–30).

To live a redeemed life to its fullest is to invite and expect resentment and reaction from the world. When Christians are not persecuted in some way by society, it generally means they are reflecting rather than confronting that society. And when we please the world, we can be sure that we grieve the Lord (cf. James 4:4; 1 John 2:15–17). Make sure you are living apart from the world and its allurements.

Ask YOURSELF

How do you experience persecution in your life, perhaps at work, within your family (including parents and in-laws), or among the various people you routinely associate with? How do you typically respond to it—if not directly, at least in the thoughts you entertain?

MARCH 17

The Cost of Discipleship

*Blessed are those who have been persecuted for the sake of
righteousness, for theirs is the kingdom of heaven.*

Matt. 5:10

OUR LORD MADE IT CLEAR from His earliest teaching that following Him was costly. Those who entered His kingdom would suffer for Him before they would reign with Him.

The cost of discipleship is billed to our account in many different ways. A believer today might be expected to hedge on the quality of his work to increase company profits. To follow one's conscience in obedience to the Lord might cost him his job or at least a promotion. A Christian housewife who refuses to listen to gossip or to laugh at the crude jokes of her neighbors may find herself ostracized. Some costs will be great and some will be slight. But by the Lord's and the apostles' repeated promises, faithfulness always has a cost, which true Christians are willing to pay.

In the early days of the church, the price paid was often the ultimate. To choose Christ might mean choosing death by stoning. To choose Christ could mean torture by any number of excessively cruel and painful methods. That was the very thing Christ had in mind when He identified His followers as those willing to bear their crosses. That is His call to be ready to die, if need be, for the cause of the Lord (Matt. 10:35–39; 16:24–25).

Are you willing to pay that cost?

Ask YOURSELF

What are our usual reasons for *not* being willing to pay the cost of discipleship? Fear? Reputation? A stronger desire to be liked than to be lumped together with Christ's followers? Ask yourself, "What makes me more strongly attached to these excuses than to bearing the name of my Lord?"

ANTICIPATING PHYSICAL PERSECUTION

Blessed are those who have been persecuted for the sake of righteousness,
for theirs is the kingdom of heaven.

MATT. 5:10

*T*HE GREEK WORD THAT IS translated "persecuted" and "persecute" in Matthew 5:10–12 has the basic meaning of chasing, driving away, or pursuing. From that meaning developed the connotations of physical persecution, harassment, abuse, and other unjust treatment.

The believer who possesses the qualities described in the first seven beatitudes will be willing to face persecution "for the sake of righteousness." He will have an attitude of self-sacrifice for the sake of Christ. He is exemplified by a lack of fear and shame and the presence of courage and boldness. The tense of the Greek verb indicates that the believer has a continuous willingness to endure persecution if it is the price of godly living.

Under the demands of this beatitude many Christians break down in their obedience to the Lord; here is where the genuineness of their response to the other beatitudes is most strongly tested. It is where we are most tempted to compromise the righteousness we have hungered and thirsted for. It is here where we find it convenient to lower God's standards to accommodate the world and thereby avoid conflicts and problems we know obedience will bring.

But God does not want His gospel altered under pretense of its being less demanding, less righteous, or less truthful than it is. He does not want witnesses who lead the unsaved into thinking that the Christian life costs nothing.

Do a spiritual inventory and make sure you are willing to pay the cost for the sake of righteousness.

Ask YOURSELF

What causes us to wish that Christian faith weren't so costly? When our hearts lead us to compromise in order to avoid detection and possible derision, what lies are we really telling ourselves? And why doesn't the secretive safety provided by these actions leave us feeling satisfied?

EXPECTING VERBAL INSULTS

Blessed are you when people insult you and persecute you,
and falsely say all kinds of evil against you because of Me.

MATT. 5:11

*B*EYOND PHYSICAL PERSECUTION, Jesus encouraged believers with blessing for having insults cast against them. The Greek word for "insult" carries the idea of reviling, upbraiding, or serious insulting. To insult someone is to throw abusive words in the face of an opponent, to mock viciously.

To be an obedient citizen of the kingdom is to court verbal abuse and reviling. As He stood before the Sanhedrin after His arrest in the Garden of Gethsemane, Jesus was spat upon, beaten, and taunted with the words, "Prophesy to us, You Christ; who is the one who hit You?" (Matt. 26:68). As He was being sentenced to crucifixion by Pilate, Jesus was again beaten, spit upon, and mocked, this time by the Roman soldiers (Mark 15:19–20).

Faithfulness to Christ may even cause friends and loved ones to say things that cut and hurt deeply. But remember, it is clear that the hallmark of a blessed person is righteousness. Holy living is what provokes persecution of God's people. Such persecution because of a righteous life is joyous.

Make sure you are doing all you can to live faithfully for Christ.

*Ask*YOURSELF

How would you define the joys and blessings that flow from being misunderstood and mistreated? What do we unwittingly choose to miss by responding to the words, actions, and demeaning looks of persecution with anger, bitterness, hate, retaliation, or any other less-than-godly reaction?

FORESEEING FALSE ACCUSATIONS

Blessed are you when people insult you and persecute you,
and falsely say all kinds of evil against you because of Me.

MATT. 5:11

*F*AITHFULNESS TO CHRIST WILL bring enemies of the gospel who will "falsely say all kinds of evil against" us. Whereas "insults" are abusive words said to our faces, these "evil" things are primarily abusive words said behind our backs.

Jesus' critics said of Him, "Behold, a gluttonous man and a drunkard, a friend of tax collectors and sinners!" (Matt. 11:19). If the world said that of the sinless Christ, what things can His followers expect to be called and accused of?

Slander behind our backs is harder to take, partly because it is harder to defend against than direct accusations. It has opportunity to spread and be believed before we have a chance to correct it. Those who slander us can do much harm to our reputations before we're even aware that we've been slandered.

We can't help regret being slandered, but we shouldn't grieve about it. Instead, we should count ourselves blessed, as our Lord assures us we will be, when the slander is "because of Me." We have no surer evidence of the Lord's blessing than to be cursed for His sake. It should not seriously bother us when men's curses fall on the head that Christ has eternally blessed.

Are you prepared to accept the slander you might receive because you are a Christian?

Ask YOURSELF

We can sometimes invite persecution by being unduly abrasive and difficult, so that others do not persecute us as much for our faith as for the tacky way we express it. How can we tell the difference? Are people being offended by Christ or just by us? There is certainly no blessing in being obnoxious.

PROMISE FOR THE PERSECUTED

Blessed are those who have been persecuted for the sake of righteousness, for theirs is the
kingdom of heaven. . . . Rejoice and be glad, for your reward in heaven is great;
for in the same way they persecuted the prophets who were before you.

MATT. 5:10, 12

*J*ESUS PRONOUNCES A DOUBLE blessing on those who are persecuted for the sake of righteousness, which is for His own sake. The specific blessing promised is that "theirs is the kingdom of heaven."

Jesus said, "Truly I say to you, there is no one who has left house or brothers or sisters or mother or father or children or farms, for My sake and for the gospel's sake, but that he will receive a hundred times as much now in the present age, houses and brothers and sisters and mothers and children and farms, along with persecutions; and in the age to come, eternal life" (Mark 10:29–30).

First, Jesus promises us blessings here and now. Not every believer is rewarded in this life with the things of this life. But every believer is rewarded in this life with the comfort, strength, and joy of His indwelling Lord. He is also blessed with the assurance that no service or sacrifice for the Lord will be in vain.

Next, there is also a millennial aspect to the kingdom blessing. When Christ establishes His thousand-year reign on earth, we will be co-regents with Him over that wonderful, renewed earth (Rev. 20:4).

Finally, there is the reward of the eternal kingdom, the blessing of all blessings of living forever in our Lord's presence and enjoying it to the utmost. The ultimate fruit of kingdom life is eternal life.

*Ask*YOURSELF

How do we keep these blessings and promises before us when the fire of persecution really heats up? How have you experienced the favor and reward of God even in the midst of situations in which you felt unjustly abused and ridiculed?

POSTURE FOR GLADNESS

*Rejoice and be glad, for your reward in heaven is great; for in the same way
they persecuted the prophets who were before you.*

MATT. 5:12

THE CHRISTIAN'S RESPONSE TO persecution and affliction should not
be to retreat and hide. Jesus told us we are the "salt of the earth" and the "light of the
world" (Matt. 5:13–14). For our salt to flavor the earth and our light to lighten the
world, we must be active in the world. The gospel is not given to be hidden but to enlighten. "Let your light shine before men in such a way that they may see your good
works, and glorify your Father who is in heaven" (v. 16).

When we become Christ's salt and light, our salt will sting the world's open
wounds of sin, and our light will irritate its eyes that are accustomed to darkness.
But even when our salt and light are resented, rejected, and thrown back into our
face, we should "rejoice, and be glad."

The meaning of "be glad" is to exult, to rejoice greatly, to be overjoyed. Jesus
used the imperative mood, thus *commanding* us to be glad. Not to be glad when we
suffer for Christ's sake is to be untrusting and disobedient.

The world can take away a great deal from God's people, but it cannot take away
their joy and their happiness. When people attack us for Christ's sake, they are really
attacking Him (cf. Gal. 6:17; Col. 1:24). And their attacks can do us no more permanent damage than they can do to Him.

So rejoice in the privilege we have been given to be salt and light, no matter the
reaction.

Ask YOURSELF

Gladness joins many of the other qualities that make up the beatitudes, character traits that are unnatural enough to be impossible without the Holy Spirit's empowerment. So, what does it tell you when gladness bubbles up from within you?
How can fear of persecution rival the joy of knowing that Christ is living and active
in your heart?

REASONS FOR GLADNESS

Rejoice and be glad, for your reward in heaven is great; for in the
same way they persecuted the prophets who were before you.

MATT. 5:12

JESUS PROVIDES US WITH TWO reasons for our rejoicing and being glad when we are persecuted for His sake.

First, He says, "Your reward in heaven is great." Whatever we do for the Lord now, including suffering for Him—*especially* suffering for Him—reaps eternal dividends.

But God's dividends aren't ordinary dividends. They are not only "eternal" but also "great." We often hear, and perhaps are tempted to think, that it is unspiritual and crass to serve God for the sake of rewards. But that is one of the motives God Himself gives for serving Him. We first of all serve and obey Christ because we love Him, just as on earth He obeyed the Father because He loved Him. But it was also because of "the joy set before Him" that Christ Himself "endured the cross, despising the shame" (Heb. 12:2). It is neither selfish nor unspiritual to do the Lord's work for a motive that He Himself gives and has followed.

Second, we are to rejoice because the world "persecuted the prophets who were before" us in the same way that it persecutes us. Persecution is a mark of our faithfulness just as it was a mark of the prophets' faithfulness. When we suffer for Christ's sake, we know beyond a doubt that we belong to God because we are experiencing the same reaction from the world that the prophets experienced. So realize that if you are persecuted, you belong in the line of that great company of righteous servants.

Ask YOURSELF

What's your immediate reaction to the idea that we labor for the "reward" of God's blessing? God knows our hearts. He has given us desires to register our growth and progress in the faith. As long as the reward we seek is more of Jesus and to see Him glorified, should we be averse to wanting return on our faithful investment?

SALT AND LIGHT—THE NATURE OF BELIEVERS

You are the salt of the earth; but if the salt has become tasteless, how can it be made salty again?
It is no longer good for anything, except to be thrown out and trampled under foot by men.
You are the light of the world. A city set on a hill cannot be hidden; nor does anyone light
a lamp and put it under a basket, but on the lampstand, and it gives light to all who
are in the house. Let your light shine before men in such a way that they may see your
good works, and glorify your Father who is in heaven.

MATT. 5:13–16

*I*N THESE FOUR VERSES THE Lord summarizes the function of believers in the world—influence. This is a mandate for Christians to influence the world. The Beatitudes are not to be lived in isolation or only among fellow believers, but everywhere we go.

In verses 13 and 14, the pronoun "you" is emphatic. The idea is, "You are the only salt the earth knows and the only light the world sees." The world's corruption won't be retarded and its darkness won't be illumined unless God's people are its salt and light. "You" in both verses is plural; that means the whole body, the church, is called to be the world's salt and light.

By definition, an influence must be different from that which it influences, and Christians must be different from the world they are called to influence. We cannot influence the world for God if we are worldly ourselves, nor can we give light to it if we retreat to places and ways of darkness ourselves.

Ask YOURSELF

Is there anything that's currently taking the bite out of your saltiness, or dimming the brightness of your light? Deal openly with the Lord about these things, asking Him to rid you of their influence so that you can be used of God to influence others.

THE FUNCTION OF SALT

You are the salt of the earth; but if the salt has become tasteless, how can it be made salty again?
It is no longer good for anything, except to be thrown out and trampled under foot by men.

MATT. 5:13

*S*ALT HAS ALWAYS BEEN VALUABLE in human society, often much more so than it is today. But the particular characteristics of salt that Jesus was referring to in this passage have resulted in various suggestions.

Some interpreters point out that salt is white and therefore represents purity. As the "pure in heart" (v. 8), Jesus' disciples are to be pure before the world and are to be God's means of helping purify the rest of the world.

Others emphasize the characteristic of flavor. Just as many foods are tasteless without salt, the world is drab and tasteless without the presence of Christians.

Because salt stings when placed on a wound, some interpreters believe Jesus meant to illustrate that Christians are to sting the world, prick its conscience, and thus make it uncomfortable in the presence of God's gospel.

Salt also creates thirst. So others believe God intends for His people to live before the world in such a way that others will be made aware of their spiritual dehydration.

While all of these interpretations are reasonable, it's likely Jesus was primarily referring to salt as a preservative. Christians are a preserving influence in the world; they retard moral and spiritual spoilage. As God's children and as temples of His Holy Spirit, we represent God's presence in the earth. We are the salt that prevents the entire earth from degenerating even faster than it already is.

Ask YOURSELF

In what ways are you and your church personifying the various properties of salt, whether by words, actions, or outreaches? Think very specifically. Which of these examples are proving to be the most effective at this, and why?

THE POSITIVE NATURE OF LIGHT

You are the light of the world. A city set on a hill cannot be hidden;
nor does anyone light a lamp and put it under a basket, but
on the lampstand, and it gives light to all who are in the house.

MATT. 5:14–15

*I*N ITS FULLEST SENSE, GOD'S light is the full revelation of His Word—the written Word of Scripture and the living Word of Jesus Christ. As the light of the world, Jesus is telling us to proclaim God's light in a world engulfed in darkness, just as our Lord came "to shine upon those who sit in darkness and the shadow of death" (Luke 1:79). Christ is the true light and we are His reflections.

By its nature, light must be visible to illuminate. Both in the daytime and at night, "a city set on a hill cannot be hidden." By day its houses and buildings stand out on the landscape, and at night the many lights shining out of its windows make it impossible to miss. A secret Christian is as incongruous as a hidden light. Lights are meant to illuminate, not to be hidden; to be displayed, not to be covered.

God did not give the gospel of His Son to be the secret, hidden treasure of a few, but to enlighten every person (John 1:9). Just as God offers His light to the whole world, so must His church. It is not our gospel but God's, and He gives it to us not only for our own sakes but also the entire world's.

As a true believer, you *are* salt and light, and you must fulfill that identity.

Ask YOURSELF

How does this command of Christ operate in a culture that's as sensitive to religious tolerance as ours is today? How does one hold high the true light of the gospel when the prevailing belief declares that all ways to God are equally illuminating?

TRUE SALT AND LIGHT ARE PURE

You are the salt of the earth; but if the salt has become tasteless, how can it be
made salty again? It is no longer good for anything, except to be thrown out and
trampled under foot by men. You are the light of the world. A city set on a hill cannot be
hidden; nor does anyone light a lamp and put it under a basket, but on the
lampstand, and it gives light to all who are in the house.

MATT. 5:13–15

*W*ITH GREAT RESPONSIBILITY, there is often great danger. We can't be an influence for purity in the world if we have compromised our own purity. We can't sting the world's conscience if we continually go against our own. We can't be used of God to retard the corruption of sin in the world if our lives become corrupted by sin. To lose our saltiness is not to lose our salvation, but we will lose our effectiveness.

Light, too, is in danger of becoming useless. Like salt, it can't lose its essential nature. A hidden light is still light, but it is useless light. That's why people do not "light a lamp and put it under a basket, but on the lampstand, and it gives light to all who are in the house." A light that is hidden under a basket can't even be used to read by; it helps neither the person who hides it nor anyone else.

Don't hide your light for fear of offending others, whether out of indifference or lovelessness or any other reason. If you do, you demonstrate unfaithfulness to the Lord.

Ask YOURSELF

The demands of purity call for more than merely the eradication of sin and shameful habits, but also for replacing impurity with active, living, breathing righteousness. What are some specific acts of obedience and service to which God is calling you at this hour, in this generation?

SHINING THE LIGHT

Let your light shine before men in such a way that they may see
your good works, and glorify your Father who is in heaven.

MATT. 5:16

*L*ETTING OUR "LIGHT SHINE before men" allows them to see our "good works," the beauty the Lord has worked in us. To see good works by us is to see Christ in us. That's why Jesus says, "Let your light shine." It is not something we create or make up, but something we allow the Lord to do through us. It is God's light; our choice is whether to hide it or let it shine.

We allow God's light to shine through us so God will receive the praise. Our intent should be that in what we are and what we do, others may see God and "glorify [our] Father who is in heaven."

Our good works should magnify God's grace and power. That is the supreme calling of life: glorifying God. Everything we do is to cause others to give praise to God, the source of all that is good. The way we live ought to lead those around us to glorify our heavenly Father.

However, when what we do causes people to be attracted to us rather than to God, to see our human character rather than His divine character, we can be sure that what they see is not His light. Make sure your deeds point people to God, the author of those deeds.

Ask YOURSELF

As we've seen before, some will respond to your good deeds with derision and persecution, but others will shower praise on you for your acts of Christian character. How do you respond to those who give you credit for your servant's heart and faithful obedience? How do you deflect that praise to God so it doesn't nestle down in your own heart?

How Jesus Understood the Law and the Prophets

Do not think that I came to abolish the Law or the Prophets;
I did not come to abolish but to fulfill.

MATT. 5:17

*I*S THERE AN ABSOLUTE BASIS FOR truth, for law, for morals, for real right and wrong? The absolute, Jesus says, is the law of the eternally sovereign God. God laid down His absolute, eternal, abiding law and made it known to humanity. And as God's own Son, Jesus declared unequivocally that He did not come to teach or practice anything contrary to that law even in the slightest way, but to uphold it entirely.

Jesus obviously had a high regard for the law, but at the same time He taught things completely contrary to the traditions. His teachings did not lower scriptural standards but upheld them in every way. He not only elevated God's standard to the height it belonged, but also lived at that humanly impossible level.

The law and the prophets represent what we call the Old Testament, the only written Scripture at the time Jesus preached. Because Matthew does not qualify his use of law, we are safe to say that it was God's whole law—the commandments, statutes, and judgments; the moral, judicial, and ceremonial—that Jesus came not to abolish but fulfill. It was also the other Old Testament teachings based on the law, and all their types, patterns, symbols, and pictures that He came to fulfill. Jesus Christ came to accomplish every aspect and every dimension of the divinely authored Word.

Ask YOURSELF

Knowing how hard it is for us to maintain holy attitudes and behaviors for more than a few hours at a time, marvel again at the extreme power of Jesus Christ, who endured every temptation to maintain His perfect purity on earth. And marvel anew that such supernatural righteousness has been imputed to us!

How Jesus Fulfilled the Law—Moral and Judicial

Do not think that I came to abolish the Law or the Prophets;
I did not come to abolish but to fulfill.

MATT. 5:17

*T*HE MORAL LAW WAS GOD'S foundational code. Jesus fulfilled that law by His perfect righteousness. He obeyed every commandment, met every requirement, and lived up to every standard.

But most important, Jesus fulfilled the Old Testament by *being* its fulfillment. He did not simply teach it fully and exemplify it fully—He *was* it fully. He did not come simply to teach righteousness and to model righteousness; He came *as* divine righteousness. What He said and what He did reflected who He *is*.

God's judicial law was given to provide unique identity for Israel as a nation that belonged to Jehovah. The laws relating to agriculture, settlement of disputes, diet, cleanliness, dress, and such things were special standards by which His chosen people were to live before the Lord and apart from the world. This judicial law Jesus fulfilled on the cross.

Jesus' crucifixion marked Israel's ultimate apostasy in the final rejection of her Messiah and the interruption of God's dealing with that people as a nation. With that, the judicial law passed away because Israel no longer served as His chosen nation.

Praise God, He will someday redeem and restore Israel (Rom. 9–11), but in the meanwhile the church is His chosen body of people on earth (1 Peter 2:9–10). All the redeemed—those who receive the work of the cross—are His chosen ones.

Ask YOURSELF

There is no way, of course, for us to duplicate the perfect performance of Jesus, but by surrendering in daily, ongoing ways to His Holy Spirit, we can see Christ's character exuding from us in steady practice. Have your own failures and experiences caused you to deny this truth? Submit to Him afresh today.

JESUS CHRIST IS SUPERIOR TO THE CEREMONIAL LAW

Do not think that I came to abolish the Law or the
Prophets; I did not come to abolish but to fulfill.

MATT. 5:17

*T*HE CEREMONIAL LAW GOVERNED the form of Israel's worship. When Jesus died on the cross, He fulfilled that law as well as the judicial. Sacrifice was the heart of all Old Testament worship, and as the perfect sacrifice, Jesus brought all the other sacrifices to an end. While He was on the cross, "the veil of the temple was torn in two from top to bottom" (Matt. 27:51). Christ Himself became the new and perfect way into the Holy of Holies, into which any man could come by faith.

In this way, the Levitical, priestly, sacrificial system ended. Though the temple was not destroyed until A.D. 70, every offering made on its altar after Jesus died was needless. Symbolically, they had no more significance. Of course, the Tabernacle and Temple sacrifices that were offered even *before* Christ's death *never* had power to cleanse from sin. They were only pictures of the Messiah-Savior's work of cleansing, pictures that pointed to that supreme manifestation of God's mercy and grace.

The ceremonial law ended because it was fulfilled. Since the reality had come, the pictures and symbols had no more place or purpose. From Genesis 1:1 through Malachi 4:6, the Old Testament is Jesus Christ. It was inspired by Christ, it points to Christ, and it is fulfilled by Christ.

*Ask*YOURSELF

What does the magnificence of God's story stir in you as you consider it again— the signs and fulfillments created by God's design before the foundation of the world and forged through long centuries of human history? Sit at His feet again today in awe-filled worship.

APRIL 1

JESUS AND THE PERMANENCE OF SCRIPTURE

For truly I say to you, until heaven and earth pass away, not the
smallest letter or stroke shall pass from the Law until all is accomplished.

MATT. 5:18

*J*ESUS' TEACHINGS ARE NOT ONLY unqualifiedly authoritative ("truly I say to you"), they are permanent. He implicitly equated His words of instruction with God's eternal Word: "Heaven and earth will pass away, but My words will not pass away" (Matt. 24:35). As such, Jesus' words are on a par with the Old Testament and are timeless.

In view of that reality, how foolish of us ever to wonder about the relevancy of God's Word for us. The Bible is God's eternal Word, and even though completed nearly two millennia ago, it has much to say to us today. Scripture is and always has been "living and active and sharper than any two-edged sword, and piercing as far as the division of soul and spirit, of both joints and marrow, and able to judge the thoughts and intentions of the heart" (Heb. 4:12).

Jesus reveals that the permanence of God's Word extends to the smallest letters and the smallest parts of printed letters—neither will be erased or modified.

No other statement by the Lord more clearly states His absolute confidence in the enduring nature and inerrant quality of the Bible. It is God's own Spirit-inspired Word, down to every single word, letter, and part of letter.

Ask YOURSELF

Not necessarily by time percentages, to what extent does the Word factor into your usual day? When and why do you turn to its wisdom and instruction? What have you found to be the best ways to keep the Scriptures alive and active within you?

JESUS' RELIANCE ON SCRIPTURE

*For truly I say to you, until heaven and earth pass away, not the
smallest letter or stroke shall pass from the Law until all is accomplished.*

MATT. 5:18

*R*EPEATEDLY DURING HIS EARTHLY ministry, Jesus referred to the Old Testament as authoritative truth (e.g., Matt. 19:4; 24:38–39; Mark 12:26; Luke 11:51; 17:29; John 3:14; 8:56), always confirming its accuracy and authenticity. On one occasion, in defending His messiahship before the unbelieving Jewish leaders, He declared, "The Scripture cannot be broken" (John 10:35).

For Jesus, it was clear that God gave His Word to lead people to salvation. In His parable of the rich man and Lazarus, Abraham tells the rich man that if his brothers, whom he did not want to follow him to hell, "do not listen to Moses and the Prophets, they will not be persuaded even if someone rises from the dead" (Luke 16:31). Scripture is more than sufficient to bring sinners to salvation.

More than once, Christ used Scripture's authority to establish His own. At a Sabbath service in the Nazareth synagogue, He appealed to the book of Isaiah: "'The Spirit of the Lord is upon Me, because He anointed Me to preach the gospel to the poor. He has sent Me to proclaim release to the captives, and recovery of sight to the blind, to set free those who are oppressed, to proclaim the favorable year of the Lord.'... And He began to say to them, 'Today this Scripture has been fulfilled in your hearing'" (Luke 4:18–19, 21; cf. Isa. 61:1; Matt. 11:3–5; Mark 11:17).

Scripture's authority is Jesus' authority, and to obey Him is to obey His Word (John 6:68; 8:47).

Ask YOURSELF

What argues against our confidence in the convicting, converting power of the Word of God? What could we do to ensure that our hearts aren't blinded to this truth, to put ourselves in positions where we can see God at work through the Scriptures?

We Must Receive, Honor, and Obey the Word

For truly I say to you, until heaven and earth pass away, not the smallest
letter or stroke shall pass from the Law until all is accomplished.

MATT. 5:18

*T*O BE A FOLLOWER OF JESUS CHRIST is to accept what He says about Scripture and to wholeheartedly echo Peter's sentiment: "You have words of eternal life" (John 6:68). The privilege of knowing Christ and His Word also carries with it certain essential obligations.

First, we must receive God's Word exactly for what it is, "the word implanted, which is able to save your souls" (James 1:21). We should be completely receptive because the Word is the highest standard of truth, joy, and blessing, and it tells us of the way to salvation.

Second, we are obliged to honor the Scripture. The psalmist wrote, "How sweet are Your words to my taste! Yes, sweeter than honey to my mouth!" (Ps. 119:103; cf. Jer. 15:16). The great Reformer Martin Luther did not fear his human opponents. However, when he stood in the pulpit to expound Scripture, his knees often knocked under a sense of awe and duty to honor the Word.

Third, we must obey God's Word. The apostle Paul commanded Timothy, "Be diligent to present yourself approved to God as a workman who does not need to be ashamed, accurately handling the word of truth" (2 Tim. 2:15). A key to genuine obedience in the Christian walk is to "let the word of Christ richly dwell within" (Col. 3:16).

Ask YOURSELF

In what ways is the Scripture honored in your home? If this is an area in your family life that has been allowed to slip, what could you begin doing right away to restore the Bible to a place of regular reflection, instruction, and prominence?

APRIL 4

WE MUST DEFEND AND PROCLAIM THE WORD

For truly I say to you, until heaven and earth pass away, not the
smallest letter or stroke shall pass from the Law until all is accomplished.

MATT. 5:18

*I*N CONSIDERING OUR OBLIGATIONS to the divine Scripture, two other major obligations are crucial for the Christian. First, he or she must defend the Word of God. We should strive for the integrity, authority, and purity of the Bible. As Jude exhorts us, we must "contend earnestly for the faith which was once for all handed down to the saints" (Jude 3). Charles Spurgeon wrote this about defending the Word:

> The everlasting gospel is worth preaching even if one stood on a burning fagot and addressed the crowds from a pulpit of flames. The truths revealed in Scripture are worth living for and they are worth dying for. I count myself thrice happy, to bear reproach for the sake of the faith.

Lastly, those who love the Lord live to proclaim God's Word. Spurgeon is again relevant:

> I would stir you all up to be instant in season and out of season in telling out the gospel message, especially to repeat such a word as this: "God so loved the world that He gave His only begotten Son, that whosoever believeth in Him shall not perish but have everlasting life." Whisper it in the ear of the sick, shout it in the corner of the streets, write it on your tablet, send it forth from the press, but everywhere let this be your great motive and warrant.

Ask YOURSELF

If you're not a preacher, you may feel somewhat excluded from this biblical mandate. But in what ways can proclamation be a part of your life? What opportunities are available for you to inject God's truth into discourse or conversation?

GOD'S LAW NOT UP FOR ANNULMENT

*Whoever then annuls one of the least of these commandments, and teaches
others to do the same, shall be called least in the kingdom of heaven.*

MATT. 5:19A

𝒫EOPLE RESENT PROHIBITIONS AND demands on their behavior. Even
believers, out of ignorance, misunderstanding, or blatant disregard, sometimes want
to water down God's standards. But when anyone "annuls" (breaks, sets loose) any
part of God's Word, he or she is not following Christ's example.

Jesus did acknowledge that not all of God's commands are of equal importance.
He told a pharisaical lawyer that one divine commandment is above all others and
that another is second (Matt. 22:37–39). Thus all the other commandments fall somewhere below those two and vary in significance.

Our Lord's point here in the sermon, however, is that we must not annul—by
ignoring, modifying, or disobeying—even the smallest aspect of God's law. Some
commands might be greater than others, but none should be disregarded. Paul did
not pick and choose what he would teach. He did emphasize some issues more than
others, but he omitted nothing (Acts 20:27). And we certainly must not teach others
to disregard or disobey any portion of the law. To do so shows that our disobedience
is conscious and intentional.

Jesus does not restrict His warning to formal teachers. By example, every Christian teaches those around him to be more obedient or more disobedient. Our words
of respect for God's Word present a guide for others. To speak disparagingly of the
Word or to ignore its requirements presents testimony to others of the law's unim-
portance to us. This ought to be the furthest thing from our agenda.

𝒜𝓈𝓀YOURSELF

On what subject matters do you find yourself most tempted to comment, "I
know what the Bible says, *but . . .*"?

APRIL 6

HOW TO BE LEAST IN CHRIST'S KINGDOM

Whoever then annuls one of the least of these commandments, and teaches
others to do the same, shall be called least in the kingdom of heaven.

MATT. 5:19A

*T*HE RESULT OF A BELIEVER'S practicing or teaching disobedience of any part of Scripture is to "be called least in the kingdom of heaven." "Called" does not refer merely to what people say about us, but what God says about us. Others usually know nothing of or don't care about our disobedience, but God always knows and cares.

It is completely God's prerogative to determine rank in His kingdom (cf. Matt. 20:23). Therefore He has a perfect right to hold those in lowest esteem who have a low esteem for the Word. This does not mean the Lord will take away the offender's salvation; they are still "in the kingdom of heaven." But it does mean they will forfeit certain blessing and reward to whatever extent they are disobedient and disrespectful. The apostle John warned his readers, "Watch yourselves, that you do not lose what we have accomplished, but that you may receive a full reward" (2 John 8).

If we ignore or reject even the most minor aspect of God's law, we devalue all of it (James 2:10) and join the ranks of God's least. It should be the highest concern of us who profess to love our Savior and Lord never to prompt Him to call us the least.

Ask YOURSELF

Few of us would admit to devaluing the Word of God, but perhaps that's because we limit to one or two the number of ways this is done. How might a person show disrespect for the Scripture's authority and teaching beyond the most obvious offenses?

POSITIVE RESPONSE TO GOD'S LAW

Whoever keeps and teaches them, he shall be called great in the kingdom of heaven.

MATT. 5:19B

*T*HOSE SAINTS WHO UPHOLD every part of God's Word in their lives and in what they teach exhibit a most positive response to His law and receive from Him the commendation "great." They see Paul as their pattern, when he told the Thessalonians, "You are witnesses, and so is God, how devoutly and uprightly and blamelessly we behaved toward you believers; just as you know how we were exhorting and encouraging and imploring each one of you as a father would his own children, so that you would walk in a manner worthy of the God who calls you into His own kingdom and glory" (1 Thess. 2:10–12; cf. 1 Tim. 4:11–12; 6:11–12).

The apostle kept and taught the entire purpose of God (Acts 20:27) and therefore ranks among the greatest in God's kingdom. If we do the same, we too will be among the greatest in heaven.

One key to our positive response to God's moral law is knowing that it's changeless and eternal. In heaven, the traits it requires will not need to be commanded, for they will simply be manifested as part of God's own character. But we do not naturally reflect those characteristics while still on earth. Thus His moral standards must continue to be taught and heeded so that we might bear Spirit-produced fruit while we wait for its ultimate fulfillment (cf. Rom. 8:2–4).

Greatness does not come by gifts, success, or popularity but by our reverence for, respect of, and obedience to the Word in daily life and how we encourage those attitudes in others.

Ask YOURSELF

What specific, noticeable things are "great" about a person who deliberately pursues obedience to the Word? How do they distinguish themselves from others in expression, attitude, and outlook?

APRIL 8

OUR RESPONSIBILITY CLARIFIED

Whoever keeps and teaches them, he shall be called great in the kingdom of heaven.

MATT. 5:19B

HE NEW TESTAMENT PRESENTS a paradox concerning God's law. On one hand, it is abolished; on the other, responsibilities to it remain. Regarding Jews and Gentiles, Paul writes that Christ "is our peace, who made both groups into one and broke down the barrier of the dividing wall, by abolishing in His flesh the enmity, which is the Law of commandments contained in ordinances, so that in Himself He might make the two into one new man, thus establishing peace" (Eph. 2:14–15). With the church's emergence, the "dividing wall" of civil ordinances disappeared.

The ceremonial law also has terminated. While Christ was on the cross, "the veil of the temple was torn in two from top to bottom" (Mark 15:38). With Jesus' death the Old Testament sacrifices became invalid and unnecessary.

In a certain sense God's moral law seems no longer binding on His children (Rom. 10:4; 6:12–15; Gal. 5:17–18). Paul harmonizes this notion when he speaks of being "without law, though not being without the law of God but under the law of Christ" (1 Cor. 9:21). In Christ, believers are anything but without the law. Whereas His law is totally different from the Old Testament moral law with its penalties for disobedience, it is not different at all from the righteous standards which that law taught.

Whenever we look at the moral law with humility and a sincere desire to obey, the law will invariably point us to Jesus Christ—as was always its ultimate intention.

Ask YOURSELF

What benefits do the teachings of the law continue to deposit in the life of the believer? If not for its guidance and its setting of boundaries, where would our human nature choose to live and operate?

APRIL 9

WARNING AGAINST EXTERNAL RIGHTEOUSNESS

For I say to you that unless your righteousness surpasses that of the scribes
and Pharisees, you will not enter the kingdom of heaven.

MATT. 5:20

*T*HE RELIGIOUS LEADERS OF Jesus' day were entirely concerned with a mere external observance of God's law, giving almost no consideration to motives or attitude. In Matthew 23:25, Jesus gives a descriptive view of such useless religion: "You are like whitewashed tombs which on the outside appear beautiful, but inside they are full of dead men's bones and all uncleanness." Because of that terrible condition, our Lord labeled the scribes and Pharisees as "hypocrites." They thought God would judge them only for what they did, not for what they thought.

But Jesus considers this sort of righteousness to be of the worst kind. Anybody who practices such "religion" is guilty of a large array of vile sins (Matt. 23:25–31). At another time Jesus warned the Pharisees, "You are those who justify yourselves in the sight of men, but God knows your hearts; for that which is highly esteemed among men is detestable in the sight of God" (Luke 16:15).

Christ's next teachings in this sermon would declare that God's first concern is with people's hearts. He condemns attitudes of anger, hatred, and lust, not merely their outward manifestations in murder and adultery (Matt. 5:22, 27–28). Similarly, anyone's deeds of righteousness, such as prayer, giving, or fasting—if not done with a humble, loving attitude—are worthless (cf. 6:5–18). Hypocrisy and externalism cannot substitute for genuine righteousness.

Ask YOURSELF

Where has hypocrisy slipped into your life? Confess every example of it today—not the temptation itself, but rather every time you have gone on to mask pride and impurity with self-righteous appearances. Deal directly with these and repent, experiencing again the freedom of living whole, genuine lives of faith.

Warning against Partial Righteousness

For I say to you that unless your righteousness surpasses that of the
scribes and Pharisees, you will not enter the kingdom of heaven.

MATT. 5:20

*T*HE RIGHTEOUSNESS PRACTICED by the religious leaders further displeased God because it was partial, falling way short of His perfect standard. Again in Matthew 23, Jesus illustrates this phony righteousness: "You tithe mint and dill and cummin, and have neglected the weightier provisions of the law: justice and mercy and faithfulness; but these are the things you should have done without neglecting the others" (v. 23).

The Jewish leaders were conscientious about making nonessential tithes of the smallest plants and seeds, yet they totally neglected showing justice and mercy to others or having heartfelt faithfulness to God.

To a large degree this sin of partial righteousness flows directly from externalism. Unregenerate people disregard justice, mercy, and faithfulness because those traits basically reflect a divinely transformed heart. Without a new heart no one can accomplish "the weightier provisions of the law."

In a separate encounter, the Lord quoted Isaiah and further warned the Pharisees of their empty and misdirected religion: "This people honors Me with their lips, but their heart is far away from Me. But in vain do they worship Me, teaching as doctrines the precepts of men" (Mark 7:6–7). Like the religious leaders and many of the people of Jesus' day, professing believers today can be constantly exposed to Scripture but only superficially responsive to it. Their watered-down, partial obedience to God's commands demonstrates their failure to grasp the profound spiritual intent of God's law and their probable unsaved condition.

Ask YOURSELF

Realize afresh today that the only obedience which interests God is total obedience—the kind that can only be accomplished through Christ's righteousness, imputed to His redeemed children. What instances of partial obedience need to be converted to full obedience in your life?

BEWARE OF REDEFINED, SELF-CENTERED RIGHTEOUSNESS

For I say to you that unless your righteousness surpasses that of the scribes
and Pharisees, you will not enter the kingdom of heaven.

MATT. 5:20

*M*ANY PEOPLE TODAY—and sadly, more and more within the church—have redefined biblical concepts to fit their own human perspectives. Like the scribes and Pharisees, religionists know they can't match God's righteousness, so they simply change the definition of holiness. A prime example from Old Testament times is how the Jews reinterpreted God's command, "Consecrate yourselves therefore, and be holy, for I am holy" (Lev. 11:44). They turned this from a call for inner holiness into a requirement to perform certain rituals.

The godly person will never rely on self-centered, redefined righteousness. Instead, he will focus on the kind of holiness Jesus taught. He will be broken about sin and mourn over the evil propensity of his heart. Such people long only for the righteousness God can give through His Spirit. They will never rely on their own strength or wisdom for what they can do spiritually.

God has always been focused on inner righteousness. When Samuel was ready to anoint David's oldest brother, Eliab, to succeed King Saul, God told him, "Do not look at his appearance or at the height of his stature, because I have rejected him; for God sees not as man sees, for man looks at the outward appearance, but the Lord looks at the heart" (1 Sam. 16:7). And that inner righteousness must be perfect: "Therefore you are to be perfect, as your heavenly Father is perfect" (Matt. 5:48). To be truly qualified for entrance into Christ's kingdom we must be as holy as God Himself.

Ask YOURSELF

Being broken over sin is certainly a crucial part of dealing with its incessant appeal and presence in our lives. But be sure you're not choosing to remain in perpetual inactivity and introspection. How well is your grieving over sin being translated into renewed obedience?

JESUS CLARIFIES MURDER'S DEFINITION

You have heard that the ancients were told, "You shall not commit murder" and
"Whoever commits murder shall be liable to the court." But I say to you that everyone
who is angry with his brother shall be guilty before the court; and whoever says to his
brother, "You good-for-nothing," shall be guilty before the supreme court;
and whoever says, "You fool," shall be guilty enough to go into fiery hell.

MATT. 5:21–22

*T*HROUGHOUT HISTORY, MOST decent people rest assured that at least
one sin they have not committed is murder. The conventional wisdom limits murder to physically taking another person's life. But Jesus' teaching on murder shatters
the self-righteous complacency of so many good people.

God's original command "you shall not commit murder" was of course scriptural (Ex. 20:13). But the Jewish practice of taking murder cases to civil court fell
well short of the biblical standard in three ways: it did not prescribe the death penalty
(Gen. 9:6), it did not take God's holy character into consideration (His role in met-
ing out judgment, the sinfulness of taking a life made in His image, or the general
disobedience to the law), and it said nothing about the heart offense of the murderer.
These omissions ignored David's statement in Psalm 51:6, "You [God] desire truth in
the innermost being, and in the hidden part You will make me know wisdom."

With the transitional words, "But I say to you," Jesus begins to point us to a
scriptural understanding of murder and its implications. Murder goes much deeper
than physically taking someone's life. It originates with evil thoughts in the heart,
and is still a serious sin, whether or not it culminates in violent action against another person.

Ask YOURSELF

If Jesus is making this harder than before, then what's so freeing about being
free from the law? Why is this more helpful than a black-and-white statute?

JESUS ON MURDER: CONTRAST TO THE RABBIS

You have heard that the ancients were told, "You shall not commit murder" and
"Whoever commits murder shall be liable to the court." But I say to you that everyone
who is angry with his brother shall be guilty before the court.

MATT. 5:21–22A

*W*ITH JUST TWO SENTENCES JESUS shatters the rabbinic view of murder, which was so complacently self-righteous. Because of their externalism and legalism, the Jews had an inflated view of themselves. But Jesus destroyed that thinking with the declaration that a person guilty of anger, hatred, cursing, or defamation against another is guilty of murder and worthy of a murderer's punishment.

All anger, hatred, etc., is incipient murder, as the apostle John writes, "Everyone who hates his brother is a murderer" (1 John 3:15a). By that biblical standard, we are all guilty of murder—after all, who has not hated someone at one time or another?

Not only does Jesus here sweep away the rubbish of the rabbinic, traditional view of murder, His total indictment blasts away any notion of self-justification so common to everyone. The way the Jews thought in Jesus' time is identical to people's prevalent thinking today. Even believers can feel proud that they are "not like other people: swindlers, unjust, adulterers" (Luke 18:11)—and we could add "murderers." Jesus in that parable and in this passage says we are all potentially capable of the worst sins, even murder, because of the sometimes evil attitudes of our hearts.

Not to consider the state of your heart and confess thoughts of anger and hatred, which can lead to taking someone's life, is not to consider that the Lord can hold you guilty of murder.

Ask YOURSELF

What benefit is found in knowing that you and I are capable of the most heinous crimes imaginable? Does recognizing this startling piece of information have an effect on your relationship with God and your resultant manner of living?

APRIL 14

SELFISH ANGER EQUALS MURDER

Everyone who is angry with his brother shall be guilty before the court.

MATT. 5:22A

*F*ROM JESUS' OWN LIFE WE know He does not forbid every form of anger. In righteous indignation He twice cleansed the temple of its defiling, profaning influences (Matt. 21:12–13; John 2:14–15). The apostle Paul instructs Christians to "be angry, and yet do not sin" (Eph. 4:26). Faithfulness to Christ sometimes demands that we exercise a righteous anger. Many of the current cultural trends, the surges of violence and grossly dishonest and immoral practices, and the unbiblical ideas promoted even within supposedly evangelical circles need to be opposed with righteous anger. That's because such things undermine the kingdom and glory of God. The psalmist wrote, "God is a righteous judge, and a God who has indignation every day" (Ps. 7:11).

In His sermon, Jesus did not speak against legitimate, righteous indignation, but against a selfish anger toward someone for doing something against us, someone who's just rubbed us the wrong way. The word the Lord used for "angry" indicates a simmering anger that a person nurtures and refuses to let die. Examples of such anger are the long-standing grudge or the smoldering bitterness that refuses to forgive someone. This kind of anger does not want reconciliation and can become so profound as to be a "root of bitterness springing up" (Heb. 12:15).

Jesus says anyone who harbors such severe anger against another person is the same as guilty before the civil court of murder and deserving of the death penalty in God's eyes.

*Ask*YOURSELF

So are there names and faces that come to mind when confronted with this stark reminder from Scripture? Is there personal anger that needs instant removal from your heart?

SLANDER EQUALS MURDER

Whoever says to his brother, "You good-for-nothing," shall be guilty before the supreme court.

MATT. 5:22B

*T*HE WORD (*RACA*) TRANSLATED by the New American Standard Bible "good-for-nothing" has been variously rendered elsewhere as "brainless idiot," "worthless fellow," "blockhead," and the like. It was a term of malicious abuse and slander that really has no precise modern translation. David graphically described persons who used such slander as those who "sharpen their tongues as a serpent; poison of a viper is under their lips" (Ps. 140:3). The Roman soldiers who tortured and crucified Jesus could well have used the term to mock and disrespect Him (cf. Matt. 27:29–31).

According to Jewish legend, a young rabbi had just come from a session with his famous teacher. He felt especially proud of how he had handled himself before the teacher. As he basked in those feelings of superiority, he passed an especially unattractive man who greeted him. The young rabbi responded, "You Raca! How ugly you are. Are all men of your town as ugly as you?"

"That I do not know," the man replied, "but go and tell the Maker who created me how ugly is the creature He has made."

To slander someone made in God's image is to slander God Himself and is the same as murdering that person. Jesus called such harsh contempt murder of the heart. The contemptuous person was as much as "guilty before the supreme court" (the Jewish Sanhedrin, which tried the most serious cases and pronounced the ultimate penalty—death). We dare not trifle with any kind of contemptuous language toward others.

Ask YOURSELF

Remember, this is not just an injunction against *speaking* unkind, judgmental words, but also of thinking them in our minds. When God has led you to seasons of victory in your thought life, how has He accomplished it? What stopped evil thoughts from ever coming up?

THE EVIL OF SAYING, "YOU FOOL"

Whoever says, "You fool," shall be guilty enough to go into fiery hell.

MATT. 5:22C

*N*O ONE WANTS TO BE CALLED a fool, and on the other side of the coin, no one should fix that label on someone else. That's especially true when we realize that the word in this verse translated "fool" is from the Greek word from which we get *moron*. The word also denotes one who is stupid or dull. Greek literature sometimes used it to refer to a godless or obstinate person. And it was perhaps parallel to a Hebrew word that means "to rebel against."

Twice the psalmist tells us "the fool has said in his heart, 'There is no God'" (Ps. 14:1; 53:1; cf. 10:4). The book of Proverbs contains many negative references and warnings to fools (1:7; 10:8, 10; 14:9). Jesus used a related but less severe term when He reprimanded the two disciples on the road to Emmaus: "O foolish men and slow of heart to believe in all that the prophets have spoken!" (Luke 24:25).

Because of these and other testimonies in God's Word, we know people engage in foolish thoughts and actions. Therefore it is not wrong for us to warn or rebuke someone who is acting or speaking foolishly and clearly opposing God's will. In fact, we are *supposed* to take this action! The Lord is warning us here, however, that it is sin to slanderously call someone a fool out of personal anger or hatred. Maliciously calling another a fool is again equivalent to murder and worthy of eternal punishment in hell if not repented of.

Ask YOURSELF

Most of our slanderous remarks are not made to others' faces but rather behind their backs. What guiding principles can you set in place to guard yourself from being ugly and unkind to others, even when speaking about them in private conversation?

Hatred Blocks Real Worship

Therefore if you are presenting your offering at the altar, and there
remember that your brother has something against you . . .

MATT. 5:23

OUTWARD ACTS OF WORSHIP ARE unacceptable to God as long as we harbor internal sin. They are particularly offensive if we retain a hateful attitude toward a brother and yet attempt to come before God.

Worship is important for most religious people today. They can spend much time in places of worship, offering prayers, giving tithes, and doing all sorts of religious activities. But, as with the scribes and Pharisees, none of it is meaningful if carried out with the wrong attitude.

Presenting an offering at the altar was a familiar scene for Jesus' listeners. On the Day of Atonement, for example, worshipers would bring animal sacrifices and give them to the priest as sin offerings. But that process must halt if the worshiper were to remember some hatred between himself and a brother. Unresolved conflict has priority over external ceremony and must be settled.

Sin between us and other brethren must be resolved before we can bridge the gap of sin between us and God. The Lord told Israel, "What are your multiplied sacrifices to Me? . . . I have had enough of burnt offerings of rams and the fat of fed cattle; and I take no pleasure in the blood of bulls, lambs or goats. . . . Wash yourselves, make yourselves clean; remove the evil of your deeds from My sight. Cease to do evil, learn to do good" (Isa. 1:11, 16–17a).

Not to be at peace with someone else and yet to attempt worship of God is a hindrance to genuine fellowship.

Ask YOURSELF

This is a call for worship to matter, and for relationship with God to be taken seriously. More than a Sunday morning verse, it's a principle demanding conciliatory action in the days prior to the Lord's day. Is there such a matter occurring in your life situation right now?

BRIDGING THE GAP TO TRUE WORSHIP

Leave your offering there before the altar and go; first be reconciled
to your brother, and then come and present your offering.

MATT. 5:24

*N*O MATTER WHO IS RESPONSIBLE for a severed relationship—and often both sides bear some guilt—it's essential to reconcile before going to God in worship. Even if you have nothing against the other person and the fault lies entirely with them, you should do everything possible to settle things. You can't change another's heart attitude, but you should desire to close the gap between yourself and the other person and hold no grudge against him or her—then you can enter freely and fully into divine worship.

Better music, more eloquent prayers, or more classic architecture—none of these will enhance true worship. Even better or more biblical preaching will not of itself improve our worship experience. However, a contrite and righteous attitude toward God and our brothers and sisters will enhance genuine worship. Sometimes the drastic measure of staying away from church for a time until a broken or strained relationship is right is the only action that will make our worship God-honoring.

Long before Jesus preached the Sermon on the Mount, Samuel said, "Has the Lord as much delight in burnt offerings and sacrifices as in obeying the voice of the Lord? Behold, to obey is better than sacrifice, and to heed than the fat of rams" (1 Sam. 15:22). After that the psalmist said, "If I regard wickedness in my heart, the Lord will not hear" (Ps. 66:18). If sin remains unconfessed and relationships broken, there will be no integrity in our worship.

Ask YOURSELF

Again, you are responsible only for the condition of your own heart, not another's. But can you honestly say today that you have made peace in your heart with those who have been at odds with you? Have you forgiven? Have you sought renewed relationship?

RECONCILING WITH OTHERS

Make friends quickly with your opponent at law while you are with him on the way, so that your opponent may not hand you over to the judge, and the judge to the officer, and you be thrown into prison. Truly I say to you, you will not come out of there until you have paid up the last cent.

MATT. 5:25–26

$\mathcal{T}$HE TIME FOR RECONCILIATION WITH others is always now, just as it is with salvation. Tomorrow may be too late. No excuse is valid to allow bitterness, anger, hatred, or any other sin to keep us separated from another person. Jesus illustrates here that we should make good on any debt or settle any grievance before it is too late and we're imprisoned.

In the Roman Empire, two opponents at law could settle an issue on the way to court, but not after a judge became involved. To avoid judgment and imprisonment, the guilty person had to pay "the last cent," or everything owed in debt.

Being thrown into prison and not being able to get out until a debt is paid is Jesus' analogy to the Father's punishment. We can't miss the Son's teaching here: we must make every effort possible, with no delay, to mend any broken relationship with a brother before we can avoid divine chastening and have a right relationship with God.

We know that because of sin, none of us is ever completely at peace or perfectly related to another. And since it's impossible to have perfectly right attitudes toward others or God, no worship is ever fully acceptable. All of Jesus' teachings in this passage and the rest of the Sermon on the Mount show us again the utterly perfect standard of God's righteousness and the absolute impossibility of our meeting that standard on our own.

Ask YOURSELF

There's no denying the pain of strained and severed relationships. But there's nothing like knowing you've done everything you can to make it right. Can you live in the Lord's peace even if nothing changes?

DESIRE, THE ROOT SIN OF ADULTERY

You have heard that it was said, "You shall not commit adultery"; but I say to you that everyone
who looks at a woman with lust for her has already committed adultery with her in his heart.

MATT. 5:27–28

*T*HE SEVENTH COMMANDMENT protects the sanctity of marriage, and anyone who relies on external righteousness to keep it is prone to break it. Just as anger equals murder, lustful desire equals adultery.

In Jesus' admonition, "looks" indicates intentional and repeated gazing. Therefore He means purposeful looking that arouses lust. In contemporary terms, it condemns a man who sees an X-rated movie, watches a salacious television show, or visits pornographic websites. It encompasses any thought or action done to arouse sexual desire.

Jesus is not referring to accidental exposure to sexual temptation. It is no sin if a man looks away from a provocative scene. It is the continued look that Christ condemns, because that demonstrates an adulterous heart. And by inference this prohibition would apply to women also, who must not gaze at men or dress in seductive ways to elicit stares.

In earliest redemptive history, Job understood these principles: "I have made a covenant with my eyes; how then could I gaze at a virgin? . . . If my step has turned from the way, or my heart followed my eyes, or if any spot has stuck to my hands, let me sow and another eat, and let my crops be uprooted" (Job 31:1, 7–8).

If the adulterous heart gives in to temptation, the godly heart will protect itself, praying, "Turn away my eyes from looking at vanity, and revive me in Your ways. Establish Your word to Your servant, as that which produces reverence for You" (Ps. 119:37–38; cf. 2 Tim. 2:22).

Ask YOURSELF

What could replace your next lustful thought or glance? Instead of focusing on what God has graciously restricted, what blessings, privileges, and freedoms can capture your attention instead?

DEALING RADICALLY WITH SIN

If your right eye makes you stumble, tear it out and throw it from you; for it is better for you to lose one of the parts of your body, than for your whole body to be thrown into hell. If your right hand makes you stumble, cut it off and throw it from you; for it is better for you to lose one of the parts of your body, than for your whole body to go into hell.

MATT. 5:29–30

*W*E MUST BE WILLING, as Jesus teaches here, to relinquish whatever is necessary to protect us from evil and preserve righteousness. Mutilation will not cleanse our hearts, but Jesus' figurative words call for dramatic severing of any impulse that could lead to sin (cf. Matt. 18:8–9).

In other words, we must deal radically with sin, as Paul says, "I discipline my body and make it my slave, so that, after I have preached to others, I myself will not be disqualified" (1 Cor. 9:27). If we don't purpose to carefully control the worldly influences around us, they will control us. Those we can't control we should not hesitate to discard.

Cutting off harmful influences will not necessarily and automatically turn a corrupt heart into a pure one. But just as external acts of murder or adultery reflect internal hearts of sin, the outward act of fleeing sinful effects reflects the inward attitude that seeks holiness and God's will rather than human pleasure.

Jesus reminds us again that His standards of righteousness are humanly impossible to attain. We have all been murderers and adulterers in our hearts, and often we don't realize this because of sin's subtlety and blinding effect. But the impossibility of measuring up to divine standards points to our need to receive a new heart and turn over our helplessness to His sufficiency.

Ask YOURSELF

How have you practiced this kind of severing in your Christian life? What familiar sins and seductions have proven so injurious in your past, it's best if they're just never in the same room with you?

JESUS ON DIVORCE

It was said, "Whoever sends his wife away, let him give her a certificate of divorce"; but I say to you that everyone who divorces his wife, except for the reason of unchastity, makes her commit adultery; and whoever marries a divorced woman commits adultery.

MATT. 5:31–32

JESUS NO MORE APPROVES OF DIVORCE than did Moses (cf. Matt. 19:6). Adultery, another reality God never condoned, is the only reason under the law that allows for dissolving of a marriage, with the guilty party to be put to death (Lev. 20:10). Because Jesus mentions this here and again in Matthew 19:9, God must have allowed divorce to replace execution as the penalty for adultery at some time during Israel's history.

Divorce is never commanded; it is always a last resort, allowed when unrepentant immorality has exhausted the patience of the innocent spouse. This merciful concession to human sinfulness logically implies that God also permits remarriage. Divorce's purpose is to show mercy to the guilty party, not to sentence the innocent party to a life of loneliness. If you are innocent and have strived to maintain your marriage, you are free to remarry if your spouse insists on continued adultery or divorce.

Jesus does not demand divorce in all cases of unchastity (immorality, primarily adultery in this context), but simply points out that divorce and remarriage on other grounds results in adultery.

Our Lord wants to set the record straight that God still hates divorce (Mal. 2:16) and that His ideal remains a monogamous, lifelong marriage. But as a gracious concession to those innocent spouses whose partners have defiled the marriage, He allows divorce for believers for the reason of immorality. (Paul later added the second reason of desertion, 1 Cor. 7:15.)

*Ask*YOURSELF

How could you be an encouragement to a couple whose marriage is on the verge of collapse? How could you show Christ's mercy to those who have been wounded the greatest?

JESUS ON VOWS AND OATHS

Again, you have heard that the ancients were told, "You shall not make false vows, but shall
fulfill your vows to the Lord." But I say to you, make no oath at all, either by heaven,
for it is the throne of God, or by the earth, for it is the footstool of His feet, or by Jerusalem,
for it is the city of the great King. Nor shall you make an oath by your head,
for you cannot make one hair white or black.

MATT. 5:33–36

*I*N THE REGULAR BUSINESS OF LIFE, people use vows and oaths—at marriage ceremonies, in the courtroom, executive oaths of office. Because human nature is prone to lying and distrust, God has provided for proper use of oaths (cf. Heb. 6:16). In describing who may enter God's presence, the psalmist says one requirement is that the person be one who "swears to his own hurt and does not change" (Ps. 15:4b; cf. vv. 2–3). Such a person's word is more important than his or her welfare.

God Himself has issued oaths in the past (Gen. 22:16–17; cf. Pss. 89:3, 49; 110:4; Jer. 11:5; Luke 1:73). He did so to impress upon people the special importance or urgency of a promise. As Hebrews notes, "Since He could swear by no one greater, He swore by Himself" (6:13). Christ often used the expression "truly" or "truly, truly" (e.g., Matt. 5:18, 26; 6:2, 5, 16; John 1:51; 3:3, 5; 5:19, 24). As with the Father's oaths, the Son's use of "truly" did not make those statements any more trustworthy than any other pronouncements. The "truly" teachings underscored the importance of certain teachings. Jesus even used an oath before the high priest Caiaphas that He was indeed God's Son (Matt. 26:63–64).

In view of the special nature of divine oaths, we should "make no oath[s] at all"—in other words, no frivolous ones that would compromise our truthfulness and integrity (cf. Pss. 119:29, 163; 120:2).

Ask YOURSELF

Could your conversation be improved with less embellishment and exaggeration? Can your word stand on its own two feet?

APRIL 24

JESUS ON GENUINE TRUTHFULNESS

But let your statement be, "Yes, yes" or "No, no"; anything beyond these is of evil.

MATT. 5:37

*K*EEPING YOUR WORD IS THE MARK of a genuine worshiper and demonstrates that you, as a child of God, hate lies. Everything in God's kingdom is sacred and all truth is His truth, so truth has no degrees or shades. Thus even what seems to be the most minor false statement dishonors God's name.

The Lord has never had any standard other than absolute truthfulness. He wants every one of us to possess "truth in the innermost being" (Ps. 51:6). And it follows that "lying lips are an abomination to the Lord" (Prov. 12:22; cf. 6:16–17; Ps. 58:3–4).

Because God has the ultimate criterion of complete truthfulness, even our most routine conversations should be truthful and dependable in every detail. Our everyday talk ought to be plain and straightforward, uncluttered by qualifiers, exaggerations, or hedges on the truth. Our word must be as good as our bond or as any vow or oath we ever make. James's admonishment agrees with Jesus' teaching, "But above all, my brethren, do not swear, either by heaven or by earth or with any other oath; but your yes is to be yes, and your no, no, so that you may not fall under judgment" (James 5:12).

Ask YOURSELF

Truth and honesty will never be your default setting until you pursue it deliberately—spending your words carefully and keeping your word completely. In what particular areas of your life is it hardest for you to keep your promises?

A PERSPECTIVE ON NON-RETALIATION

You have heard that it was said, "An eye for an eye, and a tooth for a tooth."
But I say to you, do not resist an evil person.
MATT. 5:38–39A

*C*HRISTIANS ARE TO "RESIST THE DEVIL" (James 4:7; cf. 1 Peter 5:9) and all that his evil world system stands for (Matt. 6:13; Rom. 12:9; 1 Thess. 5:22). This proves that, although Jesus refuted the Jewish leaders' wrong teaching that people should take revenge in personal matters, our Lord did not teach that His followers simply had to tolerate all sorts of sinful misconduct and evil.

The resistance of evil and wrong, if done properly, will occur within the church. Jesus' instruction on church discipline concludes with this command: "If he refuses to listen to them, tell it to the church; and if he refuses to listen even to the church, let him be to you as a Gentile and a tax collector" (Matt. 18:17; cf. 1 Tim. 5:20). A sinning member who rejects one-on-one reproof as well as reproof from two or three others and from the entire church must be excluded from the fellowship. Concerning unrepentant immorality in the church, Paul instructed—quoting the Old Testament—"Remove the wicked man from among yourselves" (1 Cor. 5:13).

In contrast to this, Jesus clarifies that His followers must not resist or take vengeance regarding supposed harm done to them personally. Such retaliation has no place in society at large, much less among Christians. Paul later wrote, "Never pay back evil for evil to anyone" (Rom. 12:17; cf. v. 19). Instead, God calls us to overcome others' bad treatment of us by doing good to them (Rom. 12:21).

*Ask*YOURSELF

What are the main reasons for this kind of rebuke and discipline? What are its goals and objectives? When do circumstances become necessary to perform it?

JESUS AND NON-RETALIATION: DIGNITY

Whoever slaps you on your right cheek, turn the other to him also.

MATT. 5:39B

*G*OD HAS CREATED EVERY HUMAN being in His image, and therefore He demands that we treat one another with basic respect, dignity, and consideration. But in a sinful world, this will not always happen, so believers can expect to suffer persecution simply because of their basic testimony (cf. Matt. 10:16–23; John 15:18–16:3). This leaves one inevitable issue to deal with: how should Christians respond to ridicule, insult, or physical abuse.

The Lord Jesus, of course, is the perfect example of how to behave when personally attacked. When the Jewish leaders and Roman soldiers physically abused Him and mocked Him prior to His crucifixion, He did not react in words or actions (Matt. 26:67–68). As Jesus hung from the cross, He prayed, "Father, forgive them; for they do not know what they are doing" (Luke 23:34).

Peter summarizes well how we should respond in view of Christ's example:

When you do what is right and suffer for it you patiently endure it, this finds favor with God. For you have been called for this purpose, since Christ also suffered for you, leaving you an example for you to follow in His steps, who committed no sin, nor was any deceit found in His mouth; and while being reviled, He did not revile in return; while suffering, He uttered no threats, but kept entrusting Himself to Him who judges righteously. (1 Peter 2:20–23)

Ask YOURSELF

When have you succeeded in practicing this kind of self-control and restraint? What happened as a result? Even if it left you feeling misunderstood and stepped upon, what value did you experience from obeying what Jesus has commanded?

JESUS AND NON-RETALIATION: SECURITY

If anyone wants to sue you and take your shirt, let him have your coat also.

MATT. 5:40

$\mathcal{M}$OST PEOPLE IN NEW TESTAMENT times owned just one coat and likely just one or two shirts. Shirts were undergarments, and coats were outer garments that also served as blankets overnight. This kind of coat was important, what the Mosaic law required be returned to its owner "before the sun sets, for that is his only covering; it is his cloak for his body" (Ex. 22:26–27).

Jesus' reference here is not to a theft, when someone wants to steal another's garment, but to a legitimate lawsuit in a legal court. In those days the courts often mandated that fines or judgments be paid in clothing. The illustration is that a genuine follower of Christ will be willing to surrender even his most valuable coat to an adversary rather than cause offense or hard feelings. The judge could not require a specific coat in payment, but the person could voluntarily give it up.

Even if a settlement against us is fairly arrived at for a certain amount, we should be willing to pay more to demonstrate sincere regret for the wrong done and the pain inflicted on another. Most of us have probably never considered this option, but it shows the love of Christ and genuineness of our faith.

$\mathcal{A}\!sk$YOURSELF

Notice again that this series of scenarios from Jesus' Sermon on the Mount consistently calls for more than the law demands. What does that tell you about the way we're supposed to respond in situations in which our personal integrity or the cause of Christ is being challenged?

JESUS AND NON-RETALIATION: LIBERTY

Whoever forces you to go one mile, go with him two.

MATT. 5:41

*T*HE CONCEPT OF LIBERTY IS much cherished in the United States and other democratic nations. The Declaration of Independence famously speaks of "life, liberty, and the pursuit of happiness." Patrick Henry of Virginia used the bold oratory, "Give me liberty or give me death!" These sentiments were derived from biblical principles, although sometimes altered from those ancient origins.

God's intention from the beginning was for mankind created in His image to live in perfect liberty, both spiritually and physically. But the Fall ruined this ideal and introduced such corrupt concepts as slavery and subjugation to totalitarian governments. Democratic governments have tried, although imperfectly, to protect the liberty of their citizens—sometimes even extending such freedoms to foreign visitors and immigrants. However, civil liberties should not supersede our duties to righteousness or our obligations to display a faithful witness.

Jesus here makes the analogy between surrendered liberties and the Roman law that could force civilians to carry a soldier's pack for a mile. Except for facing them in battle, Roman troops were not as despised by their opponents as when those people were obligated to carry the troops' packs or other equipment.

Yet our Lord teaches that we should be willing to go the extra mile for someone else—even at the expense of our cherished liberty. In so doing, we are worthy ambassadors for Christ, realizing that in Him we have an eternal liberty that can never be taken.

Ask YOURSELF

Who in your life regularly asks you to go the second mile for them? What is your usual response to their demand for your time and energy? How do you strike the balance between being sacrificial and maintaining boundaries that help you protect other godly priorities?

JESUS AND NON-RETALIATION: PROPERTY

Give to him who asks of you, and do not turn away from him
who wants to borrow from you.

MATT. 5:42

$\mathcal{S}$ECULAR PEOPLE ALSO HOLD tightly to the concept that property rights are sacred. But such self-centered possessiveness is merely another symptom of humanity's sinfulness. Even believers forget that whatever they have belongs to God and that they are simply stewards of their wealth.

We do have certain legal rights in most countries to manage property as we wish. But we must be willing to sacrifice those rights on the altar of Christian obedience and submission (cf. Rom. 12:1–2). Whenever someone wants to borrow something of ours, we ought to willingly allow him or her to do so. That person might well have a genuine need, which only we can meet.

The Lord implies here that His disciples should offer to give as soon as they sense a need, not waiting to be asked. And He is not referring to our grudgingly donating, but to generous giving that springs from a loving desire to help. Our attitude should be far more than a token charity that merely wants to salve an uneasy conscience.

Christ's words do not intend to undercut civil justice, but to destroy human selfishness, which is sin and does not belong in the hearts of true Christians. In truth, the only persons who do not selfishly or vengefully cling to their property rights are those who have died to self (cf. Gal. 2:20). The faithful believer lives for Christ and if necessary surrenders all his or her rights and dies for Him (Rom. 14:8).

Ask YOURSELF

Again, since we cannot give away everything we have, how do we deal with the requirement of adhering to this Christian command while also using sound judgment, being good stewards of our God-given resources?

APRIL 30

JESUS ON GOD'S LOVE: FOR ENEMIES

But I say to you, love your enemies.

MATT. 5:44A

*P*EOPLE TEND TO BASE LOVE ON the attractiveness and likeability of the one loved. They love the so-called beautiful people, enjoyable activities, nice houses, and sharp cars. That list could go on, but Jesus' kind of love is need oriented. In His parable of the good Samaritan (Luke 10:29, 36–37), the Samaritan showed tremendous love because he sacrificed his own convenience, safety, and finances to help a desperately needy man.

The love our Lord sets forth here is translated from the Greek *agapē*, the noblest and best New Testament love. It is the form of love that strives to meet another's utmost welfare. Such love may involve emotion, but it must involve action. Like every aspect of righteousness, love originates in the regenerate heart, but it shows its fullest potential by what it does. More than anything, this kind of love is the love God is, expresses, and provides (Rom. 5:5, 8; 1 John 4:7–12), which allows us to love as He loved.

When Christ told His apostles, "A new commandment I give to you, that you love one another, even as I have loved you" (John 13:34), He had just washed their feet as an example of *agapē* love. The apostles were self-centered, quarrelsome, envious of one another, and even sometimes challenged the Lord. Yet Jesus always did for them what was for their good. And this is how He wants all of us who claim to follow Him to show love—even for our enemies.

Ask YOURSELF

Few biblical mandates are more unnatural to our desires and experiences, but few make us a more sterling example of the difference Christ makes in an ordinary individual's life. If you are currently dealing with situations that call for this kind of love, how do you intend to express it?

JESUS ON GOD'S LOVE: FOR PERSECUTORS

Pray for those who persecute you.

MATT. 5:44B

*T*HROUGHOUT THE CENTURIES THE worst kinds of persecutions against Jesus' followers have come from religious people. Persecution has been so strong against believers because they uphold God's standards, which indict the sin and corruption of false religion. God's Word unmasks hypocrisy in a most crucial area—humanity's propensity for self-justification.

Knowing that persecution would be the world's response to the Father's truth, Christ assures us that we will be persecuted, just as He was (John 15:20). Thus His command that we pray for our persecutors is one every faithful believer will have some opportunity to obey, not just those who live in countries where Christianity is illegal or severely restricted.

The best way to have *agapē* love for those who persecute us is to pray for them. We might sense their sinfulness and intense hatred and ridicule of us. Those traits make it impossible to love the persecutors for *what* they are, but we must love them for *who* they are—sinners in need of God's forgiveness and His saving grace. So we need to pray for them that they will repent and turn to Him for salvation, as we have already done.

Bear in mind, though, that persecutors will not always and only be unbelievers. Those professing to be fellow believers can give saints real grief and difficulty, too, but—as in every case—the first step in making right those situations is prayer. Jesus knew that prayer for persecutors can begin to knit our hearts with God's in the matter of loving our enemies.

Ask YOURSELF

Which has been the hardest for you to deal with—persecution from without or from within the family of God? Why is prayer such a powerful tool in combating the hard feelings this dredges up in you?

JESUS ON GOD'S LOVE: TO SHOW OUR SONSHIP

. . . so that you may be sons of your Father who is in heaven; for He causes His sun
to rise on the evil and the good, and sends rain on the righteous and the unrighteous.

MATT. 5:45

*G*OD HIMSELF IS LOVE, AND the best evidence that we are His children through faith in Jesus Christ is our love for other believers. "By this all men will know that you are My disciples, if you have love for one another" (John 13:35; cf. 1 John 4:20). Our divine sonship is further evidenced when love leads us to pray for our opponents.

Even though the world often has a faulty understanding of what the gospel is, it knows enough about Christ and His teachings to see that believers do not obey all His commands or live consistently as He lived. People in the world who are the furthest from saving faith nevertheless often sense the divine power that underlies the loving and caring Christian life—simply because such a life that goes far enough to love enemies is so uncharacteristic of human nature.

In this way we show our family likeness, an increasing resemblance to our heavenly Father. For example, God provides His general blessings on everyone, with no respect for merit or deserving; otherwise no one could receive them. The psalmist writes, "The eyes of all look to You, and You give them their food in due time. You open Your hand and satisfy the desire of every living thing" (Ps. 145:15–16). If God is so generous, we who claim to know Him ought to show similar love and impartial concern for everyone, even those who don't like us.

*Ask*YOURSELF

Though God does possess qualities we can never attain as mortals, He has given us—by virtue of our adoption into His family—the privilege of looking more like Him in our attitudes and behaviors. Why is pursuing this so important?

JESUS ON GOD'S LOVE:
THAT WE EXCEED OTHERS' ACTIONS

For if you love those who love you, what reward do you have? Do not even the tax collectors
do the same? If you greet only your brothers, what more are you doing than others?
Do not even the Gentiles do the same?

MATT. 5:46–47

*T*HESE WORDS OF JESUS WERE perhaps the most devastating and offensive ones the religious leaders had ever heard. The Lord bluntly stripped away their hypocrisy to reveal that their love was nothing more than the ordinary self-centered love common among the despised tax collectors and Gentiles. Tax collectors were dishonest, traitorous extortioners; Gentiles were considered unfit to be people of God.

Yet the type of love displayed by the scribes and Pharisees, according to Jesus' infallible assessment, was no better than the persons' whom they so looked down upon. In essence, our Lord declared that their righteousness was no better than that of the worst and lowest of other classes and groups.

Christ urges believers to have a much higher standard of righteousness than the world's low standard. The world should notice Christians as being more honest employees and more helpful and caring neighbors. The culture should always notice that saints love as God loves: "Let your light shine before men in such a way that they may see your good works, and glorify your Father who is in heaven" (Matt. 5:16). J. Oswald Sanders once wrote, "The Master expects from His disciples such conduct as can be explained only in terms of the supernatural."

Ask YOURSELF

Yes, we can become so comfortable in our culture and so indoctrinated in its ways that we are nearly indistinguishable in our likes, our schedules, and our matters of importance. Ask yourself what makes you appear different from the unsaved world around you. Is it just by what you *don't* do, or by Jesus' active brand of love and righteousness?

JESUS ON GOD'S LOVE: TO BE LIKE THE FATHER

Therefore you are to be perfect, as your heavenly Father is perfect.

MATT. 5:48

*T*HESE WORDS EMBODY ALL the truths Jesus teaches in the Sermon on the Mount—in fact, they are the apex of all He teaches in the gospels. The ultimate goal of our redemption and the sincere, strong yearning of God's heart is for all who would trust in His Son to be like Him.

The word translated "perfect" essentially means arriving at an intended end or realizing a completion of something. The word elsewhere in the New Testament is often rendered "mature" (cf. 1 Cor. 2:6; 14:20; Eph. 4:13, etc.). But here Jesus clearly intended to convey the meaning of perfection, because He is presenting God as the ultimate, holy standard for being and doing. It is the criterion of absolute perfection.

In our own power, such supreme and divine perfection is completely impossible to attain. And if we wonder how our Savior can demand the impossible, we simply have to remember His later instruction, "With people this is impossible, but with God all things are possible" (Matt. 19:26). God always provides the means and the power to accomplish what He commands.

Simply because God's righteousness is perfect, it is impossible in human strength to attain it. However, the impossible becomes possible for those of us who trust the Lord Jesus, because God gives to us the very righteousness of Christ.

*Ask*YOURSELF

Are you willing to believe God for the impossible—that you can actually be "wise in what is good and innocent in what is evil" (Rom. 16:19)? How could you cooperate with Him today in drawing closer to this noble goal?

WHAT'S WRONG WITH FALSE GIVING?

When you give to the poor, do not sound a trumpet before you, as the hypocrites
do in the synagogues and in the streets, so that they may be honored by men.
Truly I say to you, they have their reward in full.

MATT. 6:2

*G*IVING TO THE POOR LITERALLY MEANS any act of mercy, but it came to mean more specifically the giving of money or goods to the needy. Jesus did not say "if" but "when" concerning our giving—in other words, He expects us to do so. But just as sympathy for the needy does not help them unless something is actually done toward their need, so giving money provides us no spiritual blessing unless done from the heart.

Those who, like the Pharisees, give to impress others with their piety and generosity will receive no further reward. When we give with this false motive, we receive back only what people can give; we thereby forfeit God's blessings.

Many times, of course, the pretense people use to draw attention to or make an impression with their giving is not so obvious. They know, especially if they profess to follow Christ, that other Christians will resent ostentatiousness. So they seek to make their giving "accidentally" noticed. But any strategy designed to draw attention is still a basic form of trumpet-blowing hypocrisy, which can appear in various forms. Whenever we make a point of doing our giving publicly to be noticed, rather than doing it privately simply for God's reward, we behave more like the hypocrites of Jesus' day, not like His children.

*Ask*YOURSELF

What are some of the ways that giving can be done for personal recognition, even within the decorum of outward humility? How does one guard against this need for acknowledgment? What are we forgetting when we're tempted to crave the credit for every dollar we share with others?

THE SATISFACTION OF TRUE GIVING

When you give to the poor, do not let your left hand know what your right hand is doing, so that
your giving will be in secret; and your Father who sees what is done in secret will reward you.

MATT. 6:3–4

THE MOST SATISFYING, GOD-BLESSED giving is that which we do and then forget about. We do not wait for or want recognition—we're not even concerned whether the recipient is grateful or not. The act should be so discreet that even our left hand will not realize what happened.

The Old Testament describes giving as a part of God's cycle of blessing. Proverbs says, "The generous man will be prosperous, and he who waters will himself be watered" (11:25). God blesses our giving, and when that occurs we can give some more out of the additional resources He gives. The Lord, through Moses, told the Israelites, "You shall celebrate the Feast of Weeks to the Lord your God with a tribute of a freewill offering of your hand, which you shall give just as the Lord your God blesses you" (Deut. 16:10).

Appeals from all sorts of charities, ministries, and causes—some legitimate, others illegitimate—bombard Christians today, perhaps in a greater way than ever before. Having discernment on how to allocate your giving resources can be very difficult. But first of all, you should give systematically to your local church: "On the first day of every week each one of you is to put aside and save, as he may prosper" (1 Cor. 16:2). Then you can be alert for opportunities to give other amounts directly to individuals in need.

Willing and generous giving has always and should always characterize God's faithful people.

Ask YOURSELF

Are you being faithful to contribute the firstfruits of your giving—regularly, repeatedly—to the church where you are fed each week? Does this seem like a painful thing to do, or does it instead stir gratitude within you? As you pray, ask God to lead you with wisdom, sensitivity, and generosity to other people and ministries He wants to bless through you.

PRINCIPLES OF GIVING, PART 1

When you give to the poor, do not let your left hand know what your right hand is doing, so that your giving will be in secret; and your Father who sees what is done in secret will reward you.

MATT. 6:3–4

*F*ROM THIS AND OTHER SCRIPTURE, we can learn principles to guide us in God-honoring giving. *First* of all, genuine heart-giving is an investment with God. "Give, and it will be given to you. They will pour into your lap a good measure—pressed down, shaken together, and running over. For by your standard of measure it will be measured to you in return" (Luke 6:38; cf. 2 Cor. 9:6).

Second, biblical giving should be sacrificial. We don't determine this by the amount, but by the proportion. Consider the widow and Jesus' observation: "A poor widow came and put in two small copper coins, which amount to a cent. Calling His disciples to Him, He said to them, 'Truly I say to you, this poor widow put in more than all the contributors to the treasury; for they all put in out of their surplus, but she, out of her poverty, put in all she owned'" (Mark 12:42–44).

Third, Christians of all income levels should give. If you don't give when you have little, you won't necessarily give when you're prosperous. You might give a larger amount, but not a greater proportion. Jesus' parable of the unrighteous steward teaches, "He who is faithful in a very little thing is faithful also in much; and he who is unrighteous in a very little thing is unrighteous also in much" (Luke 16:10). God is concerned not with how much you have to give, but with how much love is behind the gift.

Ask YOURSELF

Think of personal examples from your own life where this "faithful in small things" principle has proven itself true. What have you promised you'd do if only you had a little more? What has usually happened when the "more" became reality?

PRINCIPLES OF GIVING: PART 2

When you give to the poor, do not let your left hand know what your right hand is doing, so that
your giving will be in secret; and your Father who sees what is done in secret will reward you.

MATT. 6:3–4

*C*ONTINUING FROM YESTERDAY'S LIST of scriptural giving principles, four more come to mind. *First*, financial giving correlates to spiritual blessings. God will not entrust things of greater value to those who are not faithful with lesser things. Jesus asks, "If you have not been faithful in the use of unrighteous wealth, who will entrust the true riches to you?" (Luke 16:11). Men have dropped out of the ministry because they couldn't handle their finances, and others remain but see little fruit because God won't commit souls to them if they can't manage material things, including their giving.

Second, believers must personally decide their giving. True giving will flow from a righteous heart, not artificially imposed percentages. "Each one must do just as he has purposed in his heart, not grudgingly or under compulsion, for God loves a cheerful giver" (2 Cor. 9:7; cf. 8:1–2; Phil. 4:15–18).

Third, Christians must give toward the needs of others. The early Jerusalem church did not hesitate to share its resources (Acts 2:44–45), and years later Paul took a collection from Gentile churches to help meet the continued needs of believers in Jerusalem.

Finally, genuine giving demonstrates the love of Christ, not adherence to the law. The New Testament does not specify required amounts or percentages (such as the tithe) for our giving. The amount we give, which ought to be as generous as possible, will derive from our heartfelt love and our knowledge of others' needs.

Ask YOURSELF

How do you go about deciding the amounts you give? Are you satisfied that you're being obedient to the Lord in this? Remember, giving is not supposed to be a source of guilt but rather a fount of blessing and gratitude. Are you experiencing a high level of peace about your giving decisions?

True Giving Should Anticipate Rewards

When you give to the poor, do not let your left hand know what your right hand is doing, so that your giving will be in secret; and your Father who sees what is done in secret will reward you.

MATT. 6:3–4

*W*HEN YOU GIVE AS JESUS DIRECTS—lovingly, unpretentiously, and with no concern for public recognition—"your Father who sees what is done in secret will reward you." In other words, if you remember, God forgets; and if you forget, God still remembers. You should simply try to meet every need you can and leave the bookkeeping to Him. This kind of giving is just a matter of realizing that "we have done only that which we ought to have done" (Luke 17:10).

There is nothing wrong with humbly anticipating our reward for true and honest giving. God knows our hearts, attitudes, and motives, and He will not fail to reward us appropriately. After all, our sovereign Lord knows exactly what everyone is doing (Heb. 4:13).

In giving and every other realm of good works, Jesus Christ is our perfect role model (cf. Eph. 2:10). He preached and taught before crowds large and small, and He did miracles of healing, compassion, and power over nature for many to see and benefit from. But He always focused the final attention on His heavenly Father and did not seek His own glory but the Father's (John 8:49–50).

Our motive in hoping for any rewards ought to be the anticipation of placing them as offerings at the Lord's feet, like the twenty-four elders who "will cast their crowns before the throne, saying, 'Worthy are You, our Lord and our God, to receive glory and honor and power'" (Rev. 4:10–11).

Ask YOURSELF

Like with any sinful tendency you wish to conquer, the secret is daily obedience, even in the smallest ways, not wanting to give the enemy the slightest opening for victory. In what ways could the day ahead likely give you an opportunity to practice this—to seek God's reward alone?

WRONG REASON FOR PRAYER

When you pray, you are not to be like the hypocrites; for they love to stand and pray
in the synagogues and on the street corners so that they may be seen by men.
Truly I say to you, they have their reward in full.

MATT. 6:5

*O*VER THE CENTURIES, VARIOUS questionable practices and attitudes have affected the prayer life of God's people—ritualization, prescription prayers, limitations of time and place, the love of long prayers, and meaningless repetitions. But the worst fault was when God's people prayed mainly to be noticed by others, especially by fellow Jews. This fault was inherently sinful because it originated from and helped intensify pride. Such an evil, self-glorifying motive was and is the ultimate perversion of God's gift of prayer, which is intended to glorify Him (cf. John 14:13) and express our dependence on His grace.

Prayer that focuses on self is always hypocritical; it stands in sharp contrast to true prayer, which focuses on God. Hypocrites are simply actors, persons playing a role, as the Greeks did on stage with their large masks. What such persons do and say is seldom sincere, but merely designed to create an image.

The scribes and Pharisees' prayers served the same purpose as so many of their activities—to draw praise and honor to themselves. This is the type of righteousness that has no place in the kingdom of God (cf. Matt. 5:20).

The more sacred something is, such as prayer, the more Satan wants to profane it. And one way to do that is to inject pride and self-centeredness into prayer—to get believers to pray as the Pharisees did. So if you pray to be impressive to fellow believers, you are praying for the wrong reason.

Ask YOURSELF

What should be the tone and purpose of public prayer? Should it be any different from your private interactions with God? What could you do to help make sure you're addressing God and not your audience?

MAY 11

WHAT ABOUT PUBLIC PRAYER?

They love to stand and pray in the synagogues and on the street corners so that they
may be seen by men. Truly I say to you, they have their reward in full.

MATT. 6:5B

*I*N JESUS' TIME, THE SYNAGOGUES were the likeliest and most appropriate places for sincere public praying. Devout Jews also offered many prayers on street corners, if that's where they were at the appointed hour of prayer. But the word Jesus uses here indicates a major street, and therefore a major street corner where a bigger crowd would likely be. By inference the hypocrites were at fault for wanting to pray before the biggest possible audience. No location is intrinsically forbidden as a place of prayer. But it's not right to consistently choose such a spot just to attract the largest audience.

As with anything tainted by human ambition and pride, the sin of praying in the wrong place begins in the heart. Like the Pharisee in Jesus' parable (cf. Luke 18:11), the hypocrites He mentions here prayed primarily to themselves and before others, not to God—and He wants no part in that.

Some Christians have thought Jesus' warnings here rule out all forms of public prayer. But to do so was not our Lord's intention. He prayed many times with His apostles (e.g., Luke 11:1) and in the midst of much larger crowds (e.g., Matt. 14:19). The early church rejoiced and "lifted their voices to God with one accord" (Acts 4:24) after the Jewish leaders released Peter and John. Public praying also is available to us, whether in church, Sunday school, or any smaller meeting of fellow believers.

*Ask*YOURSELF

What reward do those who perform their religious practices for show actually receive? And why isn't this enough to really satisfy—even when it's paid "in full"?

PRAYER'S REAL AUDIENCE: GOD

But you, when you pray, go into your inner room, close your door and pray to your
Father who is in secret, and your Father who sees what is done in secret will reward you.

MATT. 6:6

*J*ESUS' PRIMARY INSTRUCTION ABOUT prayer here is not about the location, but about our attitude in realizing that God constitutes our audience. If you go to a quiet, private place and shut everything else out as you pray, you'll turn your focus from yourself and others and over to God exclusively. Jesus regularly got away to pray alone so He could have effective communion with His Father, the most important, singular member of His prayer audience.

Praying to God "who is in secret" doesn't mean He is not our main audience for public prayers. He is definitely there wherever and whenever we call on Him. Genuine prayer is thus in a sense always intimate. If offered rightly, even public prayer will shut us into a private moment with God, enclosed in His presence.

Our "Father who sees what is done in secret" never betrays one of our prayer confidences. Unlike the occasional breached confidence we suffer at the hands of even our closest family or friends, private prayers and secret concerns shared with God will forever remain known just to Him, unless we later want others to know. The important thing for God is not the precise words we utter in private prayer, but rather the private thoughts we express in our hearts. Only He can know these with certainty and truly care about them (cf. 1 Cor. 4:3–5).

When God is genuinely the audience of our prayers, He will faithfully and unfailingly bless and reward us.

Ask YOURSELF

What have you discovered to be the greatest blessings of prayer? If none immediately spring to mind, try imagining a life without access to God's ear and His Spirit. What would you miss most about being out of contact with Him?

MEANINGLESS REPETITION: FALSE PRAYER CONTENT

And when you are praying, do not use meaningless repetition as the Gentiles do,
for they suppose that they will be heard for their many words.

MATT. 6:7

*I*F WE'RE HONEST, ALL OF US HAVE BEEN guilty of repetitive prayers—
before meals, at prayer meetings, before bed—with little or no thought to what we
are saying or how God feels when He hears us do that. But such prayers are offensive
to God and should be to us as well.

We should understand, however, that Jesus here is not forbidding the repetition
of genuine requests. In His parable of the midnight visit, Jesus pointed to the persistent man as a model of the believer's persistent prayer to God. In another parable,
the Lord praised the godly widow's persistence before the ungodly judge: "Will not
God bring about justice for His elect who cry to Him day and night, and will He
delay long over them?" (Luke 18:7). Paul asked God three times to remove his thorn
in the flesh (2 Cor. 12:7–8).

Jesus Himself could be persistent in prayer. In the Garden of Gethsemane, He
pleaded, "My Father, if it is possible, let this cup pass from Me; yet not as I will, but
as You will" (Matt. 26:39). Christ prayed this prayer a second time, and again He
"prayed a third time, saying the same thing once more" (v. 44).

Sincere, honest repetition of needs and praises before God is not wrong or ineffective. It is the mindless, indifferent repeating of tired, cliché-filled "prayers" that
is not pleasing to Him. God wants our hearts *and* our minds properly engaged when
approaching His throne.

Ask YOURSELF

What would enliven your set times of prayer, transforming them into fresh, ex-
pressive, genuine moments with God? Even if the same words and requests are made,
what could you do to make them real and in-the-moment?

SINCERE PRAYER REQUESTS

So do not be like them; for your Father knows what you need before you ask Him.

MATT. 6:8

WE DO NOT HAVE TO BADGER or cajole God to ensure that He will hear and answer our prayers or to convince Him that our requests are sincere. Prayer is more for our benefit than God's, as Luther said, "By our praying ... we are instructing ourselves more than we are him." Our prayers, no matter how eloquent or earnest, can never really inform or persuade God. Our responsibility and privilege is simply to approach Him with sincerity, purpose, and true devotion.

We can share with God all manner of needs, burdens, and heartfelt concerns, even though He already knows everything that's on our hearts and minds. God delights to hear us and commune with us more than we ever delight to commune with Him. He loved us first and with a greater intensity than we could ever love Him. Our sincere prayer requests allow God the opportunity to more fully reveal all His wonderful attributes to us (cf. John 14:13).

The great evangelist D. L. Moody once felt so filled up and overwhelmed with God's blessings that he reportedly prayed, "God, stop." Potentially, every faithful believer today could have Moody's response to God's goodness. The Lord answers us in better ways than we want or expect—but He always answers.

Ask YOURSELF

The fact that God "knows what you need before you ask Him" can easily be construed into a rationalization for praying less. What is it about this astounding reality, however, that should actually inspire us to pray more? How does it reorient us to the true meaning of relationship with God?

The Lord's Prayer: An Overview, Part 1

Pray, then, in this way: "Our Father who is in heaven, hallowed be Your name. Your kingdom come.
Your will be done, on earth as it is in heaven. Give us this day our daily bread. And forgive us our debts,
as we also have forgiven our debtors. And do not lead us into temptation, but deliver us from evil.
[For Yours is the kingdom and the power and the glory forever. Amen.]" For if you forgive others
for their transgressions, your heavenly Father will also forgive you. But if you do not forgive
others, then your Father will not forgive your transgressions.

MATT. 6:9–15

*I*N THE WORDS OF THIS PASSAGE, Jesus provides a concise but comprehensive model outline of genuine prayer. First our Lord addresses God's glory (vv. 9–10), then He speaks to humanity's needs (vv. 11–13a). Three petitions make up each of the sections. The first three deal with God's name, kingdom, and will; the second three appeal to the Father concerning daily bread, forgiveness, and protection from temptation.

Jesus says nothing specific about *where* we should pray. During His earthly ministry, He prayed in many different places and situations, both public and private. Paul instructed his readers to pray "in every place" (1 Tim. 2:8).

There is also nothing specific about a *time* to pray. Jesus prayed at many different hours, around the clock. Scripture pictures believers praying at every conceivable occasion—at regular, habitual prayer times; at times of special danger and special blessing; before and after meals; and when arriving at or leaving a certain location.

At any time and under any circumstance, prayer is appropriate. It should be a continual, comprehensive way of life—an open communion with God (Eph. 6:18; 1 Thess. 5:17).

Ask YOURSELF

As we embark on several days of devotional discussion concerning the Lord's Prayer, try to articulate what this passage has meant to you through the years. What is in this pattern of prayer that has ministered to you in deep, unforgettable ways?

THE LORD'S PRAYER: AN OVERVIEW, PART 2

Pray, then, in this way.
MATT. 6:9A

*O*VER THE YEARS PEOPLE HAVE had misunderstandings about the Lord's Prayer (more accurately, the Disciples' Prayer) that need correcting. First, Jesus' words were not meant to be repeated as a formal prayer. The disciples had asked Him how to pray, not what to pray. And He hardly would have given them a prayer to recite after He had just warned against "meaningless repetition" (v. 7).

Second, people often don't realize that Jesus' teaching here is simply a skeleton or pattern for prayer. As believers, we are to flesh out the skeleton with our own words of worship, praise, and intercession as we come to the Father.

Third, people have seldom realized how versatile Jesus' pattern for prayer is. Each phrase reflects the relationship between Creator and creature, and each one demonstrates an attitude and spirit of prayer. Similarly, we can variously outline it to show God's glory versus our need, the threefold purpose of prayer (hallow His name, usher in His kingdom, and do His will), or to present our concerns from a past, present, and future standpoint.

We can see God's overall purpose in prayer throughout the Lord's Prayer. The primary focus is on God, which includes our adoration of Him, His worthiness, and His glory. From this model we see that prayer is not so much our asking to meet our own needs and wants, but our affirming God's sovereignty, holiness, and majesty, and conforming our desires and purposes to His will.

Ask YOURSELF

What have people forfeited the most by viewing this prayer primarily as a rote, methodical, unthinking recitation before God? Does this argue against stating it in unison at church or in other religious gatherings? Or is there value in quoting it together—as long as our hearts are attuned to its meanings?

KNOWING GOD AS FATHER

Our Father who is in heaven . . .
MATT. 6:9B

*O*NLY THOSE WHO HAVE COME TO God through Christ can call God "Father." He is the Father of unbelievers only in that He created them (cf. Mal. 2:10; Acts 17:28). It is only those who trust Jesus who have "the right to become children of God" (John 1:12; cf. Rom. 8:14; Gal. 3:26).

In the Old Testament, faithful Jews saw God as the Father of Israel, the nation He elected as His special people. Isaiah proclaimed, "You, O Lord, are our Father, our Redeemer from of old is Your name" (Isa. 63:16b; cf. Ex. 4:22; Jer. 31:9). Many of them even saw God in an intimate way as their spiritual Father and Savior (Pss. 89:26; 103:13).

But because of their disobedience toward God's commands and their embracing of false gods around them, most Jews of Jesus' time had lost the true sense of God's fatherhood and viewed Him as only the remote Deity of their ancestors.

These six words at the beginning of the Disciples' Prayer reaffirm that God is the Father of all who trust in Him. Jesus Himself used the title "Father" in all His recorded prayers except one (Matt. 27:46). Although the text here uses the more formal Greek *patēr* for Father, Jesus likely used the Aramaic *abba* when He spoke these words. *Abba* has a more personal connotation (cf. Mark 14:36; Rom. 8:15), equivalent to the English "daddy."

Because saints belong to Jesus the Son, they can come to God the Father ("Daddy") as His beloved children.

*Ask*YOURSELF

Certainly in our decadent day and age, many are increasingly growing up in homes where "father" is a person to be feared, a person who rejects, a person who demeans and devalues. How does God's identity as "Father" fill the holes left by even well-meaning dads who fall short of what their role requires?

VALUE AND IMPORTANCE OF KNOWING THE FATHER

Our Father who is in heaven . . .

MATT. 6:9B

*K*NOWING GOD AS OUR FATHER carries with it a definite list of spiritual privileges and benefits. *First,* it means we need not fear, as pagans do before their false gods or unbelievers do in their agnosticism.

Second, real knowledge of God resolves uncertainties and gives us hope. A good earthly father does what it takes to protect and provide for his children; so our heavenly Father does much more to love and sustain His children (cf. Matt. 7:11; John 10:29; 14:21).

Third, knowing the Father alleviates loneliness. Family, friends, and even other believers may reject us, but we can be sure that God never will (John 14:21; cf. Ps. 68:5–6).

Fourth, knowing God as Father settles the issue of selfishness. Jesus used the plural possessive pronoun in reference to God because we share His fatherhood with millions of other Christians. Thus we ought to pray for others, not just ourselves.

Fifth, genuine knowledge of the Father means all His heavenly resources are available to us (Eph. 1:3).

Finally, this comprehension settles the issue of obedience. If Jesus in His incarnation did only His Father's will (John 6:38), we as adopted spiritual children must also do only God's will. This proves our relationship to Him (Matt. 12:50). Yet God in His grace still loves His children who disobey (cf. Luke 15:11–24).

Being our Father reveals God's willingness to lend His ear, power, and blessings to His children, for their best and His glory.

Ask YOURSELF

Which of these six benefits of God's Fatherhood struck you as most comforting and compelling today? What needs in your life does this particular blessing of God meet? And how does it do so in ways that no person could ever accomplish?

HALLOWING GOD'S NAME

Hallowed be Your name.

MATT. 6:9C

*S*CRIPTURE (1 PETER 1:16) COMMANDS believers to be holy ("hallowed"), whereas it recognizes God as being holy. So attributing to Him the holiness that already is His is how we hallow His name.

As with every other truly righteous action, hallowing God's name must begin in the heart. Peter reminds us to "sanctify Christ as Lord in your hearts" (1 Peter 3:15). When we do this, we also sanctify Him as Lord in our lives, as we above all affirm that He exists: "for he who comes to God must believe that He is and that He is a rewarder of those who seek Him" (Heb. 11:6).

Discovering and believing scriptural truth about God is also a way to hallow His name. Any deliberate ignorance or wrong doctrine about the Father shows gross irreverence for Him. But if we want to completely hallow His name and have full reverence for Him, we must go on to have a constant awareness of the Father's presence. David was a great example of this: "I have set the Lord continually before me" (Ps. 16:8).

Perhaps the greatest way of all for us to hallow His name is by following His will—down to the smallest task—making it the entire goal of our lives to glorify God (1 Cor. 10:31).

Furthermore, we hallow God's name by drawing others to Him. "Let your light shine before men in such a way that they may ... glorify your Father who is in heaven" (Matt. 5:16; cf. Ps. 34:3).

Ask YOURSELF

Everything we do, think, say, and communicate is a reflection on the name of God, since we have been called by His name and wear it as our chief identity. When are you most likely to forget that you bear the name of Christ, that you carry the responsibility for doing nothing to defame or discredit it?

What Is God's Kingdom?

Your kingdom come.

MATT. 6:10A

"KINGDOM" IS NOT SO MUCH A geographical territory as it is a sovereign dominion. When Christians pray "Your kingdom come," they are asking God to rule through Christ's future enthronement, His coming reign over the earth. The Greek for "come" indicates a sudden, instantaneous coming and here refers to the coming millennial kingdom (Rev. 20:4). Jesus is not speaking of some indirect effort by human good works to create a godly society on earth.

God's coming kingdom will be a kingdom on earth but not a kingdom of this present world system. Jesus told Pontius Pilate, "My kingdom is not of this world" (John 18:36). No human kingdom fits with God's, which is why even the best measures to improve society are mere holding actions that only retard sinful corruption until Christ returns to establish His perfect kingdom.

Jesus came to "preach the kingdom of God" (Luke 4:43), and there is no other gospel but the good news of His kingdom. Even during His final days on earth He was faithful to teach the apostles things concerning that kingdom (Acts 1:3).

Yes, the kingdom has a past element that encompasses the Old Testament patriarchs (Matt. 8:11). The kingdom was also present during Jesus' earthly ministry because He, its king, was "in [people's] midst" (Luke 17:21). In a sense that is true today as believers are members of God's invisible kingdom. But the particular focus of our prayers regarding the kingdom should be future, as we hope for the visible one to come.

Ask YOURSELF

What will you miss the least about earthly life when the fullness of His kingdom becomes your forever reality? Doesn't that give you something to really look forward to? Let the genuine hope of this occurrence bolster your hope as you live through the coming day.

HOW HIS KINGDOM COMES

Your kingdom come.
MATT. 6:10A

*I*T IS OBVIOUS THAT CHRIST IS NOT physically ruling on earth today, but one day He will. Therefore we should pray that God would hasten that time when His Son returns to establish His earthly kingdom, defeat sin, and ensure obedience to God's will. After a thousand years, this kingdom will merge into the eternal kingdom, and His earthly and heavenly rule will be the same (see Rev. 20–21).

There are two major ways in which God's kingdom comes, and they ought to inform our prayers as we ask Him to complete His purpose. *First,* His kingdom comes by means of conversions. Thus we should pray for sinners to repent (Mark 1:14–15) and to embrace the gospel (Luke 9:61–62). Our prayers must be simply that the Spirit will add new citizens to God's kingdom.

Second, the kingdom comes through believers' commitment. If we pray as Jesus commands, we will constantly ask that our lives and those of other Christians might obediently honor and glorify God in heaven.

The kingdom that we hope and pray for is of infinite value. Jesus elsewhere teaches that it "is like a treasure hidden in the field" or like "one pearl of great value" (Matt. 13:44–46). When the kingdom fully comes at His return, God will have completely answered our prayers. As the hymn says, "Jesus shall reign where'er the sun does its successive journeys run. His kingdom spread from shore to shore, 'til moon shall wax and wane no more."

Ask YOURSELF

How focused are you on these twin elements of kingdom advance? How do these priorities show themselves in your daily choices and activities? If they are commonly missing from your field of reference, ask yourself why this is the case.

GOD'S WILL: TWO MISUNDERSTANDINGS

Your will be done, on earth as it is in heaven.

MATT. 6:10B

$\mathcal{T}$WO POLAR OPPOSITE VIEWS OF GOD'S will can cause Christians to have faulty understandings of prayer and the accomplishing of God's purposes. On the one hand, some see His will as absolutely deterministic—whatever will be, will be. They either pray little at all, figuring the divine will is inevitable, or they are resignedly obedient, praying for God's will simply because He tells them to.

Neither approach to prayer demonstrates faith. Viewing God's sovereignty in a fatalistic, prayerless way robs us of the joy of aligning our wills with His and seeing His will done as we pray in faith. And praying with passive resignation leads to a weak, unexpectant prayer life. It is one that doesn't heed Jesus' instruction in the parable of the persistent widow: "He was telling them a parable to show that at all times they ought to pray and not to lose heart" (Luke 18:1).

Other believers overemphasize the role of human will and see prayer as mainly a way to twist God's will to their own desires. They think of God's will as what He dispenses from His cosmic vending machine—they get whatever they want by inserting a claim on one of His promises. But our Lord rejects such a false, man-centered concept throughout the model prayer. Genuine prayer focuses on God's name, God's kingdom, and God's will. The emphasis remains on the Father. God is sovereign, but Jesus tells us to pray that His will be done (cf. James 5:16).

$\mathcal{A}sk$ YOURSELF

Which of these two misunderstandings has been the hardest for you to counteract? Which one do you find yourself gravitating toward in your usual dealings with God? How has this led you to defeat and discouragement in your walk with Christ? What would you gain from embracing a more biblical mind-set?

A RIGHT UNDERSTANDING OF GOD'S WILL

Your will be done, on earth as it is in heaven.

MATT. 6:10B

*T*O UNDERSTAND GOD'S WILL RIGHTLY, we need an attitude of right-eous rebellion. If we would pray that God accomplishes His will, we must reject the notion that sin is normal and therefore we must accept it. Instead we must right-eously rebel against the world's ungodliness, its unbelief of Jesus Christ, and believ-ers' disobedience. Not to do this is to abandon key biblical teachings and accept powerlessness in prayer.

Jesus was not resigned to the spiritual status quo—He preached and acted against sin. When Jewish leaders profaned God's house, "He made a scourge of cords, and drove them all out of the temple, with the sheep and the oxen; and He poured out the coins of the money changers and overturned their tables; and to those who were selling the doves He said, 'Take these things away; stop making My Father's house a place of business'" (John 2:15–16).

We further must rebel against the idea that wickedness and corruption is some-how God's will that we must passively accept. Nothing evil comes from God's hand, but only from Satan's. To ask that righteousness and God's will be done oftentimes means we have to pray for Satan's will to be undone (cf. Ps. 68:1; Rev. 6:10).

To pray with a right understanding of God's will is to pray believing that He hears and answers our prayers. Lack of such faith is one of our greatest hindrances to effective praying.

Ask YOURSELF

Yes, to pray for God's will to be done on earth, we must first make sure it is being done in us. What are some aspects of God's will that are going unheeded in your own heart, even though they are far from mysterious, very clearly laid out in Scripture? Make this your prayer today—that His will would be done in you.

THREE ASPECTS OF THE DIVINE WILL

Your will be done, on earth as it is in heaven.

MATT. 6:10B

$\mathcal{G}$OD'S WORD REVEALS THREE aspects of His will. First is His will of *purpose*—His sovereign, ultimate plan for the universe. "Surely, just as I [God] have intended so it has happened, and just as I have planned so it will stand" (Isa. 14:24; cf. Eph. 1:9–11). It has been within God's purpose to allow sin to affect the world for a time. But that situation will end precisely according to His plan and foreknowledge.

Within God's will of purpose is His will of *desire*. This will is more specific but not always fulfilled in the present age. For example, Jesus desired His people, the Jews, to be saved. However, only a relative few believed in His message. Jesus prayed, "O Jerusalem, Jerusalem, the city that kills the prophets and stones those sent to her! How often I wanted to gather your children together ... and you would not have it!" (Luke 13:34). Like the Jews, most Gentiles are also unwilling to come to Christ for salvation (John 5:40; cf. 1 Tim. 2:4; 2 Peter 3:9).

Third is God's will of *command*, which is His desire that believers obey Him fully, as only they of all people can, with the help of the Spirit (see Rom. 6:16–18). Pride is the great enemy set against all of God's will. But for us to obey His will, we must forsake self-will and "prove what the will of God is, that which is good and acceptable and perfect" (Rom. 12:2; see also v. 1).

Ask YOURSELF

Understanding the many-layered aspects of God's will is not nearly as important as being obedient to every aspect you do know. Don't you long for His purpose, desire, and command to be met with full acceptance in your own life? Submit to Him in some new way today. Conform to His will.

THE TRUE SOURCE OF BREAD

Give us this day our daily bread.

MATT. 6:11

ESUS' REFERENCE TO "BREAD" NOT only signifies food but all of our physical needs. It is amazing that the self-sufficient, infinite God of the universe would care about our physical needs—that we have enough food, clothing, shelter—and then pledge to supply those needs. Thus God is the only source of our daily bread.

When everything is going well in life, we tend to think we are managing it all ourselves. Yet even the hardest-working person owes all he or she earns to the Lord's gracious provision (see Deut. 8:18; Acts 17:24–28). God provided for humanity even before He created Adam and Eve. They were His final creation, and one of the first things He said to them was, "Behold, I have given you every plant yielding seed that is on the surface of all the earth, and every tree which has fruit yielding seed; it shall be food for you" (Gen. 1:29). God has fulfilled this statement abundantly and in unlimited ways ever since.

Yet Paul teaches that in the latter days some will "advocate abstaining from foods which God has created to be gratefully shared in by those who believe" (1 Tim. 4:3). But the apostle reminds us "everything created by God is good, and nothing is to be rejected" (v. 4).

This part of the Lord's Prayer is an affirmation—appropriate for the well-fed and those who have little. By it we can thank God that every good thing comes from His gracious hand (James 1:17).

Ask YOURSELF

What are some of the more mundane, ordinary, forgettable things you not only can ask God for today, but can also transform into a prayer of gratitude? How can you make this refresher course in God's gracious gifts become a more regular part of your conscious thoughts and prayers?

ASKING FOR GOD'S PROVISION

Give us this day our daily bread.

MATT. 6:11

"GIVE" REMINDS US OF OUR NEED to ask God for His provision. In recognition of His past and present provision we ask Him, and trust for His future furnishing of all our needs. We can ask confidently because God has richly promised. "Delight yourself in the Lord; and He will give you the desires of your heart. . . . The humble will inherit the land and will delight themselves in abundant prosperity" (Ps. 37:4, 11). God does not pledge to always meet the physical needs of everybody, but only of those who trust in Him. In Psalm 37:25, David is speaking about believers when he says, "I have been young and now I am old, yet I have not seen the righteous forsaken or his descendants begging bread."

It is clear that the "us" who can expect provision from the Father are believers. Paul echoes the same principle: "Now He who supplies seed to the sower and bread for food will supply and multiply your seed for sowing and increase the harvest of your righteousness; you will be enriched in everything for all liberality, which through us is producing thanksgiving to God" (2 Cor. 9:10–11; cf. Luke 18:29–30).

God mercifully supplies our needs daily, meaning simply our ordinary, day-by-day provision of food, clothing, money, etc. The primary means by which we receive these things is through work, but isn't it the Lord who provides even the strength for that? To accept God's provision for today without undue concern for tomorrow is a testimony of our godly contentment (cf. Matt. 6:25, 32–33).

Ask YOURSELF

If the supply we have today isn't satisfying to us and doesn't seem like enough, is the problem with our Supplier or with our own measure of demand? Pray for a humble willingness to be thankful for every blessing, without focusing on the ones He seems to be withholding.

THE PROBLEM OF SPIRITUAL DEBT

And forgive us our debts.

MATT. 6:12A

*S*IN DOMINATES THE HEARTS AND minds of lost men and women, separates them from God, and is therefore their greatest enemy and problem. It is the common denominator for every crime, immorality, pain, and sorrow—and there is no natural cure: "Can the Ethiopian change his skin or the leopard his spots? Then you also can do good who are accustomed to doing evil" (Jer. 13:23). The natural individual does not even want his or her sin cured (John 3:19).

If sin is our greatest problem, our greatest need is the forgiveness God provides. Though forgiven from sin's ultimate penalty (cf. Rom. 8:1), believers need God's constant forgiveness for sins they still commit. The apostle John cautions us, "If we say that we have no sin, we are deceiving ourselves and the truth is not in us. If we confess our sins, He is faithful and righteous to forgive us our sins and to cleanse us from all unrighteousness" (1 John 1:8–9).

Jesus' act of washing the apostles' feet (John 13:5–11) is more than a picture of humility; it also portrays God's repeated, cleansing forgiveness to His disciples. The forgiveness that secures our saving position in Christ at regeneration does not need repeating; but we need God's practical forgiveness every day to cleanse us from sin's contamination as we live in this world. Out of God's vast heart of forgiveness He is ever willing to continually pardon His children (cf. Neh. 9:17; Rom. 5:20).

Ask YOURSELF

There are probably a small number of things in your life that are clearly in violation of what you know to be right—things that are top-of-mind as you consider again the depths of our sin and our need for God's forgiveness. Deal with these in prayer today as you repent before the Father and receive His promised mercy.

The Plea for Forgiveness

And forgive us our debts.

MATT. 6:12A

$\mathcal{G}$OD WILL NOT FORGIVE OUR SINS if we do not confess them. John makes that condition clear when he declares, "If we confess our sins, He is faithful and righteous to forgive us our sins and to cleanse us from all unrighteousness" (1 John 1:9). Confession simply means we agree with God that our sins are evil and defiling and we do not want them to taint our walk with Christ.

Our sinful pride makes it difficult to confess sin, but it is the only way to the free and joyful Christian life (cf. Prov. 28:13). John Stott said, "One of the surest antidotes to the process of moral hardening is the disciplined practice of uncovering our sins of thought and outlook as well as word and deed and the repentant forsaking of the same."

We must never take God's promise of forgiveness as a license for sin or as an excuse to presume on His grace. Instead we must view forgiveness as an aid to our sanctification and be constantly thankful to the Lord for His loving forgiveness.

Your prayer ought to coincide with the Puritan one: "Grant me never to lose sight of the exceeding sinfulness of sin, the exceeding righteousness of salvation, the exceeding glory of Christ, the exceeding beauty of holiness, and the exceeding wonder of grace. I am guilty but pardoned. I am lost but saved. I am wandering but found. I am sinning but cleansed. Give me perpetual broken-heartedness. Keep me always clinging to Thy cross."

Ask YOURSELF

How can one walk in an awareness of his own wretchedness while also living in the confidence of Christ's righteousness and salvation? Actually, it is only by realizing our great need for Him that we can enjoy the grace that overwhelms our sin. Seek this biblical balance in your own life.

THE NEED TO FORGIVE OTHERS

. . . as we also have forgiven our debtors.

MATT. 6:12B

*E*VEN AS WE HAVE BEEN FORGIVEN, we need to forgive. This is the character of righteousness. But because of our sinful flesh, we are often inconsistent with that duty and need constant exhortation (cf. Rom. 7:14–25).

The Lord Jesus' own example is a powerful motivation for us to forgive others. Paul reminds us, "Be kind to one another, tender-hearted, forgiving each other, just as God in Christ also has forgiven you" (Eph. 4:32; 1 John 2:6). In view of such divine graciousness, our forgiveness of another's sin expresses one of humanity's highest virtues: "A man's discretion makes him slow to anger, and it is his glory to overlook a transgression" (Prov. 19:11).

Extending genuine forgiveness to fellow believers benefits the entire body of Christ. Few other things have so weakened the church's power than unforgiveness among believers. Notably, mutually unforgiven, unresolved sins such as conflicts among members can really hinder a church's effectiveness. The psalmist warns us, "If [we] regard wickedness in [our] heart, the Lord will not hear" (Ps. 66:18; cf. Matt. 5:23–24; 1 Cor. 1:10–13; 3:1–9).

Harboring an unforgiving attitude is just plain sinful and invites God's chastening, as does any sin (1 Cor. 11:30; Heb. 12:5–13). But forgiving others brings God's forgiveness to us, and nothing in the Christian life is more important than that. Puritan Thomas Manton said, "There is none so tender to others as they which have received mercy themselves, for they know how gently God hath dealt with them."

*Ask*YOURSELF

Is there a relationship in your own life that continues to suffer from your unwillingness to forgive, from your deliberate decision to cling to your hurt and bitterness? This would be a good day to let this burden go, forgiving any who have wronged you—the same way God has forgiven you.

AVOIDING TEMPTATION

And do not lead us into temptation.

MATT. 6:13A

*B*Y ITSELF, THE WORD RENDERED "temptation" here has a neutral connotation, unlike the English that usually indicates an inducement to sin. But in this context, with its parallel to the term "evil" at the end of the verse, Jesus likely used the word to mean an enticement to sin. Yet elsewhere Scripture tells us that God does not tempt believers to evil, while at the same time we should be thankful for various trials (James 1:2–3, 13). So why did Jesus give us this expression as a pattern for prayer?

The answer to this paradox is not as difficult as it may seem. Jesus is concerned that we truly desire to avoid the danger and trouble sin creates. Saints should so despise sin and want to escape it at all costs that they pray in advance to avoid sin rather than waiting to defeat it when tempted.

Further, we know trials can promote our spiritual growth, yet we do not want to be in a place where we experience an increased possibility of sin. Like Jesus in the Garden of Gethsemane, we should pray, "My Father, if it is possible, let this cup pass from Me; yet not as I will, but as You will" (Matt. 26:39). The prospect of taking sin upon Himself repulsed our Savior, but He was willing to do so to fulfill His Father's will and secure the salvation of sinners. Whatever testing we might have to endure is nothing by comparison.

*Ask*YOURSELF

In addition to asking God not to "lead us into temptation," we must be aware of instances in which we walk headlong into it ourselves. Ask God for the spiritual strength to avoid those very familiar forms of sin that we too often approach without fear. Aren't you ready to start gaining victory over them?

TRUSTING GOD FOR PROTECTION

. . . but deliver us from evil.

MATT. 6:13B

*I*F YOU REALIZE THE GREAT DANGER that temptation poses to your soul, this petition will be a plea for God to provide a protection you can't give for yourself. You will ask God to watch over your entire being so that in whatever you do or say, see or hear, and wherever you go, He will guard you from sin.

Joseph understood that even though ungodly forces intend certain things for our evil, God can use those things for good (Gen. 50:20). But we may not react to every such situation as Joseph did. Therefore we must seize the promise that "God is faithful, who will not allow you to be tempted beyond what you are able, but with the temptation will provide the way of escape also, so that you will be able to endure it" (1 Cor. 10:13; cf. John 17:15).

When you sincerely pray "deliver us from evil," you implicitly submit to your only protection from sin, God's Word. "Submit therefore to God. Resist the devil and he will flee from you" (James 4:7). Submitting to God is in essence submitting to His Word. "Your word I have treasured in my heart, that I may not sin against You" (Ps. 119:11).

In a fallen world we are inadequate to deal with sin's powerful effects. Therefore we must confess the weakness of our flesh and the absolute powerlessness of our own resources to rescue us from sin's grasp.

Ask YOURSELF

Let this be a new day of triumph for you—a fresh start with God, knowing that His eternal might is greater than the allure of any sinful desire. Why continue on in ways that invariably lead to guilt, coldness, and defeat in your life? Choose the way that leads to unknown adventures with the Lord. Be delivered from evil as you take hold of the Father's hand and just walk away.

JUNE 1

POSTSCRIPT ON FORGIVENESS

If you forgive others for their transgressions, your heavenly Father will also forgive you.
But if you do not forgive others, then your Father will not forgive your transgressions.

MATT. 6:14–15

*B*ELIEVERS SHOULD FORGIVE OTHERS because they have received forgiveness from God themselves (cf. Eph. 1:17). We can't claim to know God's parental forgiveness—that which keeps our fellowship with the Lord rich and open—apart from forgiving others in heart and word.

Paul had this in mind when he wrote, "I found mercy, so that in me as the foremost [of sinners], Jesus Christ might demonstrate His perfect patience" (1 Tim. 1:16). An unforgiving spirit not only is inconsistent for one who has been totally forgiven by God, but also brings the chastening of God rather than His mercy.

Jesus states the truth of verse 14 in a negative way when He says, "But if you do not forgive others, then your Father will not forgive your transgressions." The sin of an unforgiving heart and a bitter spirit (Heb. 12:15) forfeits blessing and invites judgment.

We must seek to manifest the forgiving spirit of Joseph (Gen. 50:19–21) and of Stephen (Acts 7:60) as often as needed (Luke 17:3–4). To receive pardon from the perfectly holy God and then refuse to pardon others when we are sinful people is the epitome of abuse of mercy. "Judgment will be merciless to one who has shown no mercy; mercy triumphs over judgment" (James 2:13). So be sure you are practicing forgiveness of others.

Ask YOURSELF

What breaks down in your relationship with God when you withhold forgiveness from those who have wronged or mistreated you? How does it choke out your openness and freedom in the Lord's presence?

JUNE 2

JESUS AND FASTING

*Whenever you fast, do not put on a gloomy face as the hypocrites do, for they neglect their
appearance so that they will be noticed by men. Truly I say to you, they have their reward in full.*

MATT. 6:16

*T*HE GREEK WORD FOR "FAST" literally means not to eat, to abstain from
food. But by the time of Christ, fasting had been perverted and twisted beyond what
was scriptural and sincere. Fasting had become a ritual to gain merit with God and
attention before men—it was largely a hypocritical religious show.

Many Pharisees fasted twice a week (Luke 18:12), usually on the second and
fifth days of the week. They picked those days supposedly because on them Moses
received the tablets of Law from God on Mount Sinai. But they also happened to be
the two major Jewish market days, when cities and towns were crowded with farm-
ers, merchants, and shoppers, where public fasting would have the largest audiences.

Those wanting to call attention to their fasting would "put on a gloomy face" and
"neglect their appearance in order to be seen fasting by men." They would wear old
clothes, sometimes purposely torn and soiled, mess up their hair, cover themselves
with dirt and ashes, and even use makeup to look pale and sickly.

But this kind of fasting is a sham and mockery. Those whom Jesus condemned
for fasting "in order to be seen by men" were pretentiously self-righteous. God was
of little concern in their motives or their thinking, and so He had no part in their reward. The reward they wanted was recognition by men, and that's what they got.

Ask YOURSELF

Are you sometimes guilty of feeling superior to others by the faithful way you
observe various spiritual disciplines and religious expectations? What do these pride-
ful feelings and comparisons take away from the purity of your times with God?
How do they complicate your worship?

PROPER FASTING AND PRAYER

But you, when you fast, anoint your head and wash your face so that your
fasting will not be noticed by men, but by your Father who is in secret;
and your Father who sees what is done in secret will reward you.

MATT. 6:17–18

JESUS' STATEMENT "WHEN YOU FAST" indicates that fasting is normal and acceptable in the Christian life. He assumes His followers will fast on certain occasions, especially in times of testing, trial, or struggle.

Fasting is appropriate during times of sorrow. On occasions of deep grief, fasting is a natural human response. Most people don't feel like eating at those times. Other things that motivate fasting have included overwhelming danger, penitence, and the receiving or proclaiming of a special revelation from God. And fasting often accompanied the beginning of an important task or ministry.

In every scriptural account, genuine fasting is linked with prayer. You can pray without fasting, but you cannot fast biblically without praying. Fasting is an affirmation of intense prayer, a corollary of deep spiritual struggle before God. It is never an isolated act or ceremony or ritual that has some inherent efficacy or merit.

Fasting is also always linked with a pure heart and must be associated with obedient, godly living. This is the attitude that will motivate the one fasting not to attract attention to his deprivation and spiritual struggle. Fasting is not to be a display for anyone, including God. Genuine fasting is simply a part of concentrated, intense prayer and concern for the Lord, His will, and His work. Jesus' point is that the Father never fails to notice fasting that is heartfelt and genuine, and He never fails to reward it.

Ask YOURSELF

Has fasting ever been a part of your life and relationship with God? If so, what have those experiences taught you about Him . . . and about yourself and your need for Him? If you've never actually participated in fasting, what might be some appropriate times and ways for you to practice it?

JUNE 4

JESUS ON WEALTH

Do not store up for yourselves treasures on earth, where moth and rust destroy,
and where thieves break in and steal. But store up for yourselves treasures in heaven,
where neither moth nor rust destroys, and where thieves do not break in or steal;
for where your treasure is, there your heart will be also.

MATT. 6:19–21

*T*HE FOCUS OF JESUS' TEACHING here is this: "Do not lay up treasures for yourself." The Greek word for "lay up" connotes the idea of stockpiling or hoarding—it pictures wealth that isn't being used, things kept mainly to show off one's plenty.

Be sure of this, though: Jesus is not advocating poverty as a means of spirituality. Both the Old and New Testaments recognize the right to material possessions, including money, land, animals, houses, clothing, and anything else acquired honestly. In fact, the foundational truth underlying the commands not to steal or covet is the right of possessing personal property.

God expects and commands His people to be generous. But He also expects and commands that we not only be thankful for the blessings He gives but also derive pleasure from them—including the material blessings. The Lord "richly supplies us with all things to enjoy" (1 Tim. 6:17). This verse is specifically directed to "those who are rich in this present world," yet it does not command them to divest themselves of their wealth. Rather, it warns them not to be conceited about it or to trust in it. It's how we use our possessions for kingdom purposes that counts.

Ask YOURSELF

How would you define your general attitudes toward money? What is its purpose in the believer's life? How are we supposed to handle it? What are some of the greatest abuses or misunderstandings of money that have plagued your life or distorted your freedom with it?

Using Wealth Wisely

Do not store up for yourselves treasures on earth, where moth and rust destroy,
and where thieves break in and steal. But store up for yourselves treasures in heaven,
where neither moth nor rust destroys, and where thieves do not break in or steal;
for where your treasure is, there your heart will be also.

Matt. 6:19–21

*T*HERE IS A GREAT POTENTIAL FOR your possessions to become idols when you accumulate them for yourself. But possessions that are wisely, willingly, and generously used for kingdom purposes can be a means of accumulating heavenly possessions. When they are hoarded and stored, they not only become a spiritual hindrance but also are subject to loss through moth, rust, and thieves.

In ancient times, wealth was frequently measured in part by clothing. The best clothes were made of wool, which the moths loved to eat. Wealth was also often held in grain. The Greek word for "rust" means "an eating." That's the application here, since grain was often ruined by rats, mice, worms, and insects. Also, almost any kind of wealth can be stolen. Many people in those days buried their nonperishable valuables in the ground, away from the house, often in a field.

Nothing we own is completely safe from destruction or theft. But when our time, energy, and possessions are used to serve others and to further the Lord's work, they build up heavenly resources that are completely free from destruction or theft.

Make sure you are living by this principle: "Honor the Lord from your wealth, and from the first of all your produce; so your barns will be filled with plenty and your vats will overflow with new wine" (Prov. 3:9–10).

Ask YOURSELF

How many of your worries revolve around financial issues? What kind of stress and strain does this place on your mind and spirit—whether your problem involves being anxious about the prospects of the money you have, or anxious about the money you don't have?

WEALTH AND HEART ATTITUDES

The eye is the lamp of the body; so then if your eye is clear, your whole body will be full of light.
But if your eye is bad, your whole body will be full of darkness. If then the light
that is in you is darkness, how great is the darkness!

MATT. 6:22–23

EXPANDING ON THE PREVIOUS three verses, Jesus uses the eye as an illustration of the heart. The lamp, or lens, of the body is the eye; that's how we receive light. The heart is the eye of the soul, and it is through our hearts that God's truth, love, peace, and every spiritual blessing comes to us.

Words closely related to the word for "clear" include liberality and generosity. So the implication is that if our heart is generous (clear), our spiritual life will be flooded with spiritual understanding.

However, if our eye is diseased or damaged, no light can enter, and our "whole body will be full of darkness." If our hearts are burdened with material concerns, we'll become "blind" and insensitive to spiritual concerns. The eye is our window—when it's clear, light shines through; but when it's corrupt, it prevents light from entering.

The eye that is bad is the heart that is selfishly indulgent. The person who is materialistic and greedy is spiritually blind. Because he has no way of recognizing true light, he thinks he has light when he doesn't. It's because he's self-deceived that Jesus says, "How great is the darkness!"

This principle is both simple and sobering: the way we look at and use our money is a sure barometer of our spiritual condition.

Ask YOURSELF

Blind spots are certainly easy to develop in our hearts, whether about money or any other aspect of belief and practice. How can you safeguard yourself from letting your personal blind spots become ingrained attitudes, poisoning your ability to see clearly what God wants to do in your life?

JUNE 7

SERVING ONLY ONE MASTER

No one can serve two masters; for either he will hate the one and love the other,
or he will be devoted to one and despise the other. You cannot serve God and wealth.

MATT. 6:24

*J*UST AS WE CANNOT HAVE OUR treasures both in earth and in heaven or our bodies both in light and in darkness, we cannot "serve two masters." The Greek word for "masters" is often translated "lord," and often refers to a slave owner.

By definition, a slave owner has total control of the slave. For a slave there is no such thing as partial or part-time obligation to his master. He owes full-time service to his master. He is owned and totally controlled by and obligated to his master. To give anything to anyone else would make his master less than his master. It is impossible to "serve two masters" and fully or faithfully be the obedient slave of each.

In this way we can't claim Christ as Lord if our allegiance is to anything or anyone else, including ourselves. And when we know God's will but resist obeying it, we give evidence that our loyalty is to someone or something other than Him. But the person whose master is Jesus Christ can say that when he eats or drinks or does anything else, he does "all to the glory of God" (1 Cor. 10:31). Make your allegiance to Christ your priority each and every day.

*Ask*YOURSELF

What alternative "masters" compete the hardest for your devotion? How has the inviolable truth of this "no man can serve two masters" statement been proven true in your life and in your observation of others? But why do we seem so intent on trying to have it that way anyway?

WORRY IS A SIN

For this reason I say to you, do not be worried about your life, as to what you will eat
or what you will drink; nor for your body, as to what you will put on.
Is not life more than food, and the body more than clothing?

MATT. 6:25

*F*OR CHRISTIANS TO WORRY IS TO BE disobedient and unfaithful to God. Nothing in our lives, internal or external, justifies our being anxious when God is our Master.

Worry is basically the sin of distrusting the promise and providence of God, and yet it is a sin Christians commit perhaps more frequently than any other. In the Greek, the tense of Jesus' command includes the idea of stopping what is already being done. We are to stop worrying and never start again.

The English term *worry* comes from an old German word meaning to strangle, or to choke. That's exactly what worry does—it's a type of mental and emotional strangulation that probably causes more mental and physical afflictions than any other single cause.

The substance of worry is nearly always extremely small compared to the size it forms in our minds and the damage it does in our lives. It's been said that worry is a thin stream of fear that trickles through the mind that, when encouraged, will cut a channel so wide that all other thoughts will be drained out.

If worrying is a pattern in your life—stop now. In the days to follow you'll learn why you should trust your Father and stop worrying.

Ask YOURSELF

Would you categorize yourself as a worrier? If so, what do you think has driven you to choose the perceived relief of worry over the actual relief of trust in God? If not, what has tipped your heart in favor of less worry and more confidence and contentment?

REASONS TO BE CONTENT

For this reason I say to you, do not be worried about your life, as to what you will eat
or what you will drink; nor for your body, as to what you will put on.
Is not life more than food, and the body more than clothing?

MATT. 6:25

*W*ORRY IS THE OPPOSITE OF contentment, which should be a believer's normal and consistent state of mind. You should be able to say with Paul, "I have learned to be content in whatever circumstances I am. I know how to get along with humble means, and I also know how to live in prosperity; in any and every circumstance I have learned the secret of being filled and going hungry, both of having abundance and suffering need" (Phil. 4:11–12).

A Christian's contentment is found only in God—in His ownership, control, and provision of everything we possess and will ever need. Since God owns everything, what we now have and what we will ever have belongs to Him.

Daniel understood the Lord's control of everything: "Let the name of God be blessed forever and ever, for wisdom and power belong to Him. It is He who changes the times and the epochs; He removes kings and establishes kings; He gives wisdom to wise men and knowledge to men of understanding" (Dan. 2:20–21).

And if we hadn't heard it from Daniel, we should know it from one of the ancient names of God—Jehovah-Jireh, which means, "the Lord who provides."

Whatever the Lord gives us belongs to Him. Therefore, it is our responsibility to thank Him for it and to use it wisely and unselfishly for as long as He entrusts us with it.

Ask YOURSELF

What keeps "enough" from being enough for us? How do we define the level of property or possessions we need in order to feel satisfied with our supply? Why are these measurements so often faulty and skewed away from sound biblical understanding?

JUNE 10

EXAMPLE OF THE BIRDS

Look at the birds of the air, that they do not sow, nor reap nor gather into barns,
and yet your heavenly Father feeds them. Are you not worth much more than they?

MATT. 6:26

*M*ANY BIRDS LIVE IN NORTHERN Galilee, and it's likely some flew by as Jesus was teaching. As an object lesson, Jesus called attention to the fact that birds do not have intricate and involved processes for acquiring food.

Like every creature, birds receive their life from God. And He provides them with an abundance of food resources and the instinct to find those resources for themselves and their offspring. The Lord asked Job, "Who prepares for the raven its nourishment when its young cry to God?" (Job 38:41). The obvious answer is: God does.

If God is so careful to provide for such relatively insignificant creatures as birds, how much more will He take care of those He created in His own image and who have become His children through faith?

This doesn't mean Jesus is suggesting that birds do nothing to feed themselves. But they never worry about where their next meal is going to come from. They gather food until they have enough, and then go about whatever other business they may have until time for the next meal.

Use this example of a bird's worry-free life and adopt the same attitude for yourself.

Ask YOURSELF

It really is worth reiterating that birds don't sit around waiting for their needs to be met. Keep your eye to an open window one morning, and you'll see just how industrious they are. How does this help you understand Jesus' words better? In what ways have laziness and other lacks of good character increased your worry quotient?

EXAMPLE OF THE FLOWERS

And why are you worried about clothing? Observe how the lilies of the field grow; they do not
toil nor do they spin, yet I say to you that not even Solomon in all his glory clothed himself
like one of these. But if God so clothes the grass of the field, which is alive today and tomorrow
is thrown into the furnace, will He not much more clothe you? You of little faith!

MATT. 6:28–30

*M*ANY OF THE PEOPLE JESUS spoke to likely had little clothing to their
name. So He pointed again to their surroundings, this time to flowers, to assure them
of God's concern and provision.

"The lilies of the field" may have been a general term used for the beautiful wild-
flowers that graced the fields and hillsides of Galilee. Such decorations of nature
make no effort to grow and have no part in designing or coloring themselves. The
naked eye can see much of the amazing detail, shading, and coloring of a flower, yet
under a microscope it shows itself to be even more marvelous and intricate than people in Jesus' day could ever have imagined.

The simple point is that not even Solomon, one of most resplendent kings the
world has ever known, could clothe himself like one of those little flowers growing
abundantly on the hillside.

If Jesus told those who had but one simple garment not to worry about their
clothing, what would He say to us? If God bothers to array the grass of the field with
beautiful but short-lived flowers, how much more is He concerned to clothe and
care for His very own children?

Ask YOURSELF

Nature is indeed a constant reminder not only of the wonder and splendor of
God, but also of His daily provision. Perhaps the radical policies of today's green generation—a fervor that borders on and often becomes an idolatrous worship of the
earth—can make us wary of learning from the world around us. But creation is a
gift of God to us, designed to help us look to Him as our source.

Worry Is Not a Trivial Sin

*But if God so clothes the grass of the field, which is alive today and tomorrow
is thrown into the furnace, will He not much more clothe you? You of little faith!*
MATT. 6:30

*I*T SEEMS ODD, DOES IT NOT, that we who have freely put our eternal destiny into Christ's hands would at times refuse to believe that He will provide what we need to eat, drink, and wear. Faith should extend to the ordinary, just as it extends to the extraordinary.

Worry is not a trivial sin because it strikes a blow both at God's love and integrity. Worry declares our heavenly Father to be untrustworthy in His Word and His promises. To claim belief in the inerrancy of Scripture yet in the next moment express worry is to deny that very belief. Worry reveals that we are mastered by our circumstances and by our own finite perspective and understanding rather than God's Word. Worry is therefore not only debilitating and destructive but also maligns and impugns God.

When a believer is not fresh in the Word every day so that God is in his mind and heart, then Satan moves into the vacuum and plants worry. And worry pushes the Lord even further from our minds.

Paul counsels us as he did the Ephesians, "I pray that the eyes of your heart may be enlightened, so that you will know what is the hope of His calling, what are the riches of the glory of His inheritance in the saints, and what is the surpassing greatness of His power toward us who believe. These are in accordance with the working of the strength of His might" (Eph. 1:18–19).

Ask YOURSELF

Have you ever seriously considered the unspoken statement you make when worry defines your reaction to life's uncertainties? If you understood the root beliefs that fuel the fires of anxiety, what effect would this knowledge have on your level of fretfulness?

SEEKING GOD'S KINGDOM FIRST

But seek first His kingdom and His righteousness, and all these things will be added to you.

MATT. 6:33

WHEN CHRISTIANS THINK LIKE the world and crave things in the world, they will worry like the world, because a mind not focused on God is a mind that has cause to worry. The faithful, trusting, and reasonable Christian is "anxious for nothing, but in everything by prayer and supplication with thanksgiving [lets his] requests be made known to God" (Phil. 4:6).

The antidote to worry that results in contentment is to make God and His kingdom your priority. Jesus is saying, "Rather than seeking and worrying about food, drink, and clothing like unbelievers do, focus your attention and hopes on the things of the Lord, and He will take care of all your needs."

Seeking God's kingdom means losing ourselves in obedience to the Lord and pouring out our lives in the eternal work of our heavenly Father. To seek God's kingdom is to seek to win people into that kingdom that they might be saved and God might be glorified.

We are also to seek His righteousness. Instead of longing after the things of this world, we ought to hunger and thirst for the things of the world to come, which are characterized above all else by God's perfect righteousness and holiness. We not only are to have heavenly expectations but also holy lives: "What sort of people ought you to be in holy conduct and godliness, looking for and hastening the coming of the day of God" (2 Peter 3:11–12).

Ask YOURSELF

Seeking first the kingdom can be little more than a mental slogan for us until we define what this means in real-life, everyday terms. Spend some time today focusing on what a kingdom priority looks like at home, at work, at church, at the gym, at the market, in all the places your routine takes you.

Don't Worry about Tomorrow

So do not worry about tomorrow; for tomorrow will care for itself.
Each day has enough trouble of its own.

MATT. 6:34

*M*AKING REASONABLE PROVISIONS for the future is sensible, but to "worry about tomorrow" is foolish and unfaithful. God is the God of tomorrow as well as the God of today and eternity. "The Lord's lovingkindnesses indeed never cease, for His compassions never fail. They are new every morning; great is Your faithfulness" (Lam. 3:22–23).

People are so committed to worrying that, if they can't find anything in the present to worry about, they think about possible problems in the future. So Jesus assures us, "Tomorrow will care for itself." This is not the careless philosophy of the hedonist who lives only for his present enjoyment. It is the conviction of the child of God who knows tomorrow will care for itself because it is in his heavenly Father's hands.

"Each day has enough trouble of its own" is not a call to worry about that trouble—it's an invitation to concentrate on meeting the temptations, trials, opportunities, and struggles we have today, relying on our Father to protect and provide as we have need. There is enough trouble in each day without adding the distress of worry to it.

God promises His grace for tomorrow and for every day thereafter and through eternity. But He does not give us grace for tomorrow now—He gives His grace only a day at a time as it is needed, not as it may be anticipated.

So begin today to focus on the issues of today. Don't start dwelling on tomorrow until it becomes today.

*Ask*YOURSELF

What else might Jesus have in mind by commanding us to maintain our full attention on the day, the hour, the moment we're currently living in? What do we lose by living in either the past or the future?

JESUS' DEFINITION OF JUDGING

Do not judge so that you will not be judged.

MATT. 7:1

*O*NE OF THE CENTRAL MESSAGES of Jesus' Sermon on the Mount to His followers is for them to be discerning and perceptive in what they believe and what they do. All Christians need to make every effort to judge between truth and falsehood, between the internal and the external, between reality and sham, and between true righteousness and false righteousness.

Every message we hear is to be judged for the soundness of its doctrine. Paul told the Galatians, "But even if we, or an angel from heaven, should preach to you a gospel contrary to what we have preached to you, he is to be accursed!" (Gal. 1:8).

Not to rebuke sin is a form of hatred, not love. Refusing to warn a person about his sin is just as unloving as refusing to warn him about a serious disease he may have. The writer of Hebrews calls for a level of spiritual maturity wherein Christians "because of practice have their senses trained to discern good and evil" (Heb. 5:14).

So in Matthew 7:1, Jesus is not telling us never to think or make value judgments. He is referring to the self-righteous, egotistical judgment and unmerciful condemnation of others practiced by the scribes and Pharisees. Their primary concern was not to help others from sin to holiness, but to condemn them to eternal judgment because of actions and attitudes that did not square with their own worldly, self-made traditions.

Jesus is referring to the judgment of motives that no human being can know of another—judgment of external form. What Jesus is forbidding is self-righteous, hasty, unmerciful, prejudiced, and unwarranted condemnation based on human standards and human understanding.

*Ask*YOURSELF

This is one Bible verse our culture feels good about knowing—and thrusting into the faces of Christians at every opportunity. But how do you see this concept twisted in people's dealings with others and in matters of morality?

JUNE 16

WRONG JUDGMENT: AN ERRONEOUS VIEW OF GOD

Do not judge so that you will not be judged.

MATT. 7:1

*B*ELIEVERS ARE NOT TO MAKE unrighteous and unmerciful judgment on others because it manifests a wrong view of God. With the phrase "so that you will not be judged," Jesus reminds the scribes and Pharisees that they are not the final court. To judge another person's motives or to stand in the place of condemnation is to play God. "For not even the Father judges anyone, but He has given all judgment to the Son" (John 5:22). During the millennial kingdom Christ will share some of that judgment with us (Matt. 19:28), but until that time we blaspheme God whenever we take the role of judge on ourselves.

"Who are you to judge the servant of another?" asks Paul. "To his own master he stands or falls" (Rom. 14:4). Paul was little concerned about how other people judged him, nor was he concerned about how he judged himself. "I am conscious of nothing against myself," he says, "yet I am not by this acquitted; but the one who examines me is the Lord" (1 Cor. 4:4).

Except as they may be continually teaching false doctrine or following standards that are clearly unscriptural, we are never to judge a person's ministry, teaching, or life—and certainly not his motives—by some self-styled standard.

Whenever we assign people to condemnation without mercy, we pass judgment that only God is qualified to make. Our Lord does not call for men to cease to be examining and discerning, but to renounce the presumptuous temptation to try to be God.

*Ask*YOURSELF

Why is the desire to judge and size up such an alluring appetite of ours? What does our tendency to enjoy it tell us about ourselves? What would need to occur inside before we saw an increased resistance to practice it?

WRONG JUDGMENT: AN ERRONEOUS VIEW OF OTHERS

For in the way you judge, you will be judged; and by
your standard of measure, it will be measured to you.

MATT. 7:2

*M*OST PEOPLE FEEL FREE TO judge other people harshly because they erroneously think they are somehow superior. The Pharisees considered themselves exempt from judgment because they believed they perfectly measured up to the divine standards. The problem was that these weren't divine standards—they were mere human standards they had established far short of God's holy and perfect law.

When we assume the role of final, omniscient judge, we imply that we are qualified to judge—that we know and understand all the facts, all the circumstances, and all the motives involved. Therefore, when we assert our right to judge, we will be judged by the same standard of knowledge and wisdom we claim is ours. If we set ourselves up as judge over others, we cannot plead ignorance of the law in reference to ourselves when God judges us. We are especially guilty if we do not practice what we ourselves teach and preach.

Other people are not under us, and to think so is to have the wrong view of them. To be gossipy, critical, and judgmental is to live under the false illusion that those whom we so judge are somehow inferior to us.

This kind of judgment is a boomerang that will come back on the one who judges. Self-righteous judgment becomes its own gallows, just as the gallows Haman erected to execute the innocent Mordecai was used instead to hang Haman (Esther 7:10).

Ask YOURSELF

One of the more notable qualities of our sinful human nature is that the sins we seem quickest to judge in others are the ones we struggle the hardest with ourselves. Why do you think this is the case? What brings about this touchy sensitivity and indignance?

Wrong Judgment: An Erroneous View of Ourselves

Why do you look at the speck that is in your brother's eye, but do not notice the log that is in your own eye? Or how can you say to your brother, "Let me take the speck out of your eye," and behold, the log is in your eye? You hypocrite, first take the log out of your eye.

MATT. 7:3–5A

*W*HEN WE JUDGE CRITICALLY we also manifest an erroneous view of ourselves. The "speck" Jesus refers to is not something insignificant—it was likely a twig or splinter. Though small in comparison to a log, it was not a good thing to have in your eye. Jesus' comparison is not between a very small sin or fault and one that is large, but between one that is large and one that is gigantic. His primary point is that the sin of the critic is much greater than the sin of the person he is criticizing.

The wretched and gross sin that is always blind to its own sinfulness is self-righteousness. It looks directly at its own sin and still imagines it sees only righteousness.

The very nature of self-righteousness is to justify self and condemn others. Self-righteousness is the worst of all sins because it trusts in self rather than God. It trusts in self to determine what is right and wrong and to determine who does what is right or wrong.

Too, the term "notice" conveys serious, continual meditation. Until you have thought long and hard about your own sin, how can you confront another with his shortcomings?

*Ask*YOURSELF

Again, the thought conveyed here is not that we are forbidden from ever pointing out the sins of another, aiding him toward repentance and a desire for God's forgiveness. But our hearts are so suspect, we must regularly keep our sins confessed and to the surface. How do you practice this discipline in your own life?

CHALLENGING A BROTHER

Then you will see clearly to take the speck out of your brother's eye.

MATT. 7:5B

*H*ERE IS JESUS' CORRECTIVE TO erroneous judgment: first of all we confess our own sin, which is often the sin of self-righteousness and of a condemning spirit toward others, and ask for God's cleansing. When our sin is cleansed, when the log is removed from our eye, then we can see our brother's sin clearly and be able to help him. We will also see everything more clearly—God, others, and ourselves. We will see God as the only Judge, others as needy sinners who are just like us. We will see our brother as a brother on our own level and with our own frailties and needs.

David reflects the right balance of humility and helpfulness in Psalm 51: "Create in me a clean heart, O God, and renew a steadfast spirit within me.... Restore to me the joy of Your salvation and sustain me with a willing spirit. Then I will teach transgressors Your ways, and sinners will be converted to You" (vv. 10, 12–13). Jesus told Peter that after he had recovered from his moral defection, he could then "strengthen [his] brothers" (Luke 22:32).

All confrontation of sin in others must be done out of meekness, not pride. We can't play the role of judge—passing sentence as if we were God. We can't play the role of superior—as if we were exempt from the same standards we demand of others. We must not play the hypocrite—blaming others while we excuse ourselves.

Ask YOURSELF

When have you seen this interchange done in a way that honored God, considered self, and truly benefited others? What were the key factors that contributed to the purity and peace of it? How was the rebuke handled by the one being confronted? What would make the difference if that person were you?

OF DOGS AND SWINE

Do not give what is holy to dogs, and do not throw your pearls before swine,
or they will trample them under their feet, and turn and tear you to pieces.
MATT. 7:6

*I*T IS CLEAR FROM THIS VERSE that Jesus doesn't exclude every kind of judgment—here He commands a specific type. But to obey His command, you need to know who the dogs and swine represent.

In biblical times dogs were largely half-wild mongrels that acted as scavengers. They were dirty, greedy, snarling, and often vicious and diseased. No responsible Jew would ever throw to a dog a piece of holy meat that had been consecrated as a sacrifice in the temple. Since no man was allowed to eat this meat, how much less should it have been thrown to wild, filthy dogs.

Swine were considered by the Jews to be the epitome of uncleanness. Like the scavenging dogs, those swine were greedy, vicious, and filthy.

Dogs and swine represent those who, because of their great perversity and ungodliness, refuse to have anything to do with the holy and precious things of God except to trample them under their feet, turning and tearing God's people to pieces.

Jesus' point is that certain truths and blessings of our faith are not to be shared with people who are totally antagonistic to the things of God. Such people have no appreciation for what is holy and righteous. They will take that which is holy, the pearls of God's Word, as foolishness and an insult. We need not waste God's holy Word on those who both reject it and mock it.

Ask YOURSELF

What are some specific situations in your own daily experience where the wisdom of this statement really comes into play? What should you watch for in others to see whether they're perhaps becoming receptive to Christ and His Word? Until then, what's the best way to stay true to your faith in their presence?

ASKING FOR WISDOM

Ask, and it will be given to you; seek, and you will find; knock, and it will be opened to you. For everyone who asks receives, and he who seeks finds, and to him who knocks it will be opened.

MATT. 7:7–8

*O*UR HEAVENLY FATHER IS generous to us and promises we have access to His eternal and unlimited treasure to meet our own needs as well as the needs of others. Even when we have been cleansed of our own sin, we need divine wisdom to know how to help a brother remove the speck from his eye.

God's wisdom is one of our greatest needs. We can't be discerning and discriminating without divine counsel from our heavenly Father; and the primary means for achieving that wisdom is prayer: "If any of you lacks wisdom, let him ask of God, who gives to all generously and without reproach, and it will be given to him" (James 1:5).

Along with God's perfect and infallible Word, we need His Spirit to interpret and illumine, to encourage and to strengthen. He does not want us to have all the answers; He wants us to be students who search the Scriptures. The Bible is a limitless store of divine truth. But apart from God Himself we can't begin to fathom its depths or mine its riches. God gives enough truth for us to be responsible, but enough mystery for us to be dependent. He gives us His Word not only to direct our lives but to draw our lives to Him.

So when you need God's wisdom to make spiritual decisions, ask God for it.

Ask YOURSELF

Part of feeling as though God isn't providing us wisdom is that we don't know how to receive it or what's required in listening for it. How has God most often supplied you with the wisdom you need to handle a certain situation?

QUALIFICATIONS TO RECEIVE GOD'S WISDOM

Ask, and it will be given to you; seek, and you will find; knock, and it will be opened to you. For everyone who asks receives, and he who seeks finds, and to him who knocks it will be opened.

MATT. 7:7–8

*T*HE PROMISES IN THESE VERSES are limited only to believers who meet certain qualifications. *First*, "everyone" refers to those who belong to the Father. Those who are not God's children can't come to Him as their Father.

Second, the one who claims this promise must be living in obedience to his Father. "Whatever we ask we receive from Him," John says, "because we keep His commandments and do the things that are pleasing in His sight" (1 John 3:22).

Third, our motive in asking must be right. "You ask and do not receive," explains James, "because you ask with wrong motives, so that you may spend it on your pleasures" (James 4:3). God does not obligate Himself to answer selfish, carnal requests from His children.

Finally, we must be submissive to His will. If we are trying to serve both God and mammon (Matt. 6:24), we can't claim this promise. "For that man ought not to expect that he will receive anything from the Lord, being a double-minded man, unstable in all his ways" (James 1:7–8).

Another possible qualification is perseverance, as indicated by the Greek imperatives ask, seek, and knock. The idea is continuance and constancy: "Keep on asking; keep on seeking; and keep on knocking."

If you meet these qualifications, be sure you're taking advantage of your access to God.

Ask YOURSELF

None of us can entirely attain to these lofty ideals, but God knows when our hearts are tender and sincere before Him, genuinely seeking His glory over our personal gain. In whatever situation you're most in need of His guidance and provision today, ask in faith while surrendering yourself.

JUNE 23

GOD'S LOVE ILLUSTRATED

What man is there among you who, when his son asks for a loaf, will give him a stone?
Or if he asks for a fish, he will not give him a snake, will he? If you then,
being evil, know how to give good gifts to your children, how much more
will your Father who is in heaven give what is good to those who ask Him!

MATT. 7:9–11

*I*F WE CLAIM TO BE GOD'S children, we should be reflecting God's character in our lives. Jesus here shows us something of what our heavenly Father's love is like.

Jesus asks two rhetorical questions. The first asks what loving father would ever give his son a stone if he asked for a piece of bread. Leading up to the second question, Jesus gives an example of a son asking his father for a fish. The father wouldn't give his son a snake, would he? The obvious answer to both is that *no* father would do that because it isn't natural to ignore the physical or spiritual needs of his son.

In contrast to sinful, human fathers, our divine, loving, merciful, gracious Father has no limit on His treasure and no bounds to His goodness. Yet even the greatest human parental love cannot compare with God's.

The truth Jesus proclaims here is that, if imperfect and sinful human fathers so willingly and freely give their children the basics of life, God will infinitely outdo them in measure and benefit. If we want God to treat us with loving generosity as His children, we should so treat others, because we are those who bear His likeness.

Ask YOURSELF

As always, our dealings with God are based on relationship—a relationship He has graciously established and continues to maintain. What threatens your own ability to view Him in this light, rather than primarily relating to Him only in religious terms—distant and detached?

THE GOLDEN RULE SUMMARIZED

In everything, therefore, treat people the same way you want
them to treat you, for this is the Law and the Prophets.

MATT. 7:12

*T*HE PERFECT LOVE OF THE heavenly Father is most reflected in His children when they treat others as they themselves wish to be treated. This verse is a summary of the Law and the Prophets. It's also a paraphrase of the second great commandment, "You shall love your neighbor as yourself" (Matt. 22:39). How we treat others is not determined by how we expect them to treat us or by how we think they should treat us, but by how we want them to treat us.

Man's basic problem is preoccupation with self. In the final analysis, every sin results from that preoccupation. We sin because we are totally selfish, totally devoted to ourselves rather than to God and to others. Unregenerate humanity can never reach the standard of selfless love on its own.

So the dynamic for living this supreme ethic must come from outside our fallen nature. It can come only from the indwelling Holy Spirit, whose firstfruit is love (Gal. 5:22). In Jesus Christ "the love of God has been poured out within our hearts through the Holy Spirit who was given to us" (Rom. 5:5). Only Christ's own Spirit can empower us to love each other as He loves us (John 13:34).

Selfless love serves for the sake of the one being served, and serves in the way it likes being served—whether it receives such service or not. This level of love is the divine level, and can be achieved only by divine help.

Ask YOURSELF

Sometimes we find ourselves grappling with such deep biblical matters that we overlook the most simple—like the Golden Rule. Try being more deliberate in the coming day to heeding this basic teaching of Jesus. See how it alters the way you approach even your routine interactions with others.

THE NARROW GATE, PART 1

Enter through the narrow gate; for the gate is wide and the way is broad that leads to
destruction, and there are many who enter through it. For the gate is small and
the way is narrow that leads to life, and there are few who find it.

MATT. 7:13–14

JESUS' SERMON ON THE MOUNT HAS been heading toward the appeal found in these two verses. Here is His call to people to make a decision about becoming a citizen of God's kingdom and inheriting eternal life, or remaining a citizen of this fallen world and receiving damnation. Every person eventually comes to this crossroads in life, where he'll need to decide on which gate to enter and which way to follow.

"Enter" is in a mood that demands a definite and specific action. Jesus pleads for people to enter the narrow gate, God's gate, the only gate that leads to life and to heaven. Throughout the sermon Jesus had contrasted the narrowness of God's internal standard of righteousness to the broad and external standards of Jewish tradition. The path to that narrow way of kingdom living is through the narrow gate of the King Himself: "I am the way, and the truth, and the life; no one comes to the Father but through Me" (John 14:6). We proclaim a narrow gospel because that is the only gospel God has given and therefore the only gospel there is.

Make sure you are proclaiming to others the narrow gospel God has given us.

Ask YOURSELF

We needn't apologize that the way to Christ is narrow and exclusive. For if it weren't for this narrow way, there would be no way. Try to avoid presenting the gospel to others in an apologetic manner, one that accommodates more human choice and preference than God's Word allows. Invite them to the true gospel alone, knowing that the Spirit of God will draw others only to the truth.

THE NARROW GATE, PART 2

*Enter through the narrow gate; for the gate is wide and the way is broad that leads to
destruction, and there are many who enter through it. For the gate is small and
the way is narrow that leads to life, and there are few who find it.*

MATT. 7:13–14

*E*NTERING THROUGH THE NARROW GATE makes a few demands on the
person passing through. First, he must enter *alone*. You can bring no one else and
nothing else with you. Some have suggested that the gate is like a turnstile: only one
person can get through at a time, and with no baggage.

The narrow gate also demands we must go through *naked*. This is a gate of *self-
denial*—you can't carry the baggage of sin and self-will. The way of Christ is the way
of the cross, and the way of the cross is self-denial: "If anyone wishes to come after
Me, he must deny himself, and take up his cross and follow Me. For whoever wishes
to save his life will lose it; but whoever loses his life for My sake will find it" (Matt.
16:24–25).

The narrow gate also demands *repentance*. Many Jews believed that merely being
a Jew, a physical descendant of Abraham, was sufficient for entrance into heaven.
Many people today believe that being in a church, or even being a good human
being, qualifies them. But the way of repentance, of turning from their own way and
their own righteousness to God's, is the only way to enter His kingdom and therefore the only way to keep from perishing.

*Ask*YOURSELF

What are the various pieces of baggage that people want to hold on to as they
enter from death to life? What are the pieces that you still have a tendency to long
for, even on this side of the narrow gate?

JUNE 27

THE TWO WAYS

Enter through the narrow gate; for the gate is wide and the way is broad that leads to
destruction, and there are many who enter through it. For the gate is small and
the way is narrow that leads to life, and there are few who find it.

MATT. 7:13–14

TWO GATES LEAD TO TWO different ways. The wide gate leads to a way that is broad; the narrow gate leads to a way that is narrow. The narrow way is the way of the godly, and the broad way is the way of the ungodly—the only two ways people can travel.

The way that is broad is the easy, attractive, inclusive, indulgent, permissive, and self-oriented way of the world. It has few rules, few restrictions, and few requirements. All you need to do is profess Jesus, or at least seem religious, and you'll be accepted into that group.

The narrow way is the hard and demanding way—the way of self-denial and the cross. When Jesus was asked, "Lord, are there just a few who are being saved?" He replied, "Strive to enter through the narrow door; for many, I tell you, will seek to enter and will not be able" (Luke 13:23–24). The Greek word for "strive" (*agonizomai*) indicates that entering the door to God's kingdom takes conscious, purposeful, and intense effort.

The narrow way is for those who want God's kingdom at any cost. Make sure that you're following Christ as Lord along that narrow way.

Ask YOURSELF

We certainly live amid a "broad way" mentality—a mind-set that can worm itself into our own ways of thinking. But what has God taught and shown you during those times when you've been most devoid of worldly restraints, when your life has been most wholly devoted to His Word and His ways?

THE WAY TO LIFE: SIMPLE, BUT NOT EASY

For the gate is small and the way is narrow that leads to life, and there are few who find it.
MATT. 7:14

*G*OD'S WAY OF SALVATION IS remarkably simple, but it is not easy. Nothing we can give or give up can earn us entrance into the kingdom. But if we long to hold on to forbidden things, it can keep us out of the kingdom.

Even though we can pay nothing for salvation, coming to Jesus Christ costs us everything we have. Jesus says, "Whoever does not carry his own cross and come after Me cannot be My disciple" (Luke 14:27).

The person who says yes to Christ must say no to the things of the world, because to be in Christ is to rely on His power rather than our own and to be willing to forsake our own way for His. It can cost persecution, ridicule, and tribulation.

When we identify ourselves with Jesus Christ, we declare war on the devil, and he declares war on us. The one whom we formerly served now becomes our great enemy, and the ideas and ways we once held dear now become our great temptations and pitfalls.

Along with warnings of suffering, the Lord also gives promises that our hearts will rejoice (John 16:22) and that we are to take courage because He has overcome the world (John 16:33). He promises to enable us to prevail over those times of suffering, not to escape them.

Ask YOURSELF

Looking back, how have you experienced growth in your total dependence upon the Lord? Though we are often so hard on ourselves and perhaps weighed down with undue guilt, our hearts should rejoice to see the Spirit taking up residence in our attitudes and practices. Worship with this in mind today.

TWO DESTINATIONS

Enter through the narrow gate; for the gate is wide and the way is broad that leads to destruction, and there are many who enter through it. For the gate is small and the way is narrow that leads to life, and there are few who find it.

MATT. 7:13–14

BOTH THE BROAD AND NARROW ways point to the good life, to salvation, heaven, God, the kingdom, and blessing—but only the narrow way actually leads there. The broad way doesn't have a road sign on it with hell as the destination. Jesus' point is that this way is marked "heaven" but it doesn't lead there.

That is the great lie of all false religions. The Lord makes clear the ultimate destinations of these two ways: the broad way leads to destruction; the narrow way leads to life. Every religion except Christianity follows the same spiritual way and leads to the same spiritual end, to hell.

There are many of those roads, and most of them are attractive, appealing, and crowded with travelers. But not a single one leads where it promises, and not a single one fails to lead where Jesus says it leads—to destruction, to total ruin and loss. It is a complete loss of well-being and the destination of all religions except the way of Jesus Christ.

But God's way—the way that is narrow—leads to eternal life, to everlasting heavenly fellowship with God, His angels, and His people. Everlasting life is a quality of life, which is the life of God in the soul of man (see Ps. 17:15).

Ask YOURSELF

Celebrate today the eternal life promised to those who embrace the call of the narrow gate and the narrow way. Be grateful that none of the carry-ons and extras will ever give us the satisfaction we hope to find in them, but that in the wake of their emptiness we will be drawn ever deeper into the One whose way is both single and secure.

TWO GROUPS

Enter through the narrow gate; for the gate is wide and the way is broad that leads to
destruction, and there are many who enter through it. For the gate is small and
the way is narrow that leads to life, and there are few who find it.

MATT. 7:13–14

"*MANY*" AND "FEW" DESCRIBE TWO groups of people. Those who enter through the wide gate and travel the broad way, toward the destination of destruction, are many. They include pagans and nominal Christians, atheists and religionists, theists and humanists, Jews and Gentiles—every person from every age, background, persuasion, and circumstance who has not come to saving obedience in Jesus Christ.

In the day of judgment many will claim to be followers of Christ: "Many will say to Me on that day, 'Lord, Lord, did we not prophesy in Your name, and in Your name cast out demons, and in Your name perform many miracles?' And then I will declare to them, 'I never knew you; depart from Me, you who practice lawlessness'" (Matt. 7:22–23). Those who are excluded will not be just atheists or rank pagans, but nominal Christians who professed to know and trust Christ but who refused to come to Him on His terms.

The group that goes through the narrow gate and travels the narrow way and is destined for life are few in number. Jesus said, "Many are called, but few are chosen" (Matt. 22:14).

Make sure you are numbered with the few and not with those who will receive Jesus' shocking declaration at the day of judgment.

Ask YOURSELF

What are some of the greatest lies that lead the mildly religious into believing they have accepted Christ into their hearts? In what ways do our churches today accommodate these? How can we work against this devious scheme of the enemy?

JULY 1

JESUS WARNS OF FALSE PROPHETS

Beware of the false prophets, who come to you in sheep's clothing, but inwardly are ravenous wolves.

MATT. 7:15

*F*ALSE PROPHETS ARE NOT SIMPLY wrong teachers, propagating a different philosophy or alternative theology. They are spiritually dangerous and we should not expose our souls and minds to their perverse, poisonous influence. These purveyors of error and heresy are spiritual beasts and far more deadly than any physical ones. Peter warns that they are "like unreasoning animals. . . . reveling in their deceptions . . . enticing unstable souls" (2 Peter 2:12, 13, 14; cf. Jude 10). Therefore, perfectly understanding all this, Jesus' admonition to "beware of the false prophets" is not merely a mention of something but a warning to be on guard against and keep our minds away from what is spiritually harmful.

For the benefit of His listeners, it was natural for Jesus to compare false prophets with wolves. In Palestine, wolves roamed the landscape seeking to prey upon stray or lagging sheep. When a wolf found a defenseless sheep, it attacked quickly and tore the sheep to pieces. Just like those merciless and ferocious animals, false teachers are always seeking new victims.

Jude's letter warns against false prophets and tells how we can safeguard ourselves against them: "Keep yourselves in the love of God, waiting anxiously for the mercy of our Lord Jesus Christ to eternal life" (v. 21). Our first priority is to be right with the Lord, living in a place of divine fellowship and sound teaching. Then we can warn others of false prophets and carefully rescue them from the damning influences (Jude 22–23).

Ask YOURSELF

Are there any spiritual half-truths that have worked on you in the past? How did they prove to be wolf-like after tricking their way into your thinking?

FALSE PROPHETS ARE DECEPTIVE

Beware of the false prophets, who come to you in sheep's clothing, but inwardly are ravenous wolves.

MATT. 7:15

*F*ALSE PROPHETS ARE MOST dangerous because of their deceptive nature. We can easily recognize and defend against an enemy that poses for what it is. But when that enemy appears as a friend, it is much harder to defend against.

Heretics and apostates make no claim to biblical truth and are recognizable. But deceivers disguise themselves as true shepherds. They give the appearance of orthodoxy and claim to teach the truth, but their intent is to deceive and destroy God's people.

Paul explains this phenomenon: "Such men are false apostles, deceitful workers, disguising themselves as apostles of Christ. No wonder, for even Satan disguises himself as an angel of light. Therefore it is not surprising if his servants also disguise themselves as servants of righteousness, whose end will be according to their deeds" (2 Cor. 11:13–15; cf. 2 Tim. 3:13). Such false prophets are demonically deceived, convinced that their perverted, distorted views are correct. They are so steeped in falsehood that darkness seems to be light, blackness white, and error truth.

This calls for genuine discernment. But how is this best done? It's by realizing that such men show themselves by what they do not say—they seldom affirm the great doctrines of the faith, but rather ignore them. In our day of confusion and indifference, we need to pray and vigilantly "test the spirits to see whether they are from God. . . . Every spirit that confesses that Jesus Christ has come in the flesh is from God" (1 John 4:1, 2).

*Ask*YOURSELF

What constitutes false teaching today? Why do such philosophies continue to find room to work in hearts and minds, even of believers? What can we do to keep them away from our churches?

DISCERNING FALSE PROPHETS: THE CHARACTER TEST

You will know them by their fruits. Grapes are not gathered from thorn bushes nor
figs from thistles, are they? So every good tree bears good fruit, but the bad tree bears bad fruit.

MATT. 7:16–17

*O*NE'S BASIC CHARACTER—attitudes, inner motives, loyalties, standards—
eventually manifests itself in his or her life. Christians produce good fruit in their attitudes and actions. But unbelievers, especially false prophets, will eventually
manifest bad fruit.

False teachers can hide their true fruit for a time behind ecclesiastical trap-
pings, evangelical vocabulary, and false fellowship. But how they behave when not
around Christians will soon enough reveal their true loyalties and convictions. Unless they exhibit "moral excellence . . . knowledge . . . self-control . . . perseverance
. . . godliness" and so forth (see 2 Peter 1:5–8), we can be sure God has not sent them
and they do not belong to Jesus Christ. Another crucial indicator of character that we
can look for, as summarized by Christ Himself, is this: "He who speaks from himself
seeks his own glory; but Hhe who is seeking the glory of the One who sent Him, He
is true, and there is no unrighteousness in Him" (John 7:18).

The teacher who emulates Christ and wants to glorify Him is a genuine servant of the Lord. But the false one, no matter how clever, can't hide for long his corrupt character—and the discerning believer will recognize this. As John Calvin
wrote, "Nothing is more difficult to counterfeit than virtue."

*Ask*YOURSELF

How does this teaching coexist with the "judge not" command from earlier in
Jesus' sermon? What happens when character judgments are treated as taboo by the
people of God? How have you witnessed this occurring?

DISCERNING FALSE PROPHETS: THE TEST OF CREED

A good tree cannot produce bad fruit, nor can a bad tree produce good fruit.

MATT. 7:18

*C*AREFUL EXAMINATION OF A FALSE prophet's teachings will always reveal unscriptural ideas and an absence of a solid, coherent theology. Often he will teach a combination of truth and error. But sooner rather than later his teachings will prove the sort of teacher he really is. As Jesus said to the Pharisees, "You brood of vipers, how can you, being evil, speak what is good? For the mouth speaks out of that which fills the heart. The good man brings out of his good treasure what is good; and the evil man brings out of his evil treasure what is evil" (Matt. 12:34–35).

The creed of the false prophet cannot withstand any careful scrutiny by the pure light of the Word. The prophet Isaiah confirms this: "To the law and to the testimony! If they do not speak according to this word, it is because they have no dawn" (Isa. 8:20).

False shepherds talk much about God's love, but not His wrath and holiness; much about how deprived of good things people are, but not about their depravity; much about God's universal fatherhood toward everyone, but not much about his unique fatherhood toward all who believe in His Son; much about what God wants to give to us, but nothing about the necessity of obedience to Him; much about health and happiness, but nothing about holiness and sacrifice. Their message is full of gaps, the greatest of which leaves out a biblical view of the saving gospel.

Ask YOURSELF

What makes us susceptible to the appealing messages of the false teachers? What are people looking for when they begin embracing error? How can we guard against this ourselves?

DISCERNING FALSE PROPHETS: SEEING THEIR CONVERTS

Every tree that does not bear good fruit is cut down and thrown
into the fire. So then, you will know them by their fruits.

MATT. 7:19–20

*W*E CAN SPOT FALSE PROPHETS by the kind of people they attract. Their converts will have the same kind of superficial, self-centered, unbiblical orientation as they do. Of this sort of attraction Peter says, "Many will follow their sensuality, and because of them the way of the truth will be maligned" (2 Peter 2:2). Many folks gravitate to false teachers because those men propagate what the majority of people want to hear and believe (cf. 2 Tim. 4:3).

God has not ordained false prophets, but within His will He allows them to exist. And it is within His purpose that false factions develop. "For there must also be factions among you, so that those who are approved may become evident among you" (1 Cor. 11:19). Factions often attract followers of false teachers. And in a sense, this protects genuine saints by separating the chaff from the wheat in the church.

Ultimately, the Lord makes sure that the converts of false prophets, who do not bear good fruit, get cut down and thrown into the fire of judgment. Peter says they are "bringing swift destruction upon themselves" (2 Peter 2:1; cf. Jer. 23:30–40; John 15:2, 6). A watchful, discerning, vigilant believer, armed with the Word of truth, will be able to isolate false teachers and withdraw from them, because he or she "will know them by their fruits."

Ask YOURSELF

Discussions like these often get us labeled as haughty and narrow-minded. How do you handle these kinds of accusations? Why will some people never understand your concern for the church's purity?

AN EMPTY PROFESSION OF FAITH

Not everyone who says to Me, "Lord, Lord," will enter the kingdom
of heaven, but he who does the will of My Father who is in heaven will enter.

MATT. 7:21

*H*ERE JESUS IS SPEAKING OF THE devotedly religious who think they are saved but aren't. The Lord will continue these warnings later about spiritual self-deception—the foolish, unprepared virgins (Matt. 25:1–12) and the goats who did not really serve Him (Matt. 25:32–33, 41–46).

Many factors deceive people regarding salvation. *First*, some have a false assurance. They rely on past "decisions for Christ," apart from the Spirit's convicting work. But our salvation is made secure by increasing evidences of fruitfulness (2 Peter 1:3–11).

Second, many fail to examine themselves (cf. 2 Cor. 13:5; 1 John 1:8–9), instead gliding through life unconcerned about sins. One who has no desire to come to God for continued cleansing is likely not saved.

Third, a person can be deceived even in the midst of much religious activity. Hearing sermons, reading the Bible, and attending Bible studies are good, but such things may insulate someone from true worship.

Fourth, many attempt to rationalize their salvation, thinking that their good deeds outweigh their bad ones. But apart from God, we cannot do anything righteous (Pss. 14:1–3; 53:1–3; Rom. 3:12).

We could mention many other spiritual delusions, all of which involve failure to enter the narrow gate with repentance, submission to Christ, humility, and a desire for holiness. The important thing, however, is not to wonder about all those possibilities but to enter God's one true way to salvation.

Ask YOURSELF

Is the validity of your salvation ever in doubt in your mind? Do you see yourself in any of the examples given above? Then anchor your faith today in the sure word and promises of God, and walk in the confidence of eternal life, bought and paid for by Jesus Christ.

JESUS' RESPONSE TO EMPTY WORDS

Many will say to Me on that day, "Lord, Lord, did we not prophesy in Your name, and
in Your name cast out demons, and in Your name perform many miracles?" And then
I will declare to them, "I never knew you; depart from Me, you who practice lawlessness."

MATT. 7:22–23

$\mathcal{O}$N FIRST READING, THESE ARE some of the most startling, convicting words Jesus ever uttered. The key issue for Him is obedience to His Word and will. He later declared, "If you continue in My word, then you are truly disciples of Mine" (John 8:31; cf. Rom. 6:16; Col. 1:22–23; Heb. 5:9).

All the empty words and professions of respect for Christ and the shallow works of supposed dedication now come to condemn all disobedient claimers to the Lord. When Jesus tells them, "I never knew you," it does not mean He didn't know their identities, but in essence, "I didn't know you as My disciples, and you didn't really know Me as Lord and Savior. You chose your kingdom, but it wasn't My kingdom."

A life that professes to be a Christian but in no way actually reflects His holiness does not possess true salvation. Such a profession comes from a dead faith that results in no good works (James 2:17).

It's not that faithful disciples will not stumble and sin sometimes; otherwise Jesus would not have taught about forgiveness of debts (Matt. 6:12) and confession of sins (cf. 1 John 1:9). Believers cannot expect perfection in this life, but they should expect to be heading in that direction.

Those who persist in lawlessness show that they are not Christians. No matter how orthodox and outwardly fervent, religious activity that doesn't stem from repentance of sin and manifest a desire for obedience to Christ is still rebellion against God's law.

Ask YOURSELF

It's not bragging on ourselves but on Christ when we admit to areas of spiritual growth and victory over sin. In what ways are you seeing yourself increasingly conformed to the nature of Christ?

SIMILARITIES BETWEEN WISE AND FOOLISH BUILDERS

*Everyone who hears these words of Mine and acts on them, may be compared to a
wise man who built his house on the rock. . . . Everyone who hears these words of Mine and
does not act on them, will be like a foolish man who built his house on the sand.*

MATT. 7:24, 26

*A*N IMPORTANT WAY TO DISCERN between true believers and those
who merely profess faith in Christ is to consider Jesus' illustration of the hearers and
builders. The crucial element to understand is the foundations upon which people
build hopes. While there are clear distinctions, there are also some interesting similarities. *First*, both kinds of builders hear the gospel. They both outwardly recognize
the way of salvation.

Second, hearing the gospel both groups build a house, which represents their
lives. Each type of builder has confidence that his or her house will stand. Each also
believes their manner of living is right and pleasing to the Lord—"Christian" in form
and manner.

Third, both parties erect their houses in the same general location. That is, their
life situations are basically the same. Perhaps they are members of the same church,
hear the same preaching, attend the same Bible study, and have fellowship with the
same friends.

In summary, so much seems to be alike for the builders Jesus describes. By inference, we could say both live much the same sorts of lives—morally respectable,
acceptably religious, theologically orthodox, good supporters and servants in their
church, and even good community citizens. But the ultimate outcome of life will be
radically different for the two.

Ask YOURSELF

How do these similarities cloud people's awareness of spiritual need? What distinctions should be visible and obvious when comparing the lives of believers and
unbelievers?

Differences in Foundations

Everyone who hears these words of Mine and acts on them, may be compared to a
wise man who built his house on the rock. . . . Everyone who hears these words of Mine and
does not act on them, will be like a foolish man who built his house on the sand.

MATT. 7:24, 26

*D*IFFERENCES BETWEEN WISE AND foolish builders are more important than the similarities. The greatest differences are the types of foundations the builders choose. One selects a solid expanse of bedrock—stable and unmovable. The other selects sand—unstable and very movable.

The house built on a foundation of rock is a life that believes and obeys Jesus' sermon and places all its hope in God. The sand, by contrast, represents paying little or no attention to the Word. The house built on that foundation is a life that relies on self-righteousness and trusts in changeable human opinions.

The indicator of real discipleship is not merely hearing and professing, but believing and doing. True converts fit James's picture: "One who looks intently at the perfect law, the law of liberty, and abides by it, not having become a forgetful hearer but an effectual doer, this man will be blessed in what he does" (James 1:25). False disciples, however, fit the other picture James paints: "merely hearers who delude themselves. For if anyone is a hearer of the word and not a doer, he is like a man who looks at his natural face in a mirror; for once he has looked at himself and gone away, he has immediately forgotten what kind of person he was" (vv. 22–24).

We can be assured of salvation only when we build on the rock of truth and obedience, not on the standards of human opinions and speculations.

Ask YOURSELF

Do you have a current undertaking—no matter how large or small—that's tempting you to hurry up and build without spending much time on the foundation? What will every effort or enterprise suffer from if more thought is given to wallpaper than to substructure?

DIFFERENCES IN HOUSES

The rain fell, and the floods came, and the winds blew and slammed against that house; and yet it did not fall, for it had been founded on the rock. . . . The rain fell, and the floods came, and the winds blew and slammed against the house; and it fell—and great was its fall.

MATT. 7:25, 27

*W*ITH MOST TASKS IN LIFE, IT COMES down to two choices: doing it the easy, convenient way, or choosing the difficult but rewarding way. In Jesus' illustration, the foolish man chooses the easy way to build his house, but the wise man chooses the hard way. The former settles for a convenient section of sand in a desirable location, but the latter searches diligently for a rock foundation on which to build.

Why is the easy way so attractive? *First*, it is appealing to those in a hurry who want only to please themselves. Within the church, the foolish don't care how their methods line up with God's Word. They just want quick results—simple to see and easy to measure. Thus the foolish are satisfied with easy evangelism and cost-free discipleship.

Second, people prefer the easy way because they are superficial. Such ministry requires little planning and effort and not much concern for quality results. That house is all about instant gratification rather than the enduring reward found in plumbing the spiritual depths.

Jesus had another description of the superficial, foolish person as one "who hears the word and immediately receives it with joy; yet has no firm root in himself, but is only temporary, and when affliction or persecution arises because of the word, immediately he falls away" (Matt. 13:20–21). By contrast, the genuine believer counts the cost, builds the wise house, and then "work[s] out [his] salvation with fear and trembling" (Phil. 2:12).

Ask YOURSELF

Think of an "easy way" you've taken in your life. What convinced you to do it? Think also of a time when you truly did things the "right way." Examine the difference in results.

DIFFERENCES IN WITHSTANDING THE STORM

The rain fell, and the floods came, and the winds blew and slammed against that house;
and yet it did not fall, for it had been founded on the rock. . . . The rain fell, and the floods
came, and the winds blew and slammed against the house; and it fell—and great was its fall.

MATT. 7:25, 27

EVERYONE'S RELIGION, WHETHER true or false, will be tried one day. That test will determine with great finality who are the wheat and who are the tares—in other words, the unredeemed will be revealed from the redeemed. When the storm of final test comes, those whose houses are on the bedrock of Jesus Christ and His Word will be spared "from the wrath to come" (1 Thess. 1:10). However, those whose houses are on the sand will not be spared, but, like the goats in Jesus' prophecy of the end times, "will go away into eternal punishment" (Matt. 25:46; cf. Ex. 12:23; Rev. 20:12, 15).

The house of the wise man—the life and ministry of the genuine believer—is spared because he has built carefully and faithfully, with a sense of substance and divine importance. After obediently doing all that God commands, he humbly realizes he was only doing his duty (Luke 17:10).

The house of the foolish man—the life and ministry of the pseudo-believer—suffers a devastating judgment from the storm and is destined for eternal punishment. Because of this inevitability, everyone who claims to be a Christian must carefully heed James's words: "Prove yourselves doers of the word, and not merely hearers who delude themselves" (James 1:22).

The greatest difference between "wise" and "foolish" resides in what promise from God they can claim. To the wise He says, in the words of the hymn, "Though all hell should endeavor to shake, I'll never, no, never, no, never forsake!"

Ask YOURSELF

Those who are foolish in planning and preparation are often foolish as well in their assessment of the damage. Why do some whose lives are falling apart not seem to notice? How can you help one you know?

RESPONSE TO THE GREATEST SERMON

When Jesus had finished these words, the crowds were amazed at His teaching;
for He was teaching them as one having authority, and not as their scribes.

MATT. 7:28–29

*T*HE RESPONSE TO THE BEST AND most astounding preaching ever—the Sermon on the Mount—was in itself very remarkable. Likely some among our Lord's audience that day believed in Him for salvation. But quite probably the number converted was small, affirming Jesus' assertion about the narrow gate: "there are few who find it" (Matt. 7:14).

The verb translated "were amazed" means to be struck out of oneself, or to be beside oneself with astonishment. The crowd was utterly flabbergasted by the power, comprehensiveness, and extraordinary insight of Christ's words. Never had people heard such a penetrating description of true righteousness or such a relentless condemnation of self-righteousness.

Even more remarkable is the way Jesus spoke with a power ("authority") that proved and reflected His sovereignty. Unlike the Jewish teachers, who quoted the rabbis words and additional sacred writings, He quoted only Scripture and spoke as the final authority on truth.

The Sermon on the Mount is important for everyone to hear. But the response to it must not conclude with mere amazement but real, saving faith. If we have read it and meditated upon its instructions and imperatives, we also need to move from astonishment to obedience. Such obedience entails moving from intellectual knowledge of the narrow gate and way to actually entering the gate by faith and following the way to eternal life.

Ask YOURSELF

Think back on the many lessons taken from Jesus' Sermon on the Mount. Which have struck you with new force? Which are your children in greatest need of hearing? Don't let His Word grow quiet within you.

JESUS AND THE LEPER, PART 1

When Jesus came down from the mountain, large crowds followed Him. And a leper came to Him and bowed down before Him, and said, "Lord, if You are willing, You can make me clean."

MATT. 8:1–2

$\mathscr{L}$EPROSY WAS A MOST FEARED AND contagious disease in the ancient world. Spongy, tumor-like swellings grew on the face and body, and eventually leprosy affected the internal organs and bones.

In ancient Israel lepers were vivid object lessons regarding sin. Like leprosy, sin infects the entire person (cf. Eph. 2:1) and is ugly, corrupting—incurable without extraordinary means.

Several things stand out about the leper who came to Jesus for healing. *First,* he came to Him with confidence. He obviously sensed Jesus' love and tenderness and somehow knew the Lord did not mind associating with him. The leper's primary concern was his tremendous need and Christ's all-sufficient ability and willingness to meet it.

Second, the leprous man approached Jesus with reverence. His boldness in calling out to Jesus and coming near derived not from presumption but from humble adoration. The word rendered "bowed down" means to prostrate oneself and is also translated "worship" in the New Testament (cf. Acts 7:43; Rev. 4:10). The leper's attitude suggests he addressed Jesus as Lord, not simply as "sir" but in recognition of His deity. He knew that as God's Son, Jesus could heal his horrible disease.

Ironically, this man is a striking contrast to the Jewish leaders. They were always clean and lavishly attired, but inwardly were corrupt and unbelieving. The man with leprosy, on the other hand, was outwardly repulsive in appearance, but inwardly he was worshipful and full of sincere faith.

$\mathscr{Ask}$YOURSELF

Noting the analogy between sin and leprosy, imagine if sin's effects actually did show themselves on our faces and skin. How would this affect our behavior and obedience? What does that tell us about the deceitfulness of sin and how to counteract it?

JESUS AND THE LEPER, PART 2

*When Jesus came down from the mountain, large crowds followed Him. And a leper came
to Him and bowed down before Him, and said, "Lord, if You are willing, You can make me clean."*

MATT. 8:1–2

*S*EVERAL MORE STRIKING FEATURES marked the leper who came to Jesus.
The man came expectantly but not demandingly, therefore he approached the Lord
with humility. It's clear he wanted to be healed, but he did not explicitly ask Jesus for
this miraculous favor. That was almost too much for the leper to presume, hence his
statement, "Lord, if You are willing, You can make me clean." What a contrast to the
attitude of those in some religious circles today who boastfully claim divine healing
as if God should automatically grant it.

The leprous man also came in sincere faith—one that displays the firm conviction that God is able to work on our behalf, but yet a conviction accompanied by
submission to His sovereign will. He knew that although Jesus was able to instantly
cure his leprosy, He was not obligated. The man's faith was much like that of Daniel's
friends who told the king, "If it be so, our God whom we serve is able to deliver us
from the furnace of blazing fire; and He will deliver us out of your hand, O king. But
even if He does not, let it be known to you, O king, that we are not going to serve
your gods or worship the golden image that you have set up" (Dan. 3:17–18). In the
same way, the leper would also accept whatever outcome Jesus provided.

Ask YOURSELF

"Expectantly but not demandingly." How would this posture change the way
you're currently praying over a pressing matter—not by discounting faith and being
guilty of doubt and double-mindedness, but by boldly placing yourself and others
under Christ's capable safekeeping?

JESUS' TOUCH AND INSTANTANEOUS HEALING

Jesus stretched out His hand and touched him, saying, "I am willing;
be cleansed." And immediately his leprosy was cleansed.

MATT. 8:3

THE MOSAIC LAW FORBADE the Jews from touching lepers, because they were unclean (Lev. 5:3) and would expose healthy people to ceremonial and physical contamination. But lepers, in their social ostracism, yearned for even a brief, up-close contact with another person besides a fellow leper.

Jesus could have healed this man with just a single word, but He made a point of touching him. This action was truly amazing—not in a spectacular, sensational manner, but simply because the Son of Man would lovingly reach out and reach down to touch an outcast of outcasts as no one else would.

The Lord bestowed instantaneous healing: "immediately his leprosy was cleansed." When He touched the man's defiled body, his disease simply disappeared. (Christ could have chosen to heal in stages, as He sometimes did [Mark 8:22–26; John 9:6–7], but there was no necessity to do so.) The picture for the eyewitnesses would have been dramatic. A bent-over, withered derelict, with skin ravaged by scaly, ugly sores, would suddenly stand up. His limbs were now perfectly normal, his face smooth and unscarred, his eyes clear and bright, and his voice strong and confident.

Modern medical science, with all its wonderful expertise and abilities to cure, can never equal the miraculous restoration Jesus provided.

Ask YOURSELF

Are there certain people you are wary of touching—either by physical embrace or even eye contact? What gives us the right of being too good or polished or educated or privileged to look lovingly into the face of another, to offer ourselves and our acceptance?

A Testimony to the Jews

*Jesus said to him, "See that you tell no one; but go, show yourself to the priest
and present the offering that Moses commanded, as a testimony to them."*

MATT. 8:4

*F*OLLOWING TIMES OF GREATEST blessing and triumph, our Lord often tests us to see if our faith is obedient. In the case of the cleansed leper, Jesus commanded him to fulfill the ritual requirements of the law and let the priests attest to his healing (cf. Lev. 14). This responsibility had to precede any celebrations of his newfound health or telling others about his cure.

Perhaps Jesus told the man not to tell others of this healing so that people would not merely give adulation to Him as a miracle worker. Furthermore, He would not have wanted this event to encourage any speculation that He was a political deliverer. Christ was still in His period of humiliation, and any exaltation of Him by the crowd would have been premature within the Father's plan.

However, the major reason for Jesus' command to the healed man to respect the Mosaic requirements was to testify to the crowd, particularly the Jewish leaders. He blasted their hypocrisy, superficiality, and unscriptural methods, but He did not want to communicate that He had no regard for God's law at all. When the priest declared the man healed—and the evidence would be obvious—it would allow Jesus' miracle to be verified by the Jewish establishment. That would give added weight to His credibility as Messiah, as One who "did not come to abolish but to fulfill" (Matt. 5:17).

Ask YOURSELF

How would you describe your spiritual state after a season of great accomplishment or at the culmination of a long struggle that has ended in victory? Is this a time when you deliberately focus on the basics of Christian faith, or when you decide to take a break for a while?

PHYSICAL HEALINGS AND SPIRITUAL CLEANSING

". . . as a testimony to them."

MATT. 8:4C

CHRIST'S MIRACULOUS HEALINGS were significant in His earthly ministry. They displayed genuine concern for human need and testified that He was God. But several times Jesus stated, "Which is easier, to say, 'Your sins are forgiven,' or to say, 'Get up and walk'? But so that you may know that the Son of Man has authority on earth to forgive sins" (Matt. 9:5–6; cf. Mark 2:9; Luke 5:23). The healing miracles simply illustrated the cleansing of sin, which was Jesus' primary purpose within God's redemptive plan.

Curing leprosy was an especially powerful illustration, because its physical destructiveness parallels sin's spiritual destructiveness. The Lord's healing of leprosy restored people to human fellowship, just as His cleansing of sin restores them to *divine* fellowship.

The church today often fails to confront individuals with the horrible destructiveness of their sin. Instead of "coming to Christ" by making an emotional, feel-good decision, people need to realize their sins and bring them to God for cleansing. True conversion occurs when, like the leper, sinners confess their need and humbly seek His restoration. Like the leprous man, sinners flee to Christ as their only hope for rescue from their helpless condition of lostness.

Paralleling the healing again, Jesus' first requirement for new converts is their obedience to His Word. Only after demonstrating a new life of righteousness can they give proper testimony to what the Savior has done.

Ask YOURSELF

Is it fair to say that sinfulness is often a precursor to sickness? There is certainly no universal answer to this question, but how can you use times of limitation, weakness, or confinement to let God examine your heart and deepen your desire to follow Him?

JESUS' TESTIMONY OF A CENTURION'S FAITH

Jesus said to him, "I will come and heal him." But the centurion said, "Lord, I am not worthy
for You to come under my roof, but just say the word, and my servant will be healed."...
Now when Jesus heard this, He marveled and said to those who were following,
"Truly I say to you, I have not found such great faith with anyone in Israel."

MATT. 8:7–8, 10

$\mathcal{T}$HE CENTURION HERE—an officer in charge of a hundred soldiers—
was undoubtedly a God-fearing Gentile. Jesus knew his heart and did not need to
hear a direct request from anyone for healing of the servant. And indeed the centurion was so humble, he felt unworthy to have Jesus come into his house.

That the centurion twice called Jesus "Lord" shows a lot more than simple cour-
tesy. The soldier was affirming that Christ was the Son of God, able to heal the man's
paralyzed servant. He knew that only a powerful word from Jesus, uttered inside or
outside the house, would be adequate.

In His humanity Jesus was amazed that the Roman centurion showed more
real faith than He had found in many Jews. Although a number of Jews had already
believed in the Lord, none had manifested the kind of sincerity, sensitivity, humility, love, and deep faith this Gentile had just displayed. On several occasions Jesus
would reprimand even the Twelve for their lack of faith (Matt. 8:26; John 14:9).

The good news of salvation originated from Israel (Matt. 1:1–23). But that benefit comes to all who believe, not just to a certain ethnic group. God ordained in His
redemptive plan that the Savior, His own Son, be born, live, and die as a Jew. But the
fact that any Jew makes it to heaven will not be because he or she was a Jew like
Jesus, but because of saving faith. This principle applies to everyone of every na-
tionality.

Ask YOURSELF

How do you respond to the call for greater faith—especially like that of someone in a different class or station than you? Are you resentful of the implication?
Convinced you can never be that way? Or are you driven to your knees in a prayerful appeal for faith at all costs?

JESUS' REALITY CHECK ON SALVATION

I say to you that many will come from east and west, and recline at the table with
Abraham, Isaac and Jacob in the kingdom of heaven; but the sons of the kingdom will
be cast out into the outer darkness; in that place there will be weeping and gnashing of teeth.

MATT. 8:11–12

*J*ESUS' WORDS TO THE JEWS IN Capernaum shattered their proud spiritual worldview, contradicting everything the rabbis had taught about salvation. Their apocryphal literature pictured a great heavenly feast in which only Jews would be present in the end.

Jesus, however, drastically revised that scene and declared that many Gentiles would be included and many Jews excluded. His Jewish listeners thought they still had exclusive possession of God's kingdom promises and privileges. But because many of them rejected Messiah when He came, they disqualified themselves from salvation blessings and destined themselves to the condemnation of outer darkness. (Part of the frightening supernatural quality of hell is that it is a place of pain, torment, and fire that lasts for eternity in total darkness—a combination not found in the present world.)

The Jews enjoyed many blessings (Rom. 3:1–2), but being physical descendants of Abraham did not guarantee salvation. True salvation is for all who are children of Abraham's spiritual faith, those whom God adopts as His children (Rom. 8:14–17; Gal. 3:7–9, 26–29). When many Jews, especially the leaders, rejected Jesus as Messiah, they proved they were not true, spiritual children of Abraham, but actually children of the devil (John 8:42–44). As such, Jesus in effect said, they forfeited God's promised blessings and any hopes of entering heaven, unless they repented. That was the radical, sobering clarification Christ brought to the Jews' profound misunderstanding of the nature of salvation.

*Ask*YOURSELF

Again, we must look within to isolate any self-righteous tendencies that place others in categories and inflate our inherent worth before God. Ask Him to bring such sins of pride and presumption to the surface, where they can be identified and disposed of.

JESUS HEALS PETER'S MOTHER-IN-LAW

When Jesus came into Peter's home, He saw his mother-in-law lying sick in bed with
a fever. He touched her hand, and the fever left her; and she got up and waited on Him.
MATT. 8:14–15

*T*HROUGH THE CENTURIES, most male Jews have displayed much preju-
dice toward women, as evidenced by the old prayer, "Lord, I thank Thee that I was
not born a slave, a Gentile, or a woman." But here Jesus, just as with the leper and the
Gentile centurion, shows mercy and compassion to an outsider—a woman—someone not favored by the Jewish establishment. He cuts through the unscriptural attitude of proud Jewish men to demonstrate again that physical health, race, status, or
a person's sex gained no advantage with Him.

When Jesus arrived at Peter's home with some of the disciples, Peter's mother-
in-law was ill, and Mark adds, "Immediately they spoke to Jesus about her" (Mark
1:30). Luke the physician notes that she had "a high fever" (Luke 4:38), though none
of the narratives says what caused her illness. That the fever was high suggests she
was seriously ill and maybe in danger of death.

Christ once again responded without delay and healed Peter's mother-in-law
immediately. She was not only a woman but also a Jew, which meant that although
the Lord had warned the Jews about presuming upon salvation, He had not completely forsaken them, as ministry to Peter's relative powerfully showed. The fact
that salvation was available to faithful Gentiles did not mean it was now unavailable
to faithful Jews. Paul later wrote, "God has not rejected His people whom He
foreknew. . . . In the same way then, there has also come to be at the present time a
remnant according to God's gracious choice" (Rom. 11:2, 5).

Ask YOURSELF

Among all religions, none has a higher view of women than does Christianity.
And yet, it's fair to ask ourselves if chauvinism is present within our hearts. Christ
honored women. So should we.

HEALINGS AND THE EXISTENCE OF DISEASE

When evening came, they brought to Him many who were demon-possessed; and He cast out the spirits with a word, and healed all who were ill. This was to fulfill what was spoken through Isaiah the prophet: "He Himself took our infirmities and carried away our diseases."

MATT. 8:16–17

*J*ESUS PERFORMED HEALING miracles for reasons far more profound than to wipe out all disease, which did happen in Palestine while He ministered. *First*, He healed to personally participate in humanity's suffering and illness. He knew people's inner feelings of agony, bewilderment, despair, and frustration because of disease, and He wanted to sympathize. He vicariously experienced those elements, "for we do not have a high priest who cannot sympathize with our weaknesses" (Heb. 4:15).

Second, Christ healed people because He experienced the awful effects of disease's root cause, sin. He could not see the pain of disease and death without feeling sin's pain. Jesus wept for Lazarus (John 11:34–36) not from sadness but from feeling the sting of sin and evil that brings death to everyone. Sin and sickness both operate as effects of the Fall, and only divine power can cure either.

Third, our Lord "took our infirmities and carried away our diseases" as a preview of His kingdom's most wonderful elements—the permanent removal of sin, sorrow, and disease (cf. Rev. 21:1–4). His redeeming work to remove the penalty and guilt of sin for His own would be complete. Just as with His transfiguration, in which He pulled back the veil over His flesh and gave three disciples a glimpse of His divine glory, Jesus gave those healed and all who witnessed a gracious preview of His eternal kingdom.

Ask YOURSELF

The question is not whether or not Jesus can heal, but rather why He chooses to sometimes withhold the healing we seek. When He does, what eternal purposes might He have in mind?

THE CONVINCING NATURE OF JESUS' HEALING MINISTRY

This was to fulfill what was spoken through Isaiah the prophet:
"He Himself took our infirmities and carried away our diseases."
MATT. 8:17

*J*ESUS CHRIST DIED FOR THE SINS of all who trust Him, yet believers still sin. By His resurrection He conquered death, yet Christians still die. He overcame suffering and illness, yet believers still have pain and disease. Jesus' main purpose in the atonement was to conquer sin and death, not just to conquer physical suffering. That latter fulfillment is still in the future (cf. Rom. 8:22–25; 13:11).

It is hard to argue that Jesus' healing ministry and crucifixion now mean that Christians should no longer expect illness. If that argument is true, then we should expect not to die—but that's false. Again, the gospel is all about forgiveness from sin, not deliverance from disease (cf. 1 Peter 2:24).

In view of the convincing nature of Jesus' healing ministry, it's hard to understand why anyone who heard or saw any of those miracles would not receive Him. It is especially hard to fathom that God's own people, with all their special blessings—the law, the prophets, the covenant—would mostly reject the Son of their God. But from the outset of Christ's incarnation, John speaks of this rejection: "Those who were His own did not receive Him" (John 1:11).

Any denial of Jesus flies in the face of the facts, whether such unbelief was by people in Jesus' day or by skeptics today. As His healing ministry progressed, the proofs of His divinity, power, mercy, and goodness became obvious beyond contradiction. They all demand a saving faith in the one true Savior and Lord.

Ask YOURSELF

How do you think you would have responded to the ministry of Christ, had you been there to witness it firsthand? Are the reasons for doubting Him today any different than they were then?

JESUS CHRIST'S AMAZING MINISTRY

This was to fulfill what was spoken through Isaiah the prophet:
"He Himself took our infirmities and carried away our diseases."

MATT. 8:17

*E*VEN EXCLUDING THE MIRACULOUS healings, Jesus' ministry was unprecedented and amazing. "Never has a man spoken the way this man speaks" (John 7:46). The man born blind, whom Jesus healed, told the Jewish leaders, "Since the beginning of time it has never been heard that anyone opened the eyes of a person born blind. If this man [Christ] were not from God, He could do nothing" (John 9:32–33).

When Jesus healed the paralytic, the onlookers "were awestruck, and glorified God" (Matt. 9:8), and after He expelled a demon they said, "Nothing like this has ever been seen in Israel" (v. 33). When He stood before Pilate, Jesus did not say a word in His own defense, "so the governor was quite amazed" (Matt. 27:14).

Everything about our Lord was astonishing, excellent, and humanly beyond explanation. It is hard to understand how anyone who witnessed His preaching and miracles, or has even just read about Him in the gospels, can still refuse to accept and obey Him. Some are drawn by His charisma and power, and they marvel at the things He taught and did, but they still take nothing to heart and don't believe. Sometimes they are willing to call themselves Christians, but they need a commitment that is more than superficial—one that perseveres in faith to the end.

Ask YOURSELF

Think of all the things that are truly amazing about Christ. If you were asked what you love the most about Him, what would you say? You never want to be at a loss to share the specific ways He makes life distinctly abundant.

STRONG PROFESSION IS NOT ALWAYS SINCERE

Then a scribe came and said to Him, "Teacher, I will follow You wherever You go."
Jesus said to him, "The foxes have holes and the birds of the air have nests,
but the Son of Man has nowhere to lay His head."

MATT. 8:19–20

*T*HE ISSUE OF COMMITMENT IS one to be evaluated very carefully. The scribe here was an authority on Jewish law and a close ally of the Pharisees. As such he would have broken with his allies had he become one of Jesus' true disciples. He knew a decision like that would be costly, and thus he might have been testing Jesus' reaction to his words.

Normally the scribes were teachers, not followers of other teachers. And one such as this man would have been reluctant to follow a rabbi like Jesus, who was not from the scholarly class, not educated in a rabbinic school, and not loyal to Jewish religious traditions.

For this scribe to address Jesus as he did was quite out of the ordinary and probably impressive to the apostles and the crowds, since he issued the claim as a Jewish leader. It's not certain that the man ever really believed in Jesus, but he probably felt sincere in his own mind with what he professed. He was likely just as convinced as Peter that he would always follow the Lord (Matt. 26:33, 35), but neither could be sure about that, as Peter's temporary denial illustrates.

Unlike today's evangelical church, always eager to instantly embrace a prominent person who professes Christ, Jesus knew that every strong profession does not necessarily translate to strong commitment. Hence He compared His living situation to the foxes and birds as a testing of the man's true dedication, which ought to be a self-examining device for us too.

Ask YOURSELF

Think of the bold promises you've made to the Lord before and the many times you've failed to follow through. Have your past inabilities kept you from making such statements anymore? Is that what God wants you to learn from these experiences?

JESUS CHALLENGES THE SCRIBE

Then a scribe came and said to Him, "Teacher, I will follow You wherever You go."
Jesus said to him, "The foxes have holes and the birds of the air have nests,
but the Son of Man has nowhere to lay His head."

MATT. 8:19–20

*S*UPERFICIALLY, JESUS' EXPRESSION "The foxes have holes and the birds of the air have nests, but the Son of Man has nowhere to lay His head" has nothing to do with the scribe's confident words. In proverbial style He simply wanted to caution the man that even though He was God's Son, His ministry did not include comfortable living—He actually had fewer amenities than some animals.

Christ wanted the scribe to assess the sincerity of his assertion. It's easy to make a bold, impressive profession of loyalty, especially if you don't first think about the cost of commitment. Early in His ministry, our Lord knew that many did not have a genuine faith: He "was not entrusting Himself to them, for He knew all men. . . . He did not need anyone to testify concerning man, for He Himself knew what was in man" (John 2:24–25). Many were committed only to the thrill of following Jesus around and seeing miracles performed, not to His Person and saving work. They were examples of the seed that had no root but fell away soon because of adversity (Matt. 13:5–6, 20–21).

Bible commentator R. C. H. Lenski once noted that people with eager but uncertain vows of allegiance to Christianity are like those who view "the soldiers on parade, the fine uniforms, and the glittering arms and [are] eager to join, forgetting the exhausting marches, the bloody battles, the graves, perhaps unmarked."

Ask YOURSELF

Are we guilty of trying to make Christian faith so attractive that we disguise its demands and difficulties? What are the logical consequences of such a tactic on those who come to Christ without counting the cost?

NOT COUNTING THE COST

Then a scribe came and said to Him, "Teacher, I will follow You wherever You go."
Jesus said to him, "The foxes have holes and the birds of the air have nests,
but the Son of Man has nowhere to lay His head."

MATT. 8:19–20

*T*HERE IS NO RECORD THAT the eager scribe ever counted the cost of discipleship. When considering various costs such as self-denial, homelessness, and maybe suffering, the man disappears. No doubt Christ's words struck where he was most vulnerable, and he could not overcome loyalty to himself and his comfort.

Jesus never watered down the gospel message as many evangelistic appeals do today. That only compromises God's Word and does a severe disservice to those who hear such a message. The Lord, by contrast, did not mince words with the apostles: "Behold, I send you out as sheep in the midst of wolves" (Matt. 10:16). And He continued that tone at the end of His ministry: "These things I have spoken to you so that you may be kept from stumbling. They will make you outcasts from the synagogue, but an hour is coming for everyone who kills you to think that he is offering service to God" (John 16:1–2). Neither did Paul waver from stern words of reminder that "all who desire to live godly in Christ Jesus will be persecuted" (2 Tim. 3:12).

Knowing and following Jesus Christ includes thrills and joys unlike any others, but they are not the kind the world can understand or appreciate (cf. John 14:27). Living the Christian life is not simply adding Jesus on to your own lifestyle, but it entails the renouncing of your ways for His and being ready to pay the price He may require (cf. Matt. 16:24).

Ask YOURSELF

What have been some of the major costs of discipleship in your own life? How have you responded to them? Have they ultimately drawn you closer to Christ, or have you often allowed them to drive a wedge between you and the Lord?

THE BARRIER OF PERSONAL RICHES

Another of the disciples said to Him, "Lord, permit me first to go and bury my father."
But Jesus said to him, "Follow Me, and allow the dead to bury their own dead."

MATT. 8:21–22

*T*HIS MAN, PERHAPS A HANGER-ON who had followed Jesus around the countryside for a while, makes what seems at first to be a reasonable statement. His seeking permission to go and bury his father, however, did not mean his parent was already dead. It was and is a common Middle Eastern figure of speech referring to a child's (mainly a son's) responsibility to help with the family business until the father dies and the inheritance is available. Such a commitment can conceivably take a long time to fulfill. It's the same as saying, "I need to wait until I receive my inheritance."

This superficial disciple did not want devotion to Jesus to get in the way of receiving what was coming to him. He was okay with associating with the Lord by name, but his personal prosperity and well-being came ahead of serving Christ.

Jesus' reply was right on the mark with another proverbial saying, "Follow Me, and allow the dead to bury their own dead." In other words, "Let the world take care of the things of the world." We should let the spiritually dead manage their own affairs.

Believers must not pattern their thinking after the world's ways, but be disciples of Christ and bring the good news of eternal life to the world, relying on His grace and enabling.

Ask YOURSELF

Are there any plans and hopes and dreams you are still holding on to that may not square with the will of God for your life? If you had to surrender any of these for the cause of Christ, how do you think you'd react?

TRUE COMMITMENT

Another of the disciples said to Him, "Lord, permit me first to go and bury my father."
But Jesus said to him, "Follow Me, and allow the dead to bury their own dead."
MATT. 8:21–22

ℒIKE THE SCRIBE, THIS SECOND man disappears from the record after approaching Jesus. Evidently the Lord's discipleship demands were too strict and the appeal of discipleship vanished (cf. Matt. 19:16–22). Christ's instruction to follow Him simply means, "If anyone wishes to come after Me, he must deny himself, and take up his cross and follow Me" (Matt. 16:24).

The Lord Jesus always made it clear that commitment must be complete or not at all. Consider this:

> I did not come to bring peace, but a sword. For I came to set a man against his father, and a daughter against her mother, and a daughter-in-law against her mother-in-law; and a man's enemies will be the members of his household. He who loves father or mother more than Me is not worthy of Me; and he who loves son or daughter more than Me is not worthy of Me. And he who does not take his cross and follow after Me is not worthy of Me. (Matt. 10:34–38)

This is not speaking of Christian service but of salvation. God won't save anyone who comes to him with strings attached.

People have long admired Christ for His authority, moral teaching, ethical standards, love and healing, even His deity. But in spite of all that, they have failed to submit themselves to Him. J. C. Ryle has written, "The saddest road to hell is the one that runs under the pulpit, past the Bible, and through the middle of warnings and invitations."

Ask YOURSELF

How have you suffered rejection and disdain for your Christian faith? What would still be lacking in your life if you had the acceptance of others but not the acceptance of Christ?

FAITH OUT OF DESPERATION

And they came to Him and woke Him, saying, "Save us, Lord; we are perishing!"
He said to them, "Why are you afraid, you men of little faith?"
MATT. 8:25–26A

$\mathscr{S}$OMETIMES GOD HAS TO BRING us to a point of desperate need before He can get us to turn to Him. That's what happened to the disciples when the storm was about to swamp their boat. They had no other human solutions for their emergency and had to come to Jesus with their need. If He could cleanse lepers and heal every other sort of disease, maybe He could control nature.

Even the greatest believers in redemptive history have wavered in their faith in their most difficult circumstances. The psalmist asked, "Why do You stand afar off, O Lord? Why do You hide Yourself in times of trouble?" (Ps. 10:1; cf. 44:22–23). Isaiah even wondered why God seemed not able to help His people: "Awake, awake, put on strength, O arm of the Lord; awake as in the days of old, the generations of long ago" (Isa. 51:9). Much like the disciples on the lake, the prophet could not see why God was asleep when His people were dying.

God wants people to turn to Him, especially for salvation when it's a matter of spiritual life and death. We can often get out of dire situations involving finances, health, or family relations without the Lord's direct intervention. But when it comes to spiritual salvation, there is no other resource but God. After we are saved, the Father still wants to hear from us—in that way we show we have not forgotten Him, even in desperate circumstances.

$\mathscr{Ask}$YOURSELF

What do we forget on ordinary days, times when we feel like we can manage well enough on our own without God's help or provision? What would desperate faith look like on a typical, average day?

JESUS REBUKES THE FAITHLESS DISCIPLES

Why are you afraid, you men of little faith?

MATT. 8:26A

*S*OMETIMES EVENTS SEEM SO obvious to us, we wonder why others don't see the problems or difficulties just as clearly. During the storm the disciples wondered two things: why Jesus could ask them what was so frightening, and how He could not be afraid Himself. In the midst of chaos, any other response seemed absurd. They even accused Him of insensitivity: "Teacher, do You not care that we are perishing?" (Mark 4:38).

But Christ had to rebuke His men because their fear sprang from faithlessness. He basically asked them, "Haven't you been with Me long enough to see what I can do and to know you are perfectly safe? Even if you should drown, that would mean instant heaven. There's nothing to worry about." They should have remembered Psalm 89:8–9, "O Lord God of hosts, who is like You, O mighty Lord? Your faithfulness also surrounds You. You rule the swelling of the sea; when its waves rise, You still them" (cf. 46:1–3; 107:23–30).

For the disciples, Jesus would literally fulfill the psalm. And for believers today, who are aware of His power and love, there is still no need to be afraid of anything. God will see us through the most tumultuous of life's storms because He can and will take care of His children.

Ask YOURSELF

When was the last time you despaired of life and safety, feeling as though there was no escape from your current situation without divine intervention? In fact, how many of these has God allowed you to live through—and to see His capable deliverance?

TENSION BETWEEN FAITH AND DOUBT

Then He got up and rebuked the winds and the sea, and it became perfectly calm. The men were
amazed, and said, "What kind of a man is this, that even the winds and the sea obey Him?"

MATT. 8:26B–27

*I*F YOU HAVE BEEN A BELIEVER for very long, you realize that knowing about the Lord's love and powerful concern and trusting in them do not always go hand in hand. Even when we trust, it is not always complete or without trepidation. When the disciples witnessed Jesus calming the storm and waves, they were no doubt relieved but also still very much unnerved. Matthew says they "were amazed," and Mark says they were "very much afraid" (Mark 4:41). They were now perhaps more afraid of the One who had just stilled the storm than they had been of the storm itself.

Our human frailties are so much a part of us that even after God has rescued us or done something amazing on our behalf, we still have doubts and fears. Like the apostles and the greats of the Old Testament, we can be most perplexed and fearful right after experiencing God's greatness and mercy.

Our faith needs continual strengthening, as the disciples came to realize when they implored, "Increase our faith!" (Luke 17:5; cf. Mark 9:24). We know the Lord can and will provide according to His perfect will and timing, but we easily can fail to trust in that reality. If we rely on mere "little faith" rather than complete faith, we will be afraid, timid, and doubtful when difficulties arise.

Ask YOURSELF

What is a proper response to God's care, even when it arrives in undeniable power and an uncanny arrangement of events? What should gratitude be growing in us each time we see Him working on our behalf and for His kingdom's cause?

The Apostles Marvel at Jesus' Power

The men were amazed, and said, "What kind of a man is this,
that even the winds and the sea obey Him?"

MATT. 8:27

THERE ARE NO REALITIES MORE overwhelming than a glimpse of God's glory or the sense of His presence. Such occurrences make it impossible not to be utterly dumbfounded before Him.

The disciples realized after Christ stilled the storm that He indeed was God standing in their boat with them. Peter displayed the same reaction of awe and terror when he briefly walked on water after his Lord did. A storm surged up and caused Peter to panic. When Jesus rescued the disciple and calmed the storm, all the disciples in the boat worshiped Him, saying, "You are certainly God's Son!" (Matt. 14:33; cf. vv. 28–32). That is simply the proper reaction any believer should have when getting a firsthand glimpse of the Lord's power in this world.

God's servants in Scripture had far more astounding earthly encounters with His magnificence than we ever will, but their examples are instructive. Daniel, for example, after beholding the Almighty, remarked, "No strength was left in me, for my natural color turned to a deathly pallor" (Dan. 10:8; cf. Isa. 6:1, 5). When the risen Christ halted Paul (Saul of Tarsus) on his way to Damascus, "he fell to the ground" (Acts 9:4).

Our daily dependence on God and sense of His presence should be no less important for us than for the prophets and apostles of old. Isaac Watts' lyrics capture this concept well:

On thee each moment we depend,
If Thou withdraw we die.
O may we ne'er that God offend,
Who is forever nigh.

Ask YOURSELF

Pause long enough to marvel at the glory of your ever-present God. Put your feelings of awe into words of worship.

JESUS VS. DEMONS

When He came to the other side into the country of the Gadarenes, two men who were
demon-possessed met Him . . . and they cried out, saying, "What business do we have
with each other, Son of God? Have You come here to torment us before the time?"

MATT. 8:28–29

*D*EMONS CAN ATTACK PEOPLE mentally, physically, or spiritually. Spiritually, they oppose true religion, promote the false, and control the occult. Intellectually, they advocate false ideologies, insanity, and masochism. Our Lord always recognized demonized people as being victims of powers beyond their control and in need of deliverance, not condemnation or exhortation.

By calling Jesus "Son of God," the demons controlling the Gadarene men showed they knew His true identity. They recognized Him as their spiritual antagonist who had the full authority to destroy them at will. Their question "Have You come here to torment us before the time?" further recognized that there is a God-ordained schedule, not yet completed, when He will relegate them to eternal damnation. As in other subjects, the demons had a correct doctrine of last things. But such belief is mere recognition, not acceptance. James reveals that even they tremble at the consequences of unbelief: "the demons also believe, and shudder" (James 2:19).

Demons despise everything about God and His Son. Yet they can't do anything but pay Jesus the greatest deferential respect when in His presence. That supports Paul's teaching that one day at the name of Christ, "every knee will bow, of those who are in heaven and on earth and under the earth, and that every tongue will confess that Jesus Christ is Lord, to the glory of God the Father" (Phil. 2:10–11).

Ask YOURSELF

Seeing the demons so obviously in fear of Christ's dominance should encourage us that He is more than able to handle any situation. Have you been withholding a need from Him, not sure He cared or could do anything about it? Bring it boldly to Him today.

SUPREMACY OVER DEMONS

And He said to them, "Go!" And they came out and went into the swine, and the
whole herd rushed down the steep bank into the sea and perished in the waters.
MATT. 8:32

*O*UR LORD JESUS WILL ALWAYS HAVE the upper hand over demonic forces. But we should never forget that demons, as fallen angels, still possess tremendous power and strength (cf. Dan. 10:21; Rev. 12:4). For example, when God sent an angel with a message for Daniel, a demon named "the prince of the kingdom of Persia" delayed the angel for three weeks, and God had to send Michael the archangel to help the other divine messenger (Dan. 10:13).

Wicked angels are superior to humans in many ways: intelligence (Ezek. 28:3–4), strength (Mark 5:4; Acts 19:16), powers to do "signs and false wonders" (2 Thess. 2:9), and in experience (having existed much longer than mankind). As spirit beings, they are not bound by time, space, or form. Thus only Christ has sufficient power to bruise Satan's head and cast him and his forces into the lake of fire and brimstone forever (Rev. 20:3, 10). It required tremendous supernatural power to expel so many demons from the two men and into the pigs, yet He accomplished the feat in an instant.

Knowing all this, we as God's children must remember that only with His armor, especially the shield of faith, can we withstand attacks from demons (Eph. 6:16) and be victorious over their schemes.

Ask YOURSELF

How have you been taught to deal with the forces of darkness and evil? By taking them on in direct spiritual confrontation? By ignoring them or acting as if they don't exist? Let Jesus be your total confidence in all such matters of warfare.

OPPOSITION TO JESUS

The herdsmen ran away, and went to the city and reported everything, including what had happened to the demoniacs. And behold, the whole city came out to meet Jesus; and when they saw Him, they implored Him to leave their region.

MATT. 8:33–34

*I*T'S STARTLING TO REALIZE THAT SOME people do not respect Jesus as much as the demons do. But that was exactly the case for this city (probably ancient Gerasa). The populace wanted nothing to do with the Lord but actually begged Him to leave their area. Mark's account of the incident gives us more clues to their attitudes: "the people came to see what it was that had happened. They came to Jesus and observed the man who had been demon-possessed sitting down, clothed and in his right mind . . . and they became frightened" (Mark 5:14–15). As much as any hostility they may have had, they were simply scared.

As unregenerate sinners, the Gerasenes were no doubt bewildered and intimidated by Jesus. They saw His ability to control demons and animals and to restore crazed minds to sanity—and the result was complete opposition to Christ.

In sharp contrast to the attitude of the city people, one of the delivered men implored Jesus to let him go with Him (Mark 5:18). He manifested a great faith, love, and adoration for the Lord—so much so that he could not bear the thought of separation. But Jesus commanded him, "Go home to your people and report to them what great things the Lord has done for you, and how He had mercy on you" (Mark 5:19). The man was to be an evangelist to his own people, testifying that despite their present opposition to Jesus, the Son of God did not want them to perish spiritually.

*Ask*YOURSELF

Are there people in your life whose rejection of and opposition to Christ are totally baffling to you—going against all logic and every example of God's reality? How should you respond to such hardheadedness?

UNDAUNTED FAITH

Getting into a boat, Jesus crossed over the sea and came to His own city.
And they brought to Him a paralytic lying on a bed. Seeing their faith,
Jesus said to the paralytic, "Take courage, son; your sins are forgiven."

MATT. 9:1–2

CHRISTIANITY'S MOST DISTINCTIVE message is the truth that God can forgive sin. The essence of the gospel is that Christ's atoning death can free people from the penalty of sin. If Jesus can heal diseases and disabilities, He can surely provide cleansing for the consequences of sin. The men who brought the paralytic to the Lord undoubtedly believed this very strongly.

Those with crippling disabilities have always had to endure social stigma and neglect. But in the Jewish culture of Jesus' day and much earlier, the stigma was especially pronounced because everyone believed chronic ailments stemmed directly from someone's sin. Bildad told Job, "If your sons sinned against Him, then He delivered them into the power of their transgression" (Job 8:4; cf. 4:7; John 9:1–2).

The paralytic here likely had the same understanding concerning sin and disease, thus he was determined at any cost to see Jesus for forgiveness and a resultant physical healing. Christ saw the determination of his faith as his friends worked through the crowd to get the paralytic in front of Him. That aggressive approach revealed their hearts of faith. In all his physical ugliness and spiritual neediness, the man threw himself upon Jesus' mercy.

The paralyzed man came to the Lord in true humility and poverty of spirit, which God requires of all seeking hearts (Matt. 5:3). Jesus sometimes healed people of little faith, but He was especially willing to heal those of great faith, as with the men and his friends.

Ask YOURSELF

Why does God choose to work through our faith? Why would He want to include our cooperation as part of His healing activity? What might He be requiring of you as He deals with a certain need in your life?

FORGIVENESS: THE GREATEST OF ALL MIRACLES

Take courage, son; your sins are forgiven.

MATT. 9:2B

*J*ESUS' ULTIMATE WORDS TO THE paralytic, "your sins are forgiven," represent the greatest of all divine miracles and definitely the most desirable for the one who hears them. This is the holy Son of God forgiving the sins of an unholy man. He could control nature with a word, and with these words He dismissed the man's sins and graciously made him right with God.

The verb translated "are forgiven" means send away or do away with. David declares, "As far as the east is from the west, so far has He removed our transgressions from us" (Ps. 103:12; cf. Mic. 7:19). "It is a trustworthy statement, deserving full acceptance," Paul asserts, "that Christ Jesus came into the world to save sinners, among whom I am foremost of all" (1 Tim. 1:15). That means Jesus came to forgive sinners who trust in Him.

Sin is hostility and rebellion against God and His law (Lev. 26:27; 1 Tim. 1:9; 1 John 3:4). It is incurable by human power (Jer. 13:23), affects all people (Rom. 3:23), affects the total person (Eph. 2:1–3), and subjects people to hell if they do not repent (2 Thess. 1:9).

Such a bleak portrait means the best news anyone can ever receive is the word that his or her "sins are forgiven."

Ask YOURSELF

As you pray through a particular issue of need in your life right now, what are you really seeking? Are you only wanting the resolution of a conflict, the alleviation of pain, the mending of a relationship? Or does God want your eyes on even greater spiritual matters?

STUBBORN FURY AGAINST JESUS

And some of the scribes said to themselves, "This fellow blasphemes."
MATT. 9:3

*T*O CHARGE SOMEONE WITH blasphemy was truly a serious statement for ones to make in the religious culture in which Jesus ministered. But that was the outlandish accusation against Him brought by the scribes because they rejected His claim to forgive sins (Luke 5:21; cf. Mark 2:7). They knew that forgiveness comes only from God (Isa. 43:25; Mic. 7:18–19), but because they didn't believe Jesus was God's Son, they had to conclude He was blaspheming.

Unlike the paralytic and his friends, the scribes felt no need for forgiveness—they considered themselves already righteous. They rejected Jesus' authority to forgive and further believed it wrong for someone simply to ask in faith that he or she be forgiven. For the Jewish leaders, real forgiveness came only by self-righteous and legalistic efforts to earn it.

The scribes' furious opposition to Jesus was part of a growing pattern of persecution of Him by the establishment—a situation that led to His death. The Jews themselves, ironically, were guilty of blaspheming their Messiah when they accused Him of being satanic: "He casts out the demons by the ruler of the demons" (Matt. 9:34).

Every miracle that proved who Jesus was served only to harden the hearts of the scribes and Pharisees and drive them further from belief and repentance. We can thank God that His Spirit spared us from such a condition, and pray always that our hearts remain soft toward Him.

Ask YOURSELF

Has anything occurred in your life lately to cause you to doubt God's goodness or feel unsure about His faithfulness? Why is such a conclusion always incorrect? How can you guard yourself against being subject to this kind of spiritual confusion?

JESUS STANDS AGAINST SIN'S EFFECTS

And Jesus knowing their thoughts said, "Why are you thinking evil in your hearts?
Which is easier, to say, 'Your sins are forgiven,' or to say, 'Get up, and walk'?
But so that you may know that the Son of Man has authority on earth to forgive sins . . ."

MATT. 9:4–6A

*B*ECAUSE HE IS THE SON of God, Jesus "did not need anyone to testify concerning man, for He Himself knew what was in man" (John 2:25). Christ knows all about every sin, even the unseen ones (cf. 1 Sam. 16:7; 1 Chron. 28:9), and stands firmly against them. Before God punished Ananias and Sapphira for their deception, He asked them through Peter, "Why has Satan filled your heart to lie to the Holy Spirit?" (Acts 5:3).

Similarly, in this situation, Jesus knew what His enemies were thinking and was ready to expose the evil behind their thoughts and the error of their logic regarding authority to forgive. Because sin and its symptoms are inseparable, Jesus would have to deal with sin or else He could not deal with the effects.

The Jewish leaders had no good reply or sound argument against Jesus and His divine capabilities. However, it was and is obvious: our Lord can deal with both sin and its consequences, and human beings can do neither. Only God can heal disease with a few words and forgive sins with another few words.

Christ's response to His opponents here came down to the old adage, "Actions speak louder than words." In other words, *saying* something that cannot be verified is always easier than *doing* something that can be. Jesus' foes could not verify the paralytic's forgiveness, but they were about to see proof of his healing, which forces any reasonable person to concede that Jesus does deal with sin *and* its effects.

Ask YOURSELF

Jesus knows our thoughts. As people redeemed from eternal punishment and freed to walk in abundant life, we need not fear this as a source of constant guilt. But how can we use this knowledge to discipline our hearts and purify our motives?

TRUE AUTHORITY OVER SIN

"But so that you may know that the Son of Man has authority on earth to forgive sins"
—then He said to the paralytic, "Get up, pick up your bed and go home." And he got up and went home.
MATT. 9:6–7

*I*T'S NOT UNHEARD OF FOR people to trap themselves by their own theology and logic. That's what happened with the scribes and Pharisees during this episode. They believed that disease and physical suffering were results of sin, and that removing the disease would equate with removing the sin that caused it. By that reasoning, all healing would have to include at least some forgiveness of sin—which only God can give. Jesus used this logic to prove a crucial point.

The point is clear—"the Son of Man has authority on earth to forgive sins." Essentially the Lord says, "I will again demonstrate My power to heal disease. There may be no tangible results of My forgiveness, but there are tangible, visible results when I heal." If in the minds of the Jews disease and sin are always connected, then it follows that healing and forgiveness are always connected. Therefore, so they might know He could forgive sin in the heart, which is unseen, Christ would do what they *could* see—heal the physical side-effects of sin, as represented by the paralytic.

Causing the man to walk would be proof to everyone present of Jesus' complete authority over sin and its effects—less spectacular but just as convincing as was seeing demon-filled swine run off the cliff and into the sea at our Lord's behest.

At Christ's command the man "got up and went home," an action that was a living proof of the Son's authority over infirmities and sin.

Ask YOURSELF

How does Jesus continually prove to you that His forgiveness of your sins is authentic and complete? What Scriptures give you assurance when your feelings tell you otherwise?

REVERENTIAL FEAR

But when the crowds saw this, they were awestruck, and glorified God,
who had given such authority to men.

MATT. 9:8

*T*HE WORD RENDERED "AWESTRUCK," although often translated "fear," most commonly refers to reverential awe in the New Testament. It is how someone feels who is in the presence of another, infinitely superior person.

"Awestruck" describes the reaction to numerous significant events we read about in the gospels and Acts: the shepherds hearing of Jesus' birth (Luke 2:9), the apostles when their Lord walked on water (Matt. 14:26), the guards at the tomb when the angels rolled away the stone (Matt. 28:2–4), the people in the early church right after Pentecost (Acts 2:43), and the reaction to the deaths of Ananias and Sapphira (Acts 5:5, 11).

Reverential awe of God is an essential part of the genuine Christian life (see 2 Cor. 7:1, 10–11; Phil. 2:12; 1 Peter 3:2). This attitude must undergird all important aspects of worship, ministry, love, respect, and even biblical church discipline (see 2 Cor. 5:11; Eph. 5:21; 1 Tim. 5:20).

The awe-filled response by most of the people in the crowd as they witnessed what Jesus did for the paralytic was certainly the right one, especially since it resulted in their giving glory to God. Such an attitude should never be far from us as we strive to faithfully worship and serve the Lord (cf. Acts 9:31).

*Ask*YOURSELF

How magnificent of a revelation does it take for you to be "awestruck" at God's splendor and glory? What simple, basic, everyday things are ready examples of His greatness, though disguised as something ordinary and insignificant?

MATTHEW'S POSITIVE RESPONSE

As Jesus went on from there, He saw a man called Matthew, sitting in the tax collector's booth; and He said to him, "Follow Me!" And he got up and followed Him.

MATT. 9:9

*M*ATTHEW'S GOSPEL HAS ALREADY established that Jesus offered His forgiveness to the least-loved outcasts of society. It seems evident from the context of this verse that one of those outcasts, Matthew the tax collector (this gospel's author), had been under real conviction of sin and spiritual need. He would have been very aware of Jesus' ministry in and around Capernaum, even though he might not have personally heard Him preach or had seen Him do a miracle.

Matthew likely yearned for the forgiveness that was permanently denied to him by unbelieving Judaism, which viewed him as the worst kind of reprobate and traitor. So when Christ called him, Matthew without hesitation "got up and followed Him."

Luke's account describes the moment this way: Matthew "left everything behind, and got up and began to follow Him" (Luke 5:28). Our Lord's simple but profoundly urgent call was sufficient reason for him to forsake everything he once was and owned. Matthew knew that once he left his tax collector's position he could never return to it. Of all the Twelve, he no doubt sacrificed the most in wealth to follow Jesus. Like Paul later, he affirmed that "whatever things were gain to me, those things I have counted as loss for the sake of Christ" (Phil. 3:7).

*Ask*YOURSELF

If it's been too long since the significance and honor of Jesus' call swept over you, see the excitement in Matthew's reaction to Christ. Watch him lunge at the chance to be one of Jesus' disciples. Remember again the thrill of being in your Master's service.

AUGUST 12

The Pharisees' Negative Response

*Then it happened that as Jesus was reclining at the table in the house, behold, many tax collectors
and sinners came and were dining with Jesus and His disciples. When the Pharisees saw this,
they said to His disciples, "Why is your Teacher eating with the tax collectors and sinners?"*

MATT. 9:10–11

*P*RIDEFUL RESENTMENT CAN LEAD to the most negative response to the
person and ministry of Jesus. Such was the case with the Pharisees here who were
angry and humiliated that He associated so personally with sinners and yet had not
extended to them, the religious elite, the same sort of social favor. Surely they, the pil-
lars of proper behavior and religious purity, at least deserved a banquet from this
newer Teacher, didn't they?

The Pharisees' question about Jesus' eating with sinners (or "undesirable people") was more a rhetorical rebuke than a sincere question. They were merely vent-
ing their hostility and again attempting to put Jesus on the spot. They did not even
have the courage to ask their question directly of the Lord, but hovered outside the
banquet house to find out what sort of response the disciples would get from their
Master.

The Pharisees were becoming more and more bitter and vindictive, realizing
they were at odds with practically everything Jesus was teaching. They were so convinced of their own orthodoxy and superiority that anything perceived as contrary
to their worldview was by definition heretical and unrighteous. These men were furious that Christ snubbed them yet maintained friendly relations with sinners and
outcasts.

The Pharisees' negative response to Jesus, and their misguided, unscriptural
"religion" that worked at cross-purposes to His divine ministry of redemption, is
completely the opposite of Christianity, the true and biblical religion.

Ask YOURSELF

Do you sense any hint of spiritual superiority in your heart—even the slightest
impression that your tenure as a Christian, your knowledge of the Word, or your familiarity with church decorum makes you a little more special to God than others are?

The Sick Need a Physician

When Jesus heard this, He said, "It is not those who are
healthy who need a physician, but those who are sick."
MATT. 9:12

*B*ASIC HUMAN LOGIC AND COMMON sense tells us that physically sick people need treatment from a doctor. Here Jesus simply answers the Pharisees' cynical question with the plain statement that the spiritually sick also need treatment. It's as if He said to the Jews, "If you're really so spiritually healthy, you don't need a spiritual physician. But if by their own confession, the sinners I'm eating with are the spiritually needy who must have the gospel presented, then that's why I'm ministering to them. I'm the Great Physician who can bring spiritual healing—salvation—to those who recognize their desperate need."

By analogy, no credible physician would spend all his or her time among healthy people and refuse to be with the sick. By implication, Jesus was asking the Pharisees if they—the self-proclaimed theological and religious "experts" who had all the answers for the unenlightened—were refusing to give them that medicine. This was an incredible indictment of the self-righteous, hard-hearted religionists.

The Pharisees were hypocrites who carefully fussed about the most minute matters of the law but neglected the bigger issues such as "justice and mercy and faithfulness" (Matt. 23:23). They loved themselves but hated others and revealed themselves to be without the compassion and mercy God's law requires.

We have to ask, How could the Pharisees resent the healing of those sinners God Himself desired to heal? With such an attitude they proved themselves to be sickest of all—actually dead spiritually.

Ask YOURSELF

How are we guilty of spending an undue percentage of our time providing care and attention for the spiritually sound? What is this an indicator of? What can you do to avoid this imbalance in your church and personal ministry?

AUGUST 14

Jesus Urges Compassion

But go and learn what this means: "I desire compassion, and not sacrifice."

MATT. 9:13A

*J*ESUS NEVER SHIED AWAY FROM speaking directly and bluntly if the situation demanded such talk. Here He pins the Jewish leaders to the wall by quoting from their own most honored scriptural authorities. Their own prophets rebuke them for their spiritual ignorance and their lack of obedience to God's clear commands.

Jesus paraphrases Hosea's prophetic and divinely inspired words: "I delight in loyalty rather than sacrifice, and in the knowledge of God rather than burnt offerings" (Hos. 6:6). The perfect Word of God should have been the Pharisees' supreme concern, as it should be ours, rather than the flawed words and ideas of humanity. Without true and godly compassion, all the Pharisees' rituals, ceremonies, and sacrifices were worth nothing to God. The person who is indifferent toward other people verifies that he or she is also indifferent toward God, no matter how correct their theology or impeccable their morality.

Ritual separated from righteousness and a concern for the downtrodden and lost has always been an affront to God. Through the prophet Amos, the Lord declared, "Take away from Me the noise of your songs; I will not even listen to the sound of your harps. But let justice roll down like waters and righteousness like an ever-flowing stream" (Amos 5:23–24).

Ask YOURSELF

In what ways have you let duty and religious reputation become elevated in importance beyond genuine love and compassion for others? What is so empty about the former . . . and so rejuvenating about the latter?

AUGUST 15

CHRIST CALLS ALL SINNERS TO REPENTANCE

I did not come to call the righteous, but sinners.

MATT. 9:13B

*E*VERYONE WHO IS REPENTANT, who acknowledges his or her sin and turns from it, is the object of Jesus' call. The familiar Greek word (*kaleō*) rendered here "to call" is also used of inviting someone to your home to enjoy good hospitality. This implies that Jesus did not invite the Pharisees to a meal with other sinners for the same reason He does not call any self-righteous person to salvation. In both cases, the people do not see themselves as needy, do not want to associate with those considered lower than themselves, and therefore can't identify themselves with the Lord Jesus.

Later on, Jesus told three parables to further illustrate His concern for penitent sinners. Parables of the lost sheep and lost coin show that "there will be more joy in heaven over one sinner who repents than over ninety-nine righteous persons who need no repentance" (Luke 15:7). The poignant story of the prodigal son especially illustrates the Lord's point that the Father rejoices over every person who repents, and He grieves over everyone who thinks he has no need (see Luke 15:11–32).

Christ's teaching is clear: the person who believes he or she is spiritually safe without Him has no part in His kingdom. Our Lord came to earth to call sinners to repentance, but He cannot seek and save (Luke 19:10) those who will not recognize they are lost—and the self-righteous need to reexamine their hearts concerning salvation before it's too late.

Ask YOURSELF

We never outgrow our need, though we can easily outgrow our awareness of it. What can you do to help ensure that your utter dependence on God is never far from your thoughts and attitudes?

THE DANGER OF WRONGLY-BASED RITUALS

*Then the disciples of John came to Him, asking, "Why do we and the Pharisees fast, but
Your disciples do not fast?" And Jesus said to them, "The attendants of the bridegroom
cannot mourn as long as the bridegroom is with them, can they?"*

MATT. 9:14–15A

*R*ELIGIOUS RITUAL AND ROUTINE, if not handled appropriately, will always threaten true godliness. Some practices, such as praying to saints or lighting candles for the dead, are heretical. But even biblical practices, when their forms become the center of attention, can become barriers to true righteousness. Church attendance, Bible reading, saying grace before meals, and singing hymns can become lifeless habits that exclude true worship and praise. When we apply good things such as these the wrong way, they can keep us from faithful obedience . . . and keep unbelievers from trusting in God.

Alms, prescribed prayer, and fasting were the three major expressions of piety the Jews performed in Jesus' time. The leaders took these matters quite seriously and were meticulous to practice them publicly so as to impress others with their piety (cf. Matt. 6:2, 5, 16). Thus these practices became badges of pride and hypocrisy rather than marks of humble and genuine religion before God.

Jesus' point in mentioning the bridegroom and his attendants is to show how out of place it is for His followers (attendants) to mourn and fast while He (the Bridegroom) is with them in person. Pharisaical manners and rituals are always wrong for Christians, but even good practices (such as sincere fasting), if not done properly, can hinder what the Lord wants to accomplish in our midst.

Ask YOURSELF

Should our answer to this kind of hypocrisy be the removal of all forms, disciplines, and ritual practices from our worship? Or is there value in these kinds of expressions? What would go missing from our worship if it was all spur-of-the-moment, with no cherished repetitions?

THE RIGHT PERSPECTIVE ON FASTING

But the days will come when the bridegroom is taken away from them, and then they will fast.
MATT. 9:15B

*F*ASTING IS MEANINGLESS if done merely from habit and if it doesn't derive from a deep concern over some spiritual need. And as we saw yesterday, even the best and most foundational spiritual practices, if not done with sincere motives and right purposes, are only hypocritical and pretentious.

Jesus was obviously referring to His crucifixion when He said He would be taken away from the disciples. From that time on, it would be fitting to fast and mourn. Fasting naturally comes from a broken and mourning heart, but if it is performed as a shallow, mechanical ritual only, it is displeasing to God.

Jesus' emphasis on internal matters such as forgiveness shows us that fasting must be held in the proper context of what's truly important. It also demonstrates that He brought us radically different teachings and practices from those of traditional Judaism or any other religious traditions—Catholicism, liberal Protestantism, any sects and cults—that can stress externalism, ritualism, or any man-centered habits. When we fast, Jesus wants us to do so in light of His new covenant—not the old with its forms and shadows—and in a way that increases our compassion for others, causes us to be more humble and sacrificial, and gives Him all the praise and glory.

Ask YOURSELF

Are there ways to fast besides abstaining from food? In what other ways could you experience the spiritual benefits of fasting—the clarity of communication with God, the taming of selfish desires, the renewal of priorities?

OF WINE AND WINESKINS

No one puts a patch of unshrunk cloth on an old garment; for the patch pulls away
from the garment, and a worse tear results. Nor do people put new wine into old wineskins;
otherwise the wineskins burst, and the wine pours out and the wineskins are ruined;
but they put new wine into fresh wineskins, and both are preserved.

MATT. 9:16–17

*W*HENEVER REPAIRING CLOTHING or attaching a new patch to an old garment, the tailor or seamstress must be careful to follow particular guidelines and avoid certain mistakes. In like manner, believers cannot combine outmoded and external traditions of self-righteousness and ritual with the gospel of grace and forgiveness.

With these words, Jesus illustrates the truth that the old way cannot contain His new way: "Nor do people put new wine into old wineskins; otherwise the wineskins burst, and the wine pours out and the wineskins are ruined." Old wineskins eventually dry up and crack, and if you try to pour new wine into them, they will burst and spill the wine. Fresh wine requires a fresh skin. By analogy, the only life that can contain genuine holiness is the regenerate life granted by God when the Spirit draws a person to faith and repentance, when he or she trusts Christ as Lord and Savior.

The old wineskins refer not to God's law and the Old Testament but to the rabbinical traditions that supplanted and contradicted God's truth. Thus Jesus' bringing in His new teachings in place of some old or unbiblical teachings does not mean He sets aside the divine law for some kind of ill-defined, licentious, anything-goes form of grace. The Lord unmistakably declares that He came to fulfill the Father's law, not destroy it. Law and grace, rightly understood, have always been compatible with the believer's benefit and blessing.

*Ask*YOURSELF

The subtext for this passage is that the self-righteous are focused on the value of their "wineskins," while the true believer places his worth in the value of the "new wine." What's the difference?

MARKS OF THE TRUE BELIEVER

They put new wine into fresh wineskins, and both are preserved.

MATT. 9:17B

*L*IKE NEW WINE POURED into fresh wineskins, everything stays spiritually fresh for the true believer. *First,* he or she leads a life of unquestioning obedience and follows the Lord without conditions or excuses. Not long before His ascension, Jesus told Peter, " 'Follow Me!' Peter, turning around, saw the disciple whom Jesus loved following them . . . So Peter seeing him said to Jesus, 'Lord, and what about this man?' Jesus said to him, 'If I want him to remain until I come, what is that to you? You follow Me!' " (John 21:19–22). Christians don't question Christ's will or unwisely compare themselves to other believers.

Second, like Matthew who invited sinners to his house to see Jesus, true saints have compassion on the unsaved. They want to see them saved, even though at times that desire gets supplanted by selfish concerns. Because they know "the fear of the Lord, [they] persuade men" (2 Cor. 5:11). The love of Christ will prompt them to witness to others (v. 14).

Finally, if we are truly Christ's children, we will not follow any sort of legalism or ritualism as the scribes and Pharisees did. We'll realize soon enough that these are utterly incompatible with the new life in Jesus Christ. It should also be clear to us that what was begun in the Spirit cannot be finished in the flesh (Gal. 3:3). The new wine of salvation and sanctification has no place back in the old wineskins of our life before conversion.

Ask YOURSELF

Is your life devoid of some of these freedoms? Does your heart often—or perhaps incessantly—cause Christian faith to feel as though it's just another burden or pressure rather than the pure expression of who you are? What's standing between you and abundant life?

JAIRUS'S SENSE OF NEED

*A synagogue official came and bowed down before Him, and said, "My daughter
has just died; but come and lay Your hand on her, and she will live."*

MATT. 9:18

*T*HE ACCOUNTS OF THIS INCIDENT by Mark (5:22) and Luke (8:41)
identify the synagogue official as Jairus. And everything he did in this encounter
with Jesus demonstrated his humility and sincerity. His request of the Lord was a
selfless one for something humanly impossible, and by making it he respected
Christ's power, compassion, and grace. Seemingly unworried about the reaction of
his fellow religious leaders, he knew that only Jesus could help his daughter who
had just died.

The Holy Spirit had obviously already worked in Jairus's heart to bring him to
this point. His request shows absolute faith that Jesus was able to do what was asked:
"come and lay Your hand on her, and she will live." Jairus's sense of need was so urgent that he swallowed his fear and pride and came to Jesus without hesitation or
doubt.

Often some tragedy such as this drives a person to Jesus Christ. Those who, unlike Jairus, are unaware of need in their lives will usually have no hunger for God.
That's why in evangelism, it is important to show someone their need of salvation
and therefore of Christ as the only way to receive it. Jairus saw the emptiness of
human resources in this situation and now knew Jesus was his last best hope. He
may not have approached the Lord out of the purest motive, because his prime concern was his daughter's life and his own despair. So his first thought was not solely
to glorify Christ, but he did trust Jesus for help in bringing his child back—and he
found Him truly accessible.

Ask YOURSELF

What needs do those around you have, perhaps without even knowing it? Identify several of them. As you go about your day, be aware of the needs they're expressing. And as opportunities for spiritual conversation arise, show them the answer
to their need in Christ Jesus.

JAIRUS'S TRUE FAITH

A synagogue official came and bowed down before Him, and said,
"My daughter has just died; but come and lay Your hand on her, and she will live."
MATT. 9:18

*J*AIRUS'S BELIEF THAT THE Lord Jesus could honor his request to revive his daughter from death is especially extraordinary because Jesus had not yet performed a resurrection miracle. He had performed many healing miracles, but up to this point He had not brought someone back from the dead. So there was no precedent for such a request, yet Jairus asked it in faith.

Jairus's faith surpassed that of the centurion, who believed Christ could "speak" his servant well *prior* to death (Matt. 8:9–10). It also topped that of Martha, who believed Jesus could have kept her brother Lazarus from dying, but relinquished hope once he died, even when Jesus said he would rise again (John 11:21, 23–24). With such unsurpassed faith that the Lord could resurrect his daughter by a mere touch, Jairus undoubtedly trusted Him for forgiveness of sins and newness of spiritual life, for salvation.

This episode also demonstrates that Jesus was not a religious guru with servants doing His every bidding, or a monk removed from everyday life, or a potentate at the top of a religious hierarchy who received people only through several layers of intermediaries. Instead He was the true Son of God who "became flesh, and dwelt among us" (John 1:14) and ministered personally and directly to meet believing requests of men such as Jairus.

Ask YOURSELF

Is your faith limited to the precedent of what you've seen Jesus do in the past? Or are you willing to believe Him for more than your eye has seen or your ear has heard? Bring a big need before Him today—in believing faith—and continue to watch for His answer.

AUGUST 22

JESUS' AVAILABILITY TO JAIRUS

Jesus got up and began to follow him, and so did His disciples.

MATT. 9:19

*J*ESUS WAS ALWAYS WILLING to go out of His way to serve others in the Father's name. This trait was certainly evident as Christ reached out to Jairus with accessibility and availability. There were certainly many other needy people in the region near Jairus, but the urgency of the synagogue leader's circumstances demanded that Jesus go to Jairus's home. From a distance the Lord could have sent the power to raise the man's daughter from the dead. He chose, however, to manifest selfless love and compassion by following the grieving Jairus to his home.

God is sensitive not only to the needs of the many but to the cry of individuals in need. The Holy Spirit's work through Philip in Acts 8 illustrates this principle. In the midst of a highly profitable ministry in Samaria, an angel dispatched the evangelist to Gaza (v. 26). Right away Philip met the Ethiopian eunuch, the royal official who served the queen of Ethiopia. When the Holy Spirit prompted Philip to approach the man, the evangelist found an eager seeker about the things of God and was able to lead him to saving faith in Christ (vv. 35–37).

God sometimes leads us, as He often led His own Son and the early disciples, to temporarily set aside a larger ministry to focus on the need of one person—and He wants us to be available. After all, Jesus did promise that every single individual who genuinely "comes to Me I will certainly not cast out" (John 6:37).

Ask YOURSELF

Who comes to mind when you think of someone God has called you to influence at this point in time? Avoid the temptation to withhold yourself from others, not wanting to get involved in the messiness of their needs and problems, when Jesus has called you to compassion.

Jesus Touches an Untouchable

*A woman who had been suffering from a hemorrhage for twelve years, came up behind Him
and touched the fringe of His cloak; for she was saying to herself, "If I only touch His garment,
I will get well." But Jesus turning and seeing her said, "Daughter, take courage;
your faith has made you well." At once the woman was made well.*

MATT. 9:20–22

WHEN THE GODLY SIR JAMES Simpson was on his deathbed, a friend said to him, "Well, James, soon you will be able to rest on the bosom of Jesus." But Simpson replied, "I don't know that I can quite do that, but I do think I can take hold of His garment."

In her shame at being ostracized from her family and being ceremonially unclean, the woman here wanted to be unnoticed. She merely desired to touch Jesus' garment, confident that such contact was enough to receive healing. In keeping with such confidence, she received immediate healing from her defilement.

Our Lord became aware of what had happened only as He realized that divine power had gone out from Him (Luke 8:46)—a realization that happened before He humanly knew of the woman specifically. His statement, "your faith has made you well," simply assured her and the crowd that miraculous healing had occurred. Jesus did not care that her touching Him would make Him ceremonially unclean to the Jews. The Lord was touchable even by an untouchable.

Even though the woman's expectations were likely not fully informed by Scripture—she might have superstitiously thought Christ's clothes had inherent healing powers—He spoke to her caringly and compassionately: "Daughter, take courage." In spite of other factors, the woman's faith was genuine and acceptable to the Lord. It was enough to make her well.

Ask YOURSELF

Part of the balance of Christian faith is realizing that we are unworthy to touch the hem of His garment, yet are welcomed into His full embrace as an adopted member of His family. How do these two seeming incongruities come together and balance out in your worship?

THE REDEMPTIVE ELEMENT OF JESUS' IMPARTIAL HEALINGS

Your faith has made you well.

MATT. 9:22B

*I*N MANY INSTANCES IN THE gospels, the words translated "healed," "made well," or similar variations, are from the Greek word meaning salvation or saved from sin. For instance, when blind Bartimaeus came to Jesus to regain his sight, the Lord told him, "Go; your faith has made you well" (Mark 10:52). That Bartimaeus repeatedly called Jesus "Son of David," a common messianic title, suggests that his physical healing included spiritual salvation.

In the account of the ten lepers, Luke reports that all of them "were cleansed" (Luke 17:14), but this was from a word that means essentially physical cleansing. However, of the one who glorified God and returned to give thanks, Jesus used the same expression (see v. 19) as He did to Bartimaeus and the woman with the hemorrhage. Ten men received cleansing, but only one obtained salvation. This indicates that salvation and physical healing were sometimes linked, even if in the example of the ten lepers, only one man realized both.

In addition to a strong redemptive element, Jesus' healings were impartial. That Christ ministered equally to the leading synagogue elder and the outcast woman clearly proves this. The woman's touching His garment with unclean hands did not offend Him. Nor did her presumption to obtain His help while He worked through the crowd to reach Jairus's daughter bother Him. True needs never interfered with our Lord's sovereign and impartial approach to ministry. "The Son of Man did not come to be served, but to serve, and to give His life a ransom for many" (Matt. 20:28).

Ask YOURSELF

Would you describe your feelings and interactions with others as being impartial? Are there people who (though you might never admit it aloud) are considered beneath you and unworthy of your notice and attention? Confess this as sin before the Father, and model Jesus' brand of ministry.

CHRIST'S ULTIMATE POWER OVER DEATH

When Jesus came into the official's house, and saw the flute-players and the crowd
in noisy disorder, He said, "Leave; for the girl has not died, but is asleep." And they began
laughing at Him. But when the crowd had been sent out, He entered and took
her by the hand, and the girl got up. This news spread throughout all that land.

MATT. 9:23–26

*U*NLIKE THOSE IN THE CONTEMPORARY Western world, funerals in most ancient cultures, including the Jewish one of Jesus' time, were not events with reverent music and quiet whispers. Instead funerals featured much loud wailing by professional mourners and dissonant music played by hired musicians. Because Jairus was the top leader of the local synagogue and a wealthy man, he probably hired a large number of mourners and musicians for his daughter's funeral.

Jesus surprised and annoyed the mourners by telling them to leave, claiming that the girl was not dead but asleep (cf. John 11:11). That the people's weeping turned so quickly to harsh, derisive laughter—the kind by those feeling superior to another—showed that their mourning was indeed an insincere, paid action devoid of genuine sorrow or any real faith that the Lord could raise Jairus's daughter.

Mark's account of this episode adds these details: Jesus "entered the room where the child was. Taking the child by the hand, He said to her, 'Talitha kum!' (which translated means, 'Little girl, I say to you, get up!'). Immediately the girl got up and began to walk" (Mark 5:40c–42a). Christ easily could have resuscitated her by a mere word, but His intimate interaction displayed a healing compassion far more than what was minimally necessary. And it convincingly showed His power over every enemy of mankind, including "the final enemy" of death and hades (cf. Rev. 1:18).

*Ask*YOURSELF

We can always expect faith to be met by doubters and revilers, even among those in the church—sometimes *especially* by those in the church. What kind of an impact does this have on your willingness to believe? Are you ever the cold water on anyone else's spiritual passion?

AUGUST 26

RIGHT KNOWLEDGE OF JESUS

Two blind men followed Him, crying out, "Have mercy on us, Son of David!"

MATT. 9:27

THAT THE BLIND MEN CALLED JESUS the "Son of David" means they recognized Him as the Christ. Son of David was one of the most common Jewish titles for Messiah. It was also a royal title indicating that Messiah would come from the family of King David and have a right to rule over the promised divine kingdom.

God first promised that the Deliverer for His people would be a man, the seed of a woman (cf. Gen. 3:15). Later in the Old Testament, the prophet Nathan firmly establishes the extraordinary person and work of the Son of David (2 Sam. 12–14a, 16; cf. Gen. 12:3; 21:12; 49:10). The New Testament reaffirms this great truth at the angel's Nativity announcement: "He will be great and will be called the Son of the Most High; and the Lord God will give Him the throne of His father David; and He will reign over the house of Jacob forever, and His kingdom will have no end" (Luke 1:32–33; cf. vv. 68–69; 2:4).

The reality and knowledge of Jesus' true identity stands out most vividly during His triumphal entry when the people laid branches and garments before Him and shouted, "Hosanna to the Son of David; blessed is He who comes in the name of the Lord" (Matt. 21:9).

Thus all the onlookers who heard the blind men call Jesus "Son of David" knew it was a clear confession of His messiahship. And the men's affirmation accompanied their desire for personal deliverance. Genuine salvation is available to all who have a similar right knowledge of Him.

Ask YOURSELF

Think of the names you use to refer to Christ—Lord, Savior, Redeemer, Friend. Spend a few minutes thinking through what these terms actually mean. When you speak of Him by these names in prayer, let the weight of their glory fill your words with depth and texture.

A RIGHT ATTITUDE TOWARD JESUS

Two blind men followed Him, crying out, "Have mercy on us, Son of David!"
MATT. 9:27

*T*HE ATTITUDE OF THE HEART that Christ honors and accepts is one in which the sinner understands his or her personal unworthiness. That was the attitude of the two blind men as they came to Him. They realized they didn't deserve Jesus' help, but they also must have known that "The Lord is gracious and merciful; slow to anger and great in lovingkindness. The Lord is good to all, and His mercies are over all His works" (Ps. 145:8–9; cf. Joel 2:13).

It seems reasonable to suggest that the two men came to our Lord not only for physical healing but to receive His forgiving mercy. They were no doubt burdened by a spiritual need that they knew only Jesus could meet. They approached Him with real humility, publicly throwing themselves on His abundant grace. Their attitude was perfectly aligned with that of the tax collector who mourns over his unworthiness and cries out, "God, be merciful to me, the sinner!" (Luke 18:13).

It is noteworthy that Jesus initially showed no response to the men's pleas. But as He moved along with the multitude, the blind men kept pouring out the desire of their hearts with persistence and determination. It's as if the Lord tested their faith, letting it extend to its extremity and prove its sincerity. But theirs was a Savior of mercy, granting healing and salvation to all who come with a humble, believing attitude.

Ask YOURSELF

How often do your prayers and faith begin to flag after one or two attempts at asking for help? What are some of God's reasons for requiring persistence in our pursuit of Him?

JESUS MEETS BLIND MEN'S NEEDS

The blind men came up to Him, and Jesus said to them, "Do you believe that I am
able to do this?" They said to Him, "Yes, Lord." Then He touched their eyes, saying,
"It shall be done to you according to your faith." And their eyes were opened.

MATT. 9:28–30A

*S*OMETIMES AT CONVERSION, the Lord wants sinners to give a more pub-lic profession of their trust in Him, in keeping with Paul's teaching, "If you confess with your mouth Jesus as Lord, and believe in your heart that God raised Him from the dead, you will be saved" (Rom. 10:9). This was the kind of confession Jesus drew out of the blind men, and it testified to the eyewitnesses of what He requires for sal-vation. "Yes" indicated they believed He could do what they requested of Him, and "Lord" set forth their faith that He was the promised Messiah and coming Savior, who was now in their midst.

The men's testimony proved that their understanding of Jesus was biblical, un-like many misguided and insincere followers. It distinguished them from those who thought Jesus was only a military and political deliverer, those who believed Jesus was merely a competent and charismatic human leader. Their confession empha-sized that Christ was primarily a spiritual leader, whose first concern was saving peo-ple from their sins. Though His compassion for physical suffering was genuine, it was far greater for lost souls.

Jesus prompted the blind men to openly confess their faith in Him, not so much for curing their physical blindness but for the sake of their spiritual sight. They acknowledged Him as Son of David and came asking Him for spiritual mercy and salvation, and thus they received a gift far greater than simple restoration of their eyes.

*Ask*YOURSELF

Test the strength of your concern for others' spiritual state. Is it as strong as it should be? Does your grief over their lost condition extend to your active pursuit of their repentance and trust in Jesus? What would it take to fan the flames of your evangelistic passion?

THE BLIND MEN REACH OUT

Jesus sternly warned them: "See that no one knows about this!"
But they went out and spread the news about Him throughout all that land.

MATT. 9:30B–31

*U*SUALLY BELIEVERS NEED TO SAY more, not less, about the gospel of Jesus Christ. But here our Lord had definite reasons for commanding the people to whom He had ministered most directly not to publicize what had occurred.

He did not forbid them from speaking simply because He did not want their specific healing made known or because He did not want His miracles in general to be proclaimed. The miracles were evidence of His deity and legitimate mission. Christ commanded silence because it was not time to widely publicize His messiahship, lest the news stir up premature opposition to Him or encourage revolutionary Jews to rally around Him as a political deliverer.

Jesus also did not want to overemphasize His miracles. While they were a key element of His ministry, they were not the primary reason for His incarnation. Many already were not understanding the miracles rightly: "Truly, truly, I say to you, you seek Me, not because you saw signs, but because you ate of the loaves and were filled" (John 6:26).

Another reason why the Lord may not have wanted the men heralding His messiahship was because He wanted others, especially the Jews, to look to Scripture for the fulfillment of prophecy about the Messiah.

But in spite of Jesus' command, the blind men still "went out and spread the news about Him." This was disobedient of them and was the wrong response. However, it was the sort of sin that only grateful, eager new converts would commit. The men could not resist telling everyone of their miraculous deliverance.

Ask YOURSELF

How much of your everyday conversation is taken up with what the Lord has done for you? Is it because you're trying to be sensitive to the unsaved around you? Or is it more because you just haven't thought about it that much?

CHRIST'S SAVING COMPASSION

Seeing the people, He felt compassion for them, because
they were distressed and dispirited like sheep without a shepherd.

MATT. 9:36

*J*ESUS FELT COMPASSION FOR the crowds as only the Son of God could feel.
It is among God's attributes to love and care because "God is love" (1 John 4:8). The
term for "felt compassion" literally refers to the intestines, and most often occurs in
Scripture with the figurative reference to the emotions, the way we use "heart" today.
But Jesus' concern was not just symbolic. He no doubt physically felt the symptoms
of genuine caring—ones such as aching and nausea when encountering the agony
of people's struggles with sin and hardship. In order to fulfill prophecy, "He Himself
took our infirmities and carried away our diseases" (Matt. 8:17).

Of course Jesus did not physically contract people's diseases and infirmities.
But in deep, heartfelt compassion and sympathy, He physically and emotionally suffered with all who approached Him for relief. He was not unlike the concerned father who becomes ill from worry about a desperately sick child, or for one in danger
or difficulty.

After Jesus had been in a boat following the death of John the Baptist, crowds
sought Him and He "felt compassion for them and healed their sick" (Matt. 14:14).
Shortly after that, Jesus told the Twelve of His real concern for the masses who had
no food on hand (15:30–32). But our Lord's omniscience saw an infinitely greater
need in people's lives—the profound, pervasive nature of their sin and their desperate plight of spiritual blindness and lostness. Of this horrific condition He was
most compassionate of all.

Ask YOURSELF

Without already knowing Him, this is not what most of us would expect from
the One who created the universe and continues to sustain it by His mere word. A
God who cares? Worship Him today for this gracious quality of His.

EXAMPLES OF JESUS' COMPASSION

Seeing the people, He felt compassion for them.
MATT. 9:36A

*E*XAMPLES IN THE GOSPELS OF Jesus' compassion are notable. When He saw Mary and others weeping for the deceased Lazarus, "He was deeply moved in spirit and was troubled" (John 11:33) and wept with them (v. 35). The phrase "deeply moved in spirit" connotes physical as well as emotional and spiritual anguish. As He saw Lazarus's friends and family grieving, He entered into real crying with them.

When arrested in the garden, Christ was more concerned about the disciples than Himself: "If you [soldiers] seek Me, let these go their way" (John 18:8). While on the cross He still had concern for His mother: "He said to His mother, 'Woman, behold, your son!'" (19:26).

In one of His most poignant expressions of deep compassion for others, Jesus lamented, "Jerusalem, Jerusalem, who kills the prophets and stones those who are sent to her! How often I wanted to gather your children together, the way a hen gathers her chicks under her wings, and you were unwilling" (Matt. 23:37; cf. Luke 19:41–42).

Commenting on two familiar verses about Jesus' compassion and sympathy (Heb. 4:15; 5:8), Paul Brand said,

A stupefying concept: God's Son learning through His experiences on earth. Before taking on a body, God had no personal experience of physical pain or of the effect of rubbing against needy persons. But God dwelt among us and touched us, and His time spent here allows Him to more fully identify with our pain.

Ask YOURSELF

What does Christ's compassion inspire in you? How could you be more daring and deliberate about taking His heart with you into your world of need, touching others with the love and mercy of Jesus?

MANKIND'S LOST CONDITION

They were distressed and dispirited like sheep without a shepherd.

MATT. 9:36B

ONE OF JESUS' MAIN MOTIVES for ministry was the knowledge of man's lost condition. He saw the people He lived among in the reality of their need. He was moved by their diseases and sickness, and He healed every one of them (v. 35). But He was moved even more deeply by the deepest need that most of the multitude did not even know they had—to be freed from their bondage to sin. He saw their hearts, and He knew that inwardly "they were distressed and dispirited."

Jesus saw the multitudes as being inwardly devastated by their sinful and hopeless condition. The idea behind "dispirited" is to be thrown down prostrate and utterly helpless. Jesus saw the dispirited multitudes as sheep without a shepherd to protect and care for them.

Those who claimed to be the shepherds of the multitude were the scribes and Pharisees, yet it was those very shepherds who were largely responsible for the people's confusion and hopelessness. The people were spiritually led by uncaring, unloving leaders who should have been meeting their spiritual needs. That's why Jesus calls the people "the lost sheep of the house of Israel" (Matt. 10:6)—God's chosen people who had been left to perish.

Ask YOURSELF

Begin to develop Jesus' motive for ministry as your own. Take every opportunity to introduce others to the Great Shepherd.

THE RELIGIOUS LEADERS' FALSE SOLUTION

They were distressed and dispirited like sheep without a shepherd.

MATT. 9:36B

*T*HE SCRIBES AND PHARISEES offered a religion that only added burdens instead of lifting them. For them, the common people were the object of disdain, not compassion; individuals to be exploited, not served. In that sense the scribes and Pharisees were true descendents of the false shepherds against whom the Lord railed centuries earlier through Ezekiel (34:2–4).

Many religious leaders today are still endeavoring to keep people out of the kingdom by distorting and contradicting God's Word and perverting the way of salvation. By telling people they are already saved because "a good God would never condemn anyone to hell," they lead people to be content with themselves and to see no need for repentance and salvation—thereby shutting tight the gracious door God has provided. Similarly, when people are told they can work their way into God's favor by avoiding certain sins or by performing certain good deeds or participating in some prescribed ritual, they are likewise deceived and left in their lost condition.

How wonderfully refreshing it must have been to hear Jesus say, "Come to Me, all who are weary and heavy-laden, and I will give you rest. Take My yoke upon you and learn from Me, for I am gentle and humble in heart, and you will find rest for your souls. For My yoke is easy and My burden is light" (Matt. 11:28–30). What a contrast those words were from the teaching of the scribes and Pharisees.

*Ask*YOURSELF

You may not mean to do it, but does the gospel you present to others involve more requirements than Jesus Himself placed on it? Make sure the gospel you proclaim is all about lifting their burden of sin, not loading them with more than they're carrying already.

COMING HARVEST INCLUDES IMPENDING JUDGMENT

The harvest is plentiful, but the workers are few.

MATT. 9:37B

*A*S JESUS CHANGES THE metaphor from shepherding to harvesting, He gives another motive for His ministry. He ministered because people face God's final judgment.

Jesus ministered compassionately and tirelessly because He could see the ultimate consummation of divine judgment toward which every person was headed—every one in the multitudes who did not trust in Him. Paul said, "Therefore, knowing the fear of the Lord, we persuade men" (2 Cor. 5:11).

In 2 Thessalonians, Paul paints a vivid picture of God's judgment: "The Lord Jesus will be revealed from heaven with His mighty angels in flaming fire, dealing out retribution to those who do not know God and to those who do not obey the gospel of our Lord Jesus. These will pay the penalty of eternal destruction, away from the presence of the Lord and from the glory of His power" (1:7–9).

It is easy to lose awareness of the imminence and the inevitability of God's judgment, but the Christian who loses sight of that judgment loses a major portion of his motive for witnessing.

When Jesus saw the crowds, He taught them, preached to them, and healed them—all for the ultimate purpose that they might come to Him and escape the harvest of judgment they could not otherwise avoid.

Ask YOURSELF

Think of the cost that sin has already extracted from you, here where God's mercy is still available and the promise of His restorative forgiveness is actively in force. Imagine its cost on those who will be paying its price forever. Be sure that as you witness, you don't minimize the cost sin brings.

JESUS IDENTIFIES HARVEST WORKERS

Therefore beseech the Lord of the harvest to send out workers into His harvest.

MATT. 9:38

*T*HE PRIMARY PROBLEM that hindered Jesus' ministry as He taught, preached, and healed in Palestine is the primary problem that hinders our ministry today: "the workers are few."

The workers Jesus is referring to are the people who would work in a field that was soon to be harvested—that is what the Lord is calling the disciples to do. This was the first part of our Lord's training method with the Twelve. His disciples learned that the need for the gospel to be brought into a world that is headed for judgment far surpasses the outreach itself.

Who can reach the lost, hell-bound world of sinful, hurting people who need to hear and believe the gospel? Who will tell them of their plight and lead them to the way of escape?

In His own days on earth, Christ's workers were few, and they still are today. The first need in His ministry is for workers, and one of the most important things those workers must understand is that their shortage of numbers can be increased only by God's provision and power.

God's people need to look at their world the way Jesus looked out at the multitudes in Galilee and over the city of Jerusalem. We need to observe the people around us as Ezra observed his fellow Israelites on the way from Babylon to Jerusalem (Ezra 8:15) and the way Nehemiah inspected the walls of Jerusalem before he began to rebuild them (Neh. 2:13).

Ask YOURSELF

Why are the active, evangelistic servants of God in such short supply these days? What are the causes for our silence, our indifference, our unconcern for the woeful plight of every lost man or woman we meet? As Jesus commanded, make this a specific focus of your prayer—and of your obedience.

PRAYER FOR HARVEST WORKERS

Therefore beseech the Lord of the harvest to send out workers into His harvest.

MATT. 9:38

"THE LORD OF THE HARVEST" is a title of God that represents His role as the Judge of the unsaved—those who will stand before Him in the last day and be condemned to hell. We are to plead for Him to send workers who will lovingly warn them so they may be a part of those harvested to eternal glory.

The Christian's first responsibility is not to go and start working as soon as he sees a need but to come to the Lord in prayer. Waiting on the Lord is a crucial part of serving Him. Before the disciples received the Holy Spirit at Pentecost they were not prepared to witness for Christ, and He therefore instructed them "not to leave Jerusalem, but to wait for what the Father had promised, 'Which,' He said, 'you heard of from Me'" (Acts 1:4).

It is possible to pray regularly for the salvation of a loved one, a neighbor, a friend, or a fellow employee and then to let our concern stop with our prayer. But when we earnestly pray for the Lord *to send* someone to those unsaved people, we can't help becoming open to being that someone ourselves. It is possible to pray for someone's salvation while keeping them at arm's length. But when we sincerely beg the Lord to send someone to witness to them, we place ourselves at His disposal to become one of His "workers" in that ministry. Be prepared to take on that role.

Ask YOURSELF

Who among your family, your friends, or the associates among whom you're thrust each day is in need of Christ's saving touch? Name them in prayer today . . . and at every remembrance of them. And pray that the Lord would send someone His Spirit can use to bring conviction to their souls, even if that someone is you.

THE APOSTLES SOVEREIGNLY COMMISSIONED

Jesus summoned His twelve disciples and gave them authority.

MATT. 10:1A

*W*HEN JESUS SUMMONED His twelve disciples, He was making more than a casual request. The word Matthew used is an intense term that means to call someone to oneself in order to confront him face-to-face. It is used of God's calling the Gentiles to Himself through the gospel (Acts 2:39) and of His calling His chosen men and entrusting them to proclaim the gospel (Acts 13:2; 16:10). The vocabulary implies that this summoning was connected to an official commissioning to the Lord's service.

Behind Jesus' commissioning and training of the twelve disciples are several foundational facts. *First,* these men were chosen sovereignly by God. None of the twelve initiated the idea of following Jesus and becoming His disciples, much less His apostles. It was entirely God's planning and doing. Mark tells us that Jesus "summoned those whom He Himself wanted" (Mark 3:13), and near the end of His earthly ministry Jesus reminded them, "You did not choose Me but I chose you, and appointed you" (John 15:16).

The men themselves were not consulted nor were any other men. Jesus' only consultation was with His heavenly Father. Like Abraham, Moses, David, Isaiah, and all the prophets, the twelve disciples were chosen by God's sovereign will and for His sovereign purpose, being foreordained to His service before the foundation of the world. That has always been God's way. He divinely chose Israel, He divinely chose His prophets and His apostles, and He divinely chooses those today who become the leaders of His own Body, the church.

*Ask*YOURSELF

Have you routinely thought of God's calling on your life as having this kind of urgency, intention, and purpose? Are there other priorities that are siphoning off the importance you should be placing on the tasks God has called you to accomplish in His service?

THE APOSTLES CHOSEN TO HAVE AN IMPACT

Jesus . . . gave them authority over unclean spirits, to cast them out,
and to heal every kind of disease and every kind of sickness.

MATT. 10:1

JESUS GRANTED THE TWELVE disciples God's divine authority to do exactly what He Himself had been doing. To do the kinds of works Jesus did would demonstrate they were sent by Him, just as what He did demonstrated He was sent by the Father. The book of Acts catalogs the very works Jesus gave them the authority to accomplish.

The apostles cast out many unclean spirits and healed every kind of disease and every kind of sickness. Peter and John healed a lame man at the Beautiful Gate of the temple (Acts 3:2–8). Their ministry became widespread: "At the hands of the apostles many signs and wonders were taking place among the people. . . . Also the people from the cities in the vicinity of Jerusalem were coming together, bringing people who were sick or afflicted with unclean spirits, and they were all being healed" (Acts 5:12, 16). To the man in Lystra "who had no strength in his feet, lame from his mother's womb, who had never walked," Paul said, "'Stand upright on your feet.' And he leaped up and began to walk" (Acts 14:8, 10).

The apostles manifested the kind of kingdom power that their Lord had manifested, and by their faithful obedience they turned Jerusalem and then the world upside down (Acts 17:6). Jesus promised they would do even "greater works" than His (in extent, not power), and His words began to be fulfilled.

Ask YOURSELF

Are your words and expressions of faith pointing others to Christ? Are they reflective of His distinct power and the presence of His Holy Spirit within you? If you sense yourself burning low in the power tank, where do you think the leak is occurring? Be sure that what you do points to Christ.

THE NATURE OF THE INCARNATION

*The Word became flesh, and dwelt among us, and we saw His glory, glory as of the only begotten from
the Father, full of grace and truth.*

JOHN 1:14

JOHN 1:14 IS THE MOST CONCISE biblical statement of the Incarnation. The first four words, "the Word became flesh," express the reality that in the incarnation God took on humanity; the infinite became finite; eternity entered time; the invisible became visible (cf. Col. 1:15); the Creator entered His creation. God revealed Himself to man in the creation (Rom. 1:18–21), in the Old Testament Scriptures (1 Cor. 2:7–14), and, supremely and most clearly, in Jesus Christ (Heb. 1:1–2).

Jesus Christ, God's final "Word" to mankind (Heb. 1:1–2), "became flesh."

That He actually "became" flesh affirms Jesus' full humanity.

When John says He *became* flesh, this does not mean Christ ceased being the eternal Word when He became a man. In the Incarnation the unchangeable (Heb. 13:8) God did become fully man, yet remained fully God. Think of it—He entered the realm of creatures who are limited by time and space, and experienced life as it is for those He created.

No wonder Paul wrote of the Incarnation, "By common confession, great is the mystery of godliness: He who was revealed in the flesh, was vindicated in the Spirit, seen by angels, proclaimed among the nations, believed on in the world, taken up in glory" (1 Tim. 3:16).

Ask YOURSELF

Is the doctrine of Christ's incarnation merely a subject for scholarly textbooks and sermons? Or does it have bearing on the everyday of every man and woman? How does the Incarnation affect your life and cement your salvation?

SEPTEMBER 9

THE WITNESSES TO THE INCARNATION

John testified about Him and cried out, saying, "This was He of whom I said,
'He who comes after me has a higher rank than I, for He existed before me.'"
For of His fullness we have all received, and grace upon grace.

JOHN 1:15–16

*J*OHN BROUGHT IN OTHER witnesses to the truth about the divine, preexistent, incarnate Word, the Lord Jesus Christ. He first called on John the Baptist.

That John "cried out" speaks of the bold, public nature of his witness to Jesus; he was "the voice of one crying in the wilderness, 'Make ready the way of the Lord, make His paths straight!'" (Matt. 3:3). He was the herald, proclaiming the arrival of the Messiah, and calling people to repent and prepare their hearts to receive Him. Acknowledging Jesus' preeminence, John said of Him, "He who comes after me has a higher rank than I, for He existed before me." Jesus, the Expected (literally, "coming") One (Luke 7:19–20) came after John in time; He was born six months later and began His public ministry after John began his. Yet, as John acknowledged, Jesus had "a higher rank than" he did, "for He existed before" him. This is a reference to Jesus' eternal preexistence.

The apostle also points to the witness of all believers, who "have all received" the fullness of blessing from the one who is "full of grace and truth" (v. 14). You can add your voice to that testimony by faithfully living out and proclaiming the truth of the gospel.

*Ask*YOURSELF

Spend some time today reflecting on all you have received from Christ, how "grace upon grace" has been added, multiplied, and stacked one on top of another in your life—day after day, year after year. Celebrate His grace and goodness with the measure it has been poured out on you.

THE IMPACT OF THE INCARNATION

For the Law was given through Moses; grace and truth were realized through Jesus Christ. No one has seen God at any time; the only begotten God who is in the bosom of the Father, He has explained Him.

JOHN 1:17–18

*G*OD'S LAW WAS PERMEATED with His glory and reflected His holiness and righteousness. Though God was gracious in the Old Testament, the Law was not an instrument of grace because the Law saved no one (Rom. 3:20–22; Gal. 2:16; 3:10–12). It merely convicts sinners of their inability to keep perfectly God's righteous standards, and condemns them to the eternal punishment of divine justice; thus it reveals their need for the grace of forgiveness.

Jesus Christ, however, brought the full realization of grace and truth. In Him, the truth of God's salvation was fully revealed and accomplished.

God also was made visible with a clarity never before seen or known. "No one has seen God at any time," Jesus declared of the years before His appearing (John 6:46), not merely because He is a spirit who is invisible, but more important because to do so would bring instant death. It is through Jesus Christ, the "image of the invisible God" (Col. 1:15), that God is revealed.

God, who cannot be known unless He reveals Himself, became most fully known because Jesus "explained Him." Jesus is the explanation of God. He is the answer to the question, "What is God like?"

Jesus is the only one qualified to interpret God to man, since "no one knows the Son except the Father; nor does anyone know the Father except the Son, and anyone to whom the Son wills to reveal Him" (Matt. 11:27).

Ask YOURSELF

What is something of God that He has "explained" to you recently, some facet of His nature and character that has been "revealed" to you through your interaction with Him? Aren't you glad He has chosen to make Himself known?

JOHN THE BAPTIST UNDERSTANDS HIS ROLE

He said, "I am a voice of one crying in the wilderness,
'Make straight the way of the Lord,'" as Isaiah the prophet said.

JOHN 1:23

JOHN THE BAPTIST GAINED great notoriety quickly in Israel with his baptism and his message of repentance for the forgiveness of sins. With so many people flocking to him, the Jewish authorities sent a delegation of priests and Levites to investigate him.

First they asked John, "Who are you?" His behavior was certainly not what they would have expected from the son of a priest. John's response, "I am not the Christ," only added to their confusion. When John answered in the negative to their questions if he was Elijah or the Prophet, the exasperated members of the delegation then demanded, "Who are you, so that we may give an answer to those who sent us. What do you say about yourself?" (John 1:19–22).

Rather than claiming to be someone important, he humbly referred to himself merely as "a voice of one crying in the wilderness." In answering the delegation's question about his identity, he shifted the focus away from himself and onto Christ. His quote of Isaiah 40:3, "Make straight the way of the Lord," was a challenge both to the nation and to his questioners to prepare their hearts for the coming of the Messiah.

The imagery is of a road being leveled and smoothed out in preparation for the visit of an Eastern king. John and Isaiah likened the hearts of Messiah's people to a desolate wilderness, through which a smooth, level road needed to be prepared for His coming. John was the laborer, preparing the road in advance of the King.

Ask YOURSELF

As you have opportunity to share the gospel with others, remind them that the road to Jesus is smooth and level—accessible not by special ability but by the calling, inviting grace of God. Thank God for those who pointed the way for you.

WHO IS THE LAMB OF GOD?

The next day he saw Jesus coming to him and said, "Behold, the Lamb of God who takes
away the sin of the world! This is He on behalf of whom I said, 'After me comes a
Man who has a higher rank than I, for He existed before me.'"

JOHN 1:29–30

*O*N THE DAY AFTER HE SPOKE to the delegation, John "saw Jesus coming to him." In keeping with his role as a herald, John immediately called the crowd's attention to Him, exclaiming "Behold, the Lamb of God."

The concept of a sacrificial Lamb was a familiar one to the Jewish people. All through Israel's history, God had revealed clearly that sin and separation from Him could be removed only by blood sacrifices (cf. Lev. 17:11). They were also aware that Isaiah's prophecy likened Messiah to "a lamb that is led to slaughter" (Isa. 53:7). Though Israel sought a Messiah who would be a prophet, king, and conqueror, God had to send them a Lamb. And He did.

The title "Lamb of God" foreshadows Jesus' ultimate sacrifice on the cross for "the sin of the world." With that brief statement John made it clear that the Messiah had come to deal with sin. The Old Testament is filled with the reality that the problem is sin—a problem at the heart of every person (Jer. 17:9). All men are sinful and incapable of changing the future or the present, or of repaying God for the sins of the past.

So who is the Lamb of God? He is Jesus, the only One who has the remedy to your sin problem.

*Ask*YOURSELF

We know that our sin, though dealt with ultimately and eternally, continues to be a problem for us to face and address. Are you surprised at the strength and tenacity it still wields within you? How do you go about quieting its ferocious appetite and considering yourself dead to it (See Rom. 6:11)?

THE PROPER RESPONSE TO THE LAMB OF GOD

Again the next day John was standing with two of his disciples, and he looked at Jesus as He walked, and said, "Behold, the Lamb of God!" The two disciples heard him speak, and they followed Jesus.

JOHN 1:35–37

JOHN LOOKED AT JESUS AS HE walked nearby, and repeated to his disciples what he had proclaimed to the crowds on the previous day: "Behold, the Lamb of God!" Having heard their teacher speak again those powerful words, the two disciples followed Jesus. John's willingness to unhesitatingly hand them over to Him is further evidence of his self-effacing humility and complete acceptance of his subordinate role.

That the two disciples followed Jesus does not imply that they became permanent disciples of His at this time. It is true that the Greek word for "followed" is used in John's gospel to mean, "to follow as a disciple." But it can also be used in a general sense. Andrew and John here received their first exposure to Jesus. Later, they became His permanent disciples (Matt. 4:18–22).

Since the Messiah, the Son of God—the Lamb of God—is here, the only proper response is to follow Him.

Having served his purpose as a witness to the true identity of Jesus, John the Baptist now fades from the scene (apart from a brief mention in John 3:23). The rest of the gospel focuses on the ministry of Jesus, something the Baptist himself would have approved of.

You can have the same kind of influence that John did by making sure that in addition to following Christ you also point people to Him.

Ask YOURSELF

What does "following" Jesus entail—not just in general terms but in real life? What does it mean on Friday nights when you're alone with your free time, or on Tuesday morning when you're busy with the usual routine? Think of what needs to change in moments like these if you're to be a full-time follower.

THE CORRECT RESPONSE OF SOULS SEEKING JESUS

Jesus turned and saw them following, and said to them, "What do you seek?" They said to Him,
"Rabbi (which translated means Teacher), where are You staying?" He said to them,
"Come, and you will see." So they came and saw where He was staying;
and they stayed with Him that day, for it was about the tenth hour.

JOHN 1:38–39

*A*S ANDREW AND JOHN walked after Him, "Jesus turned and saw them following, and said to them, 'What do you seek?'" He already knew what the two wanted. The Lord asked the question to challenge them to consider their motives. He did not ask them who they were seeking, but what they were seeking.

By asking "Where are You staying?" Andrew and John were not just asking where He was staying; they were courteously requesting an extended private interview with Him. The question also signaled their willingness to become His disciples.

Jesus' immediate response, "Come, and you will see," was the invitation Andrew and John were hoping for. Jesus knew their hearts, that they were honest, sincere seekers.

John does not record what they discussed that memorable evening, but the Lord undoubtedly "opened their minds to understand the Scriptures" (Luke 24:45). Whatever He said was enough to persuade them that He was indeed Israel's Messiah, as Andrew's excited testimony to his brother Peter the next day indicates (John 4:40–41).

In your service to Christ, be sure your motives are pure. Otherwise the Lord will know.

Ask YOURSELF

"What do you seek?" is a good question for us to ask ourselves as we approach the Lord, challenging our motives. What would you say you are seeking Him for? And if you're not finding it, is it because you're seeking amiss or for the wrong reasons—or perhaps seeking something God knows you don't need?

SEPTEMBER 15

NATHANAEL'S ENCOUNTER WITH JESUS

*Jesus saw Nathanael coming to Him, and said of him, "Behold, an Israelite indeed, in whom there
is no deceit!" Nathanael said to Him, "How do You know me?" Jesus answered and said to him,
"Before Philip called you, when you were under the fig tree, I saw you." Nathanael
answered Him, "Rabbi, You are the Son of God; You are the King of Israel."*

JOHN 1:47–49

*O*F ALL THE APOSTLES, NATHANAEL had one of the more interesting first encounters with Jesus. After Philip told him he had found the Messiah—"Jesus of Nazareth, the son of Joseph"—Nathanael was skeptical. His dubious reply, "Can any good thing come out of Nazareth?" reflects his incredulity that the Messiah could come from such an insignificant town. Yet he followed Philip.

As he approached, "Jesus saw Nathanael coming to Him, and said of him, 'Behold, an Israelite indeed, in whom there is no deceit!'" Jesus recognized that Nathanael's blunt, honest reply revealed his lack of duplicity and his willingness to examine Jesus' claims for himself. Nathanael was "an Israelite indeed"—he was a genuine, true disciple from the beginning.

Taken aback by Jesus' omniscient recognition of him, Nathanael was also surprised by Jesus' supernatural knowledge of information known only to him. Not only did Jesus supernaturally see Nathanael's physical location, but He also saw into his heart (cf. Ps. 139:1–4).

Whatever happened under the fig tree, Jesus' supernatural knowledge of it removed Nathanael's doubt. Overwhelmed, he acknowledged Jesus as the long-awaited Messiah.

Just think—Jesus knows you every bit as intimately as He knew Nathanael. The same acknowledgement of Christ's deity ought to be on your lips as well.

*Ask*YOURSELF

Is Jesus' intimate knowledge of you a source of fear and anxiety, or is it rather a source of comfort and security? If you're living in the first state of mind, try putting into words why anything that keeps you from the latter could possibly be worth it.

THE SIGNIFICANCE OF JESUS AT CANA

On the third day there was a wedding in Cana of Galilee, and the mother of Jesus was there; and both Jesus and His disciples were invited to the wedding.

JOHN 2:1–2

A WEDDING WAS A MAJOR SOCIAL event in first-century Palestine, and the ensuing celebration could last as long as a week. It marked the culmination of the betrothal period, which often lasted for several months. The couple was considered legally man and wife during their betrothal period. They did not, however, live together or consummate the marriage during that time (cf. Matt. 1:18). On the night of the ceremony, the groom and his friends would go to the bride's house. They would then escort her and her attendants to the groom's house, where the ceremony and banquet would be held.

John states that a particular wedding was held in Cana. That both Jesus and His mother attended suggests the wedding involved relatives or friends of the family.

By attending this wedding and performing His first miracle there, Jesus sanctified both the institution of marriage and the ceremony itself. Marriage is the sacred union of a man and a woman whereby they become one in the sight of God. The ceremony is an essential element of that union, because that's when the couple publicly vow to remain faithful to each other.

That Jesus attended the celebration also reveals the marked difference between His ministry and that of John the Baptist. Instead of being a voice in the wilderness, Jesus had the more difficult task of mingling with the crowds and ministering to them in their daily existence.

Ask YOURSELF

Does your faith travel with you into social settings like this? When your time is your own, when the conversation is light, when you feel a long way from the work-week or the usual pressures of life, are you still looking for opportunities to be used of God and helpful to others?

A New Relationship Between Jesus and Mary

When the wine ran out, the mother of Jesus said to Him, "They have no wine."
And Jesus said to her, "Woman, what does that have to do with us? My hour has not
yet come." His mother said to the servants, "Whatever He says to you, do it."

JOHN 2:3–5

*R*ETURNING TO THE WEDDING AT CANA we come across a major crisis—the wine ran out because the supply was insufficient. This potential embarrassment for the couple and their families could have stigmatized them for the rest of their lives. Mary was apparently helping to oversee the catering of the celebration and became aware of this serious problem. She anxiously said to Jesus, "They have no wine."

Jesus' abrupt reply, "Woman, what does that have to do with us?" signaled a major change in their relationship. It was an idiomatic expression that asks rhetorically what the two parties in question have in common, and has the effect of distancing them. By calling Mary "Woman" (a polite, but not intimate, form of address) instead of "Mother," Jesus politely but firmly informed her that their relationship was no longer to be what it had been while He was growing up. His public ministry had begun, and earthly relationships would not direct His actions. Mary was to relate to Him no longer as her son but as her Messiah, the Son of God, her Savior.

Undeterred by the mild rebuke, and aware that He was not saying no to the request, Mary said to the servants, "Whatever He says to you, do it." Mary shows us how we should respond to the Lord.

Ask YOURSELF

Is your relationship with Jesus such that you can receive His rebuke without taking offense or crawling into a corner? Can you respond to His truth—even a hard truth—by adjusting your life to His right way of thinking and then continuing to serve Him as faithfully as before?

THE IMPORTANCE OF THE MIRACLE AT CANA

This beginning of His signs Jesus did in Cana of Galilee,
and manifested His glory, and His disciples believed in Him.
JOHN 2:11

*W*HEN JESUS TURNED WATER INTO WINE, His purpose was not to amaze His audience with His power. His miracles met specific needs, such as opening blind eyes or deaf ears, delivering those oppressed by demons, feeding hungry people, or calming a threatening storm. This miracle met the genuine need of the family and their guests.

But even more important, this first of Jesus' signs manifested His glory (cf. 1:14)—He put His deity on display. Jesus' signs were not simply powerful displays of compassion, but were designed to reveal who He really was, since they unmistakably manifest God at work. Signs, miracles, and wonders nevertheless do not necessarily convince people to believe in the Lord and the gospel.

Amazingly, Jesus seems to have left Cana with only the disciples who had come there with Him, despite having performed a miracle, the likes of which had not happened since God created flour and oil in the days of Elijah and Elisha (1 Kings 17:8–16; 2 Kings 4:1–7). The obvious deduction that He was the Messiah escaped the people; they saw the sign, but missed what it pointed to.

His disciples, however, believed in Him. Having heard John the Baptist's testimony that Jesus was the Messiah (1:34), having heard Jesus' own words (1:39) and believed in Him (1:41), they now saw firsthand miraculous confirmation of that faith.

Ask YOURSELF

There is not a need He hasn't met in your life, even though it may appear so at times. If a "need" goes unmet, it's only because there is reason to wait or because we have incorrectly categorized our desire as a demand. As you bring your needs before Him today, you can be sure He hears you and responds.

THE SIGNIFICANCE OF TEMPLE CLEANSING

The Passover of the Jews was near, and Jesus went up to Jerusalem. And He found in the temple those
who were selling oxen and sheep and doves, and the money changers seated at their tables. And He
made a scourge of cords, and drove them all out of the temple, with the sheep and the oxen; and He
poured out the coins of the money changers and overturned their tables; and to those who were selling
the doves He said, "Take these things away; stop making My Father's house a place of business."
His disciples remembered that it was written, "Zeal for Your house will consume me."

JOHN 2:13–17

*T*HE FEAST OF PASSOVER IN JERUSALEM each year meant big business
for Jerusalem-based merchants. They sold animals necessary for the sacrifices at inflated prices to Jewish pilgrims who found it impractical to bring their own from
their homes in distant lands.

Also, every Jewish male twenty years of age or older had to pay the annual temple tax (Matt. 17:24–27). But it could be paid only by using Jewish or Tyrian coins, so
foreigners had to exchange their money for acceptable coinage. Because they held a
monopoly, money changers charged an exorbitant fee.

What should have been a place of sacred reverence and adoration had become
a place of abusive commerce and excessive overpricing.

Realizing that the purity of temple worship was a matter of honor to God, Jesus
took swift and decisive action. The intensity of His righteous indignation was unmistakable—Christ would not tolerate any mockery of the spirit of true worship.

Ask YOURSELF

Are there instances in which we have turned the worship of God into something less than it should be—perhaps into something it should never be? What kind
of heart do you intend to bring with you the next time you join with others in the
Lord's house for worship?

SEPTEMBER 20

SIGN OF THE RESURRECTION

The Jews then said to Him, "What sign do You show us as your authority for doing these things?"
Jesus answered them, "Destroy this temple, and in three days I will raise it up." The Jews then said,
"It took forty-six years to build this temple, and will You raise it up in three days?" But He was
speaking of the temple of His body. So when He was raised from the dead, His disciples remembered
that He said this; and they believed the Scripture and the word which Jesus had spoken.

JOHN 2:18–22

*T*HE JEWISH AUTHORITIES completely missed the point of Jesus' statement, incorrectly applying it to the Herodian temple. But as John points out, Jesus "was speaking of the temple of His body."

The sign He would give was His own resurrection, which even His disciples did not immediately understand (cf. 12:16). It was not until "He was raised from the dead [that] His disciples remembered that He said this; and they believed the Scripture and the word which Jesus had spoken." His death as the ultimate sacrificial Lamb would render the Jerusalem temple obsolete (cf. 4:21); and His resurrection as the triumphant Lord would lay the foundation for a new, spiritual temple in its place—namely the church (1 Cor. 3:16–17; 2 Cor. 6:16; Eph. 2:19–22).

It was not until after the resurrection that everything came into focus for the disciples. Only then did they recognize Jesus' power of resurrection as convincing proof of His deity.

Ask YOURSELF

Have you been confused recently by a section of Scripture that puzzles you with its mystery, or seems to scrape against other things you've been taught in the past? If your heart is set on learning and obeying, rather than arguing or resisting, be sure that the Holy Spirit will reveal truth as you seek Him for it.

SPURIOUS VS. SAVING FAITH

*Now when He was in Jerusalem at the Passover, during the feast, many believed in His
name, observing His signs which He was doing. But Jesus, on His part, was not entrusting
Himself to them, for He knew all men, and because He did not need anyone to testify
concerning man, for He Himself knew what was in man.*

JOHN 2:23–25

*A*FTER THE PASSOVER, JESUS remained in Jerusalem for the Feast of Unleavened Bread. During His stay He performed a number of miracles not recorded
in Scripture. As a result of those miracles, John says, "Many believed in His name."

But this faith was shallow, superficial, and disingenuous. It was not true saving
faith, as John's play on words indicates. "Believed" in verse 23 and "entrusting" in
verse 24 both come from the same Greek verb. Though they believed in Jesus, Jesus
did not believe in them; He had no faith in their faith.

Although many claimed to believe, Jesus knew that mere intellectual assent
proves nothing; even the demons have such faith (James 2:19). Jesus did not embrace the false faith manifested by those who witnessed His signs, because "He knew
all men," and therefore "did not need anyone to testify concerning man, for He Himself knew what was in man." He knows the true state of every heart. He saw in
Nathanael the heart of an honest, true seeker (1:47); He saw in these people a superficial façade—a mere outward attraction to spectacular signs (cf. 6:2). Genuine
saving faith goes far beyond that. It demands wholehearted commitment to Jesus as
the Lord of one's life (Matt. 16:24–26; Rom. 10:9). Is that the state of your heart?

*Ask*YOURSELF

It's certainly fine to admire godly people and aspire to be like them. But if you
haven't noticed already, these same ones will eventually do or say something to spoil
your image of them. We will too, if others look up to us. When you see Jesus in someone, don't strive to be like *them* but to be like *Him*.

NICODEMUS'S INQUIRY: WHAT IS THE KINGDOM?

Now there was a man of the Pharisees, named Nicodemus, a ruler of the Jews; this man came to
Jesus by night and said to Him, "Rabbi, we know that You have come from God as a teacher;
for no one can do these signs that You do unless God is with him." Jesus answered and said
to him, "Truly, truly, I say to you, unless one is born again he cannot see the kingdom of God."

JOHN 3:1–3

*N*ICODEMUS CAME TO JESUS as one of those superficial believers mentioned in John 2:23–25. But the Lord refused to accept Nicodemus's profession, which was based on the signs he had witnessed (v. 2).

Jesus went straight to the real issue—the transformation of Nicodemus's heart by the new birth, which is the act of God by which He imparts eternal life to those who are "dead in . . . trespasses and sins" (Eph. 2:1). Jesus answered his unasked question, "Unless one is born again he cannot see the kingdom of God."

By the "kingdom of God," Jesus is speaking specifically of the kingdom of salvation, the spiritual realm where those who have been born again by divine power through faith now live under the rule of God mediated through His Son. Nicodemus, like his fellow Jews, eagerly anticipated that glorious realm. But they believed that being descendants of Abraham, observing the law, and performing external religious rituals would gain them entrance into that kingdom. As Jesus made clear, no matter how religiously active someone might be, no one can enter the kingdom without experiencing the personal regeneration of the new birth.

Ask YOURSELF

What are some questions you commonly hear that purport to be genuine interest toward Christian discipleship, but in reality are dodges and smokescreens that disguise a rebellious, disinterested heart? What's the best way to respond to comments like these? What can you learn from Jesus' dealings with Nicodemus?

JESUS CHALLENGES NICODEMUS: NEW BIRTH

Jesus answered and said to him, "Truly, truly, I say to you, unless one is born again he cannot see the kingdom of God." Nicodemus said to Him, "How can a man be born when he is old? He cannot enter a second time into his mother's womb and be born, can he?"

JOHN 3:3–4

*J*ESUS' SHOCKING STATEMENT was far more than Nicodemus had expected. Incredulous, Nicodemus said to Him, "How can a man be born when he is old? He cannot enter a second time into his mother's womb and be born, can he?" Nicodemus did not misinterpret Jesus' words; he replied in the context of the Lord's analogy. How could he start all over, go back to the beginning? Jesus was telling him that entrance to God's salvation was not a matter of adding something to all his efforts but rather cancelling everything and starting all over again.

At the same time, Nicodemus clearly could not grasp the full meaning of what this meant. Jesus was making entrance into the kingdom contingent on something that could not be obtained through human effort. If spiritual rebirth, like physical rebirth, was impossible from human effort, then where did that leave this self-righteous Pharisee, since the system in which he had placed his hope was powerless to save?

Far from minimizing the demands of the gospel, Jesus challenged this most religious Jew to admit his spiritual bankruptcy and abandon everything he was trusting in for salvation.

Be sure as you proclaim the gospel that you challenge your listeners to give up what they think will get them to heaven.

Ask YOURSELF

On one hand, adherence to the law (as Nicodemus saw it) seems like a long-forgotten pursuit. But there are plenty of folks down the street or within the sound of your voice who are clinging to the hopes of their good works. How does this show itself? How can you counteract it as you witness to them?

WATER AND SPIRIT; FLESH AND SPIRIT

Jesus answered, "Truly, truly, I say to you, unless one is born of water and the Spirit he cannot enter into the kingdom of God. That which is born of the flesh is flesh, and that which is born of the Spirit is spirit. Do not be amazed that I said to you, 'You must be born again.'"

JOHN 3:5–7

*J*ESUS ANSWERED NICODEMUS'S objection by elaborating on the truth He introduced in verse 3: "Truly, truly, I say to you, unless one is born of water and the Spirit he cannot enter into the kingdom of God." "Water" and "Spirit" often refer symbolically in the Old Testament to spiritual renewal and cleansing.

It was surely Ezekiel 36:24–27 that Jesus had in mind, which shows regeneration to be an Old Testament truth with which Nicodemus should have been acquainted. Christ's point was unmistakable: Without the spiritual washing of the soul, a cleansing accomplished only by the Holy Spirit (Titus 3:5) through the Word of God (Eph. 5:26), no one can enter God's kingdom.

Jesus continued by further emphasizing that this spiritual cleansing is wholly a work of God and not the result of human effort: "That which is born of the flesh is flesh, and that which is born of the Spirit is spirit." Just as only human nature can beget human nature, so also only the Holy Spirit can effect spiritual transformation.

Even if a physical rebirth were possible, it would produce only flesh. Thus only the Spirit can produce the spiritual birth required for entrance into God's kingdom. Regeneration is entirely His work, unaided by any human effort (cf. Rom. 3:25).

Ask YOURSELF

What have you needed washing from your heart in the last several days or weeks? How have you gone about seeking the Lord's cleansing and renewal? How have you experienced the reality of His refreshment?

NICODEMUS'S DOUBT

Nicodemus said to Him, "How can these things be?" Jesus answered and
said to him, "Are you the teacher of Israel and do not understand these things?"

JOHN 3:9–10

*A*LTHOUGH HE WAS A RENOWNED, recognized, and established teacher in Israel, Nicodemus was a poor learner. His question "How can these things be?" indicates he had made little progress. Despite Jesus' further clarification, Nicodemus still could not accept what he was hearing. He could not let go of his legalistic religious system and realize that salvation was a sovereign, gracious work of God's Spirit.

Because of his position as the teacher of Israel, Nicodemus could have been expected to understand the things Jesus had said. In fact, his lack of understanding was inexcusable considering his exposure to the Old Testament. Jesus found it indefensible that this prominent scholar was not familiar with the foundational new covenant teaching, housed in the Old Testament, regarding the only way of salvation (cf. 2 Tim. 3:15). Sadly, Nicodemus serves as a clear example of the numbing effect that external, legalistic religion has on a person's spiritual perception—even to the point of obscuring the revelation of God.

Although nothing in this passage suggests Nicodemus was converted that evening (and verse 11 strongly implies that he was not), he never forgot his discussion with Jesus. Later, he boldly defended Him before the Sanhedrin (7:50–51), and helped Joseph of Arimathea prepare His body for burial (19:38–39)—actions that indicate the presence of genuine faith in his life. Somewhere after that memorable evening he spent with Jesus but before the crucifixion, Nicodemus came to understand sovereign grace and experience the reality of the new birth.

Ask YOURSELF

Perhaps there's someone (or several people) you've been talking to and praying for, deeply concerned about their spiritual condition, perhaps even a little perturbed at their stubborn resistance to the gospel. Don't give up. Don't quit asking. There is more than one Nicodemus who said no, no, no, before finally succumbing to grace.

AN OLD TESTAMENT ILLUSTRATION OF SALVATION

As Moses lifted up the serpent in the wilderness, even so must the Son of Man
be lifted up; so that whoever believes will in Him have eternal life.

JOHN 3:14–15

*T*O EMPHASIZE FOR NICODEMUS that there was no excuse for him to be ignorant of the way of salvation, Jesus appealed to a familiar incident in the Old Testament (Num. 21:5–9).

The event took place during Israel's forty years of wilderness wandering after leaving Egypt and before entering the Promised Land. As a judgment on the people's incessant complaining, the Lord sent venomous snakes to infest their camp. In desperation, the Israelites begged Moses to intercede on their behalf. And God answered Moses' prayerful petition by showing mercy to His rebellious people. He instructed Moses to make a bronze replica of a snake and raise it above the camp on a pole. Those who were bitten would be healed if they but looked at it, thereby acknowledging their guilt and expressing faith in God's forgiveness and healing power.

The point of Jesus' analogy is that just "as Moses lifted up the serpent in the wilderness, even so must the Son of Man be lifted up" (crucified; cf. 8:28; 12:32, 34). The term "must" emphasizes that Christ's death was a necessary part of God's plan of salvation. He had to die as a substitute for sinners. The stricken Israelites were cured by obediently looking to the elevated serpent, apart from any works or righteousness of their own, in complete hope and dependence on God's Word. In the same way, whoever looks in faith alone to the crucified Christ will be cured from sin's deadly bite and "will in Him have eternal life."

Ask YOURSELF

The use of analogies and common knowledge is most effective in sharing gospel truth with others. What are some of the most compelling ones God has registered in your heart? Be deliberate about getting these down, grounding them biblically, then having them mentally available to share.

JOHN 3:16—THE WORLD

For God so loved the world, that He gave His only begotten Son,
that whoever believes in Him shall not perish, but have eternal life.
JOHN 3:16

JOHN 3:16 IS UNDOUBTEDLY the most familiar and beloved verse in all of Scripture. The first thing you notice is God's motive for giving Jesus Christ (2 Cor. 9:15)—because He loved the evil, sinful world of fallen humanity. There was nothing in man that attracted God's love. Rather He loved because He sovereignly determined to do so.

It is important to note that "world" is a nonspecific term for humanity in a general sense. The statement in verse 17, "that the world might be saved through Him," proves that it does not mean everyone who has ever lived, since all will not be saved. Verse 16 cannot be teaching universal salvation, since the context promises that unbelievers will perish in eternal judgment (vv. 16–18). Our Lord is saying that for all in the world there is only one Savior (1 John 2:2), but only those who are regenerated by the Spirit and who believe in His gospel will receive salvation and eternal life through Him.

Paul, in 2 Corinthians 5:19, used "world" in a similar way: "God was in Christ reconciling the world to Himself, not counting their trespasses against them." The reason God was reconciling the world to Himself is that the world has no other reconciler. That not all will believe and be reconciled is clear from Paul's plea in verse 20: "Therefore, we are ambassadors for Christ, as though God were making an appeal through us; we beg you on behalf of Christ, be reconciled to God."

Ask YOURSELF

How else might you respond to someone who believes that "a loving God would not send anyone to hell" and therefore everyone will be saved in the end? What does this probably tell you about the person making this claim?

JOHN 3:16—THE ONLY BEGOTTEN SON

For God so loved the world, that He gave His only begotten Son,
that whoever believes in Him shall not perish, but have eternal life.

JOHN 3:16

*T*HERE ARE NO WORDS IN HUMAN language that can adequately express the magnitude of God's saving gift to the world. Even the apostle Paul refused to try, declaring this gift to be "indescribable" (2 Cor. 9:15). The Father "gave His only begotten Son"—His unique, one-of-a-kind Son. He is the one of whom He declared, "This is My beloved Son, in whom I am well-pleased" (Matt. 3:17); the one whom He "loves . . . and has given all things into His hand" (John 3:35); the one whom He "highly exalted . . . and bestowed on Him the name which is above every name" (Phil. 2:9); the one with whom He had enjoyed intimate fellowship from all eternity (John 1:1). The Father sent Him to die as a sacrifice on behalf of sinful men. "He made Him who knew no sin to be sin on our behalf," wrote Paul, "so that we might become the righteousness of God in Him" (2 Cor. 5:21).

By "sending His own Son in the likeness of sinful flesh and as an offering for sin, [God] condemned sin in the flesh" (Rom. 8:3). Just as the supreme proof of Abraham's love for God was his willingness to sacrifice his son (cf. Gen. 22:12, 16–18), so also—but on a far grander scale—the Father's offering of "His only begotten Son" was the supreme manifestation of His love for lost sinners.

Ask YOURSELF

The heart of the good news is always worth returning to and reminding ourselves of, causing us to fall down in reverential awe at every fresh glimpse of this astounding grace. As you read this cherished verse of Scripture again, let each word resonate in your spirit. Into your needy heart has come the gift of God's Son. Never get over it.

JOHN 3:16—THE OFFER OF SALVATION

*For God so loved the world, that He gave His only begotten Son, that whoever believes
in Him shall not perish, but have eternal life. For God did not send the Son into the
world to judge the world, but that the world might be saved through Him.*

JOHN 3:16–17

GOD'S GRACIOUS GIFT OF SALVATION is freely available to whoever believes in Christ. The free offer of the gospel is broad enough to encompass the vilest sinner (1 Tim. 1:15), yet narrow enough to exclude all who reject Christ (John 3:18). But to those who come to Him on His terms, Jesus said, "The one who comes to Me I will certainly not cast out" (John 6:37)—they will never perish.

To "perish" is to face God's eternal judgment. It is true that "God did not send the Son into the world to judge the world." Jesus Himself declared in John 12:47, "I did not come to judge the world, but to save the world." Yes, God will ultimately judge those who reject His Son, but this was not the mission of the Son in His first coming.

Furthermore, the point of Jesus' coming was not to redeem Israel and condemn the Gentiles, "but that the world might be saved through Him." God's gracious offer of salvation extended beyond Israel to all mankind. Once again, Nicodemus should have known this, for in the Abrahamic covenant God declared, "I will bless those who bless you, and the one who curses you I will curse. And in you all the families of the earth will be blessed" (Gen. 12:3). Gentile salvation was always God's purpose.

Ask YOURSELF

Are you ever troubled that your salvation is perhaps still in doubt, eligible for recall if you don't toe a certain line or achieve a base level of righteousness? Take heart in the promise that coming to Christ equates to never being "cast out."

BELIEF CONTRASTED WITH UNBELIEF

He who believes in Him is not judged; he who does not believe has been judged already,
because he has not believed in the name of the only begotten Son of God. This is the judgment,
that the Light has come into the world, and men loved the darkness rather than the Light,
for their deeds were evil. For everyone who does evil hates the Light, and does not come to the
Light for fear that his deeds will be exposed. But he who practices the truth comes to the Light,
so that his deeds may be manifested as having been wrought in God.

JOHN 3:18–21

ALTHOUGH GOD GRACIOUSLY has offered the world salvation through the work of Christ, that salvation is not appropriated except by penitent faith. The lost are condemned because they have "not believed in [literally, "believed into"] the name of the only begotten Son of God." While the final sentencing of those who reject Christ is still future (cf. 5:28–29), their judgment will merely consummate what has already begun.

Jesus described judgment by contrasting light and darkness. Christ is the Light—He came into the world and "enlightens every man" (John 1:9). But people refuse to come to the Light because they love the darkness where their evil deeds will not be exposed. The Light reveals their sin. But as a result, they seal their own condemnation because they reject the only One who can save them from their spiritual darkness.

In contrast, believers hate their sin and love righteousness (1 John 2:3–6), so they willingly come to the light because they have nothing to hide and no reason to fear what the light will reveal.

Ask YOURSELF

How many times a day do you participate in activities you hope no one else knows about? Aspire to the freedom of being the same person in private that you are in public—unashamed at and unexposed by the Light.

CHRIST THE SON KNOWS THE TRUTH

He who comes from above is above all, he who is of the earth is from the earth
and speaks of the earth. He who comes from heaven is above all. What He has
seen and heard, of that He testifies; and no one receives His testimony.

JOHN 3:31–32

*J*ESUS CHRIST IS THE ONE "who descended from heaven" (3:13). As such, He is "above all"—Christ is sovereign over the universe in general, and the world of humanity in particular.

In the old covenant, "God . . . spoke long ago to the fathers in the prophets" (Heb. 1:1). But in the new covenant God "in these last days has spoken to us in His Son" (v. 2). Jesus' teaching is superior to anyone else's because His knowledge is not secondhand. He is the source of divine revelation. What "He has seen and heard" in the heavenly realm, "of that He testifies" with certainty.

Yet despite Jesus' powerful, authoritative proclamation of the truth, "no one receives His testimony." The world in general rejects Jesus and His teaching. The apostle John noted this in the Prologue to his gospel: "[Jesus] was the true Light which, coming into the world, enlightens every man. He was in the world, and the world was made through Him, and the world did not know Him. He came to His own, and those who were His own did not receive Him" (1:9–11). Unbelievers willfully reject Jesus' testimony to the truth because they are dead in their trespasses and sins (Eph. 2:1) and blinded by Satan (2 Cor. 4:4).

Ask YOURSELF

When there are so many situations in which we think we know best, not to mention so many other people who have their own judgments and opinions, how do we train ourselves to keep in mind that what God says is what's true? When do you sense His authority challenged the most in your life?

CHRIST'S UNITY WITH THE FATHER AND THE SPIRIT

He who has received His testimony has set his seal to this, that God is true.
For He whom God has sent speaks the words of God; for He gives the Spirit without measure.
JOHN 3:33–34

ALTHOUGH THE MAJORITY OF PEOPLE reject Jesus' message, not everyone does. There are some who accept His testimony, believing in Him for eternal life. In the ancient world, people set their seal to something, often with a signet ring, as a sign of complete acceptance and approval. Those who have received Christ's testimony thereby verify their belief that "God is true" when He speaks through His Son.

Unlike human teachers, whose words sometimes agree with divine truth and sometimes do not, Jesus always spoke in complete harmony with the Father. Thus, those who profess to believe in God yet reject Jesus Christ are deceived. Jesus is one with the Father (John 10:30)—"He who does not honor the Son does not honor the Father who sent Him" (5:23)—and the Father said of Him, "This is My beloved Son, with whom I am well-pleased; listen to Him!" (Matt. 17:5). He is "the way, and the truth, and the life; no one comes to the Father but through [Him]" (John 14:6). To reject Jesus, then, is to call God a liar (1 John 5:10).

Jesus is also one with the Holy Spirit. Jesus infallibly spoke "the words of God" because God gave the Spirit to Him "without measure." Since "in Him all the fullness of Deity dwells in bodily form" (Col. 2:9), there were no limits to the Spirit's power working through Him.

Ask YOURSELF

When are we guilty of calling God a liar—perhaps not in regards to the salvation He's given us, but in other matters of expectation and belief? What are the great hazards of doubting His Word and discounting His truthfulness?

OCTOBER 3

ALL AUTHORITY FROM THE FATHER

The Father loves the Son and has given all things into His hand. He who believes in the Son
has eternal life; but he who does not obey the Son will not see life, but the wrath of God abides on him.
JOHN 3:35–36

ℬECAUSE OF HIS LOVE for the Son, the Father has given Him supreme
authority over all things on earth and in heaven (Matt. 11:27; 28:18; Phil. 2:9–11).
That supremacy is a clear indicator of His deity.

John's affirmation of Jesus' absolute authority demonstrated his humble attitude, even as his own heralding ministry faded into the background. Having fulfilled his mission on earth, John realized that his work would soon be finished.

But before he faded from the scene, John gave a warning and invitation that
forms a fitting climax to his ministry: "He who believes in the Son has eternal life;
but he who does not obey the Son will not see life, but the wrath of God abides on
him." The blessed truth of salvation is that the one "who believes in the Son has eternal life" as a present possession, not merely as a future hope.

But on the other hand, the one "who does not obey the Son will not see life." The
fearful reality is that "the wrath of God" continually "abides on" disobedient sinners
who refuse to believe in Jesus Christ. Condemnation is their present condition. The
idea here is not that God will *one day* condemn sinners for their disobedient unbelief; they are already in a state of condemnation (3:18; 2 Peter 2:9) from which only
saving faith in Jesus Christ can deliver them.

𝒜𝓈𝓀YOURSELF

In what ways is the wrath of God evident in the lives of unbelievers? How do
you hear it in their voice, see it in their eyes, notice it in their countenance, observe
it in their families? Some of these folks seem so nice and easy-going. What are the
more subtle forms of dissatisfaction they carry within them?

WHAT IS LIVING WATER?

Jesus answered and said to her, "If you knew the gift of God, and who it is who says to you,
'Give Me a drink,' you would have asked Him, and He would have given you living water."
She said to Him, "Sir, You have nothing to draw with and the well is deep; where then do You
get that living water? . . . Jesus answered and said to her, "Everyone who drinks of this water
will thirst again; but whoever drinks of the water that I will give him shall never thirst; but
the water that I will give him will become in him a well of water springing up to eternal life."
JOHN 4:10–11, 13–14

*J*ESUS' ENCOUNTER WITH THE Samaritan woman at the well is another opportunity for Him to teach profound spiritual truth through a metaphor. When their
conversation began, He was the thirsty one, and she the one with the water. Now
He spoke as if she were the thirsty one and He the one with the water. Her confusion is not unexpected. She did not understand Jesus was talking about spiritual realities. The "living water" He offered was salvation in all its fullness.

But she was skeptical of His ability to provide the living water He offered. So
Jesus patiently answered her skeptical question: "Everyone who drinks of this water
will thirst again; but whoever drinks of the water that I will give him shall never
thirst; but the water that I will give him will become in him a well of water springing up to eternal life." Here was Jesus offering her the living water of spiritual life to
quench her parched, needy soul.

Ask YOURSELF

What activities of Jesus in your life share some common qualities with water—
its clarity, its refreshment, its cleansing, its sustenance, its replenishment? Praise
Him for each of these things as He brings them to mind.

TRUE WORSHIP

The woman said to Him, "Sir, I perceive that You are a prophet. Our fathers worshiped
in this mountain, and you people say that in Jerusalem is the place where men ought to worship."
Jesus said to her, "Woman, believe Me, an hour is coming when neither in this mountain nor in
Jerusalem will you worship the Father. You worship what you do not know; we worship what we
know, for salvation is from the Jews. But an hour is coming, and now is, when the true worshipers
will worship the Father in spirit and truth; for such people the Father seeks to be His worshipers.

JOHN 4:19–23

*H*AVING BEEN CONVICTED of her sin and need for forgiveness, and having repented and agreed with Jesus' indictment, the Samaritan woman wondered
where she should go to meet God and seek His grace and salvation.

Jesus explains that under the new covenant, the place of worship is not the
issue, but rather the nature of worship. "An hour is coming," Jesus informed the
woman, "and now is, when the true worshipers will worship the Father in spirit and
truth. "Spirit" does not refer to the Holy Spirit but the human spirit. Worship must
be internal, not external—it must be from the heart. "Truth" calls for this heart worship to be consistent with what Scripture teaches and to be centered on Christ.

True worshipers are those who "worship the Father in spirit and truth." It is
"such people the Father seeks to be His worshipers" by sovereignly drawing them to
Himself (6:44, 65). God has called you to worship Him. Make sure your worship is
genuine.

Ask YOURSELF

What is so empty and uninspiring about worship that fails to engage the heart,
worship that is mouthed and measured rather than done like you mean it? Then why
do we resort to it so often? Why are we duped into believing that the object of our
distraction is more worthy then the rightful recipient of our praise?

THE TRUE NATURE OF GOD AND WORSHIP

*"God is spirit, and those who worship Him must worship in spirit and truth." The woman
said to Him, "I know that Messiah is coming (He who is called Christ); when that One
comes, He will declare all things to us." Jesus said to her, "I who speak to you am He."*

JOHN 4:24–26

THE PHRASE "GOD IS SPIRIT" is the classic biblical definition of the nature of God. Despite the heretical teaching of false cults, God is not an exalted man (Num. 23:19), "for a spirit does not have flesh and bones" (Luke 24:39). He is "the invisible God" (Col. 1:15), who "dwells in unapproachable light, whom no man has seen or can see" (1 Tim. 6:16). Had He not revealed Himself in Scripture and in Jesus Christ, God would be utterly incomprehensible.

Because God is spirit, those who would truly worship Him "must worship in spirit and truth." True worship does not consist of mere outward conformity to religious standards and duties; it springs from the inner spirit. It must also be consistent with the truth God has revealed about Himself in His Word. The extremes of dead orthodoxy (truth and no spirit) and zealous heterodoxy (spirit and no truth) must be avoided.

In spite of her confusion, the Samaritan woman expressed her hope that one day the Messiah would clarify all of these vexing religious questions. Imagine her surprise when the man who just a few minutes earlier had made a simple request for a drink of water claimed to be the long-awaited Messiah, and what He knew about her left her with no doubt about who He really was.

Ask YOURSELF

Why would Jesus spend so much time with this woman, letting her ask her guarded questions, waiting for her situation to be exposed, waiting to see the light come on? He didn't always appear so patient and courteous, not with everyone. What can we learn from His treatment of her?

OCTOBER 7

JESUS' SOVEREIGN CONTROL OF ALL

*At this point His disciples came, and they were amazed that He had been speaking
with a woman, yet no one said, "What do You seek?" or, "Why do You speak with her?"*

JOHN 4:27

THE DISCIPLES CAME BACK from buying food in Sychar at the exact moment Jesus revealed His messiahship to the Samaritan woman. The phrase "at this point" captures Jesus' complete mastery of the situation. Had the disciples returned earlier, they would have interrupted the conversation before it reached its dramatic conclusion; had they returned later, they would have missed hearing Jesus' declaration.

The disciples were amazed to see that Jesus "had been speaking with a woman," which was a shocking breach of societal norms. That she was a Samaritan made the Lord's action even more astonishing. And had they known the woman's immoral background, the disciples would have been completely stunned. But they respected Jesus so much that they knew better than to interrupt His conversation. Therefore they did not ask the woman, "What do You seek?" or ask Jesus, "Why do You speak with her?" They had already learned that Jesus had good reasons for doing what He did.

As He explained the truth to this woman, the Lord did not force or manipulate the conversation. Instead, He sovereignly orchestrated the timing of events so the disciples would arrive at the right moment. History is under God's absolute control, prewritten in eternity past. Therefore, Jesus Himself always acted according to the Father's timetable.

In this situation at a well in Samaria—as so often in His life—Jesus' sovereign control of events opens a window through which we can see His deity.

Ask YOURSELF

God's sovereignty is one of the aspects of His nature that disturbs some, feeling as though He's too much in their business. But what are some of the many comforts and confidences that flow from this glorious doctrine of His providence?

The Samaritan Woman's Reaction

So the woman left her waterpot, and went into the city and said to the men, "Come,
see a man who told me all the things that I have done; this is not the Christ, is it?"
They went out of the city, and were coming to Him.

John 4:28–30

*L*EAVING HER JAR AT THE WELL, the woman hurried back "into the city" and, gathering a crowd, excitedly said to the men, "Come, see a man who told me all the things that I have done." A stranger who knew all about her past was no ordinary man. Jesus' impact on her was so profound that she did not hesitate to share the news about Him—even with those familiar with her sordid reputation. Jesus had read her heart and forced her to face herself. She had already recognized her need (4:15), her sin (4:19), and who He was (4:26). Her immediate desire to witness to others was now the clinching piece of evidence that her conversion was genuine.

"This is not the Christ, is it?" The Greek construction of this question implies a negative or at least a doubtful answer. The woman described her conversation with Jesus and humbly deferred the question of His identity to the men. They were so impressed by her excitement and sincerity that they went to investigate Him for themselves. Though no specific number is given, the implication is that the woman's excited testimony had stirred up a sizeable group.

Let the testimony of this woman work as a barometer of your own desire to proclaim the gospel as the Lord gives you opportunity.

Ask YOURSELF

The incessant demands of our daily wants and needs always serves as a willing excuse for putting off Christ's command to proclaim our faith. What are some of the "waterpots" you need to put down from time to time so that you can be free and available to share what Jesus has done for you?

INTIMACY WITH THE FATHER

Meanwhile the disciples were urging Him, saying, "Rabbi, eat." But He said to them,
"I have food to eat that you do not know about." So the disciples were saying to one
another, "No one brought Him anything to eat, did he?" Jesus said to them,
"My food is to do the will of Him who sent Me and to accomplish His work."

JOHN 4:31–34

*T*HE DISCIPLES' PRIMARY concern at this point had been food. That's why they urged Jesus to eat. Jesus, however, had a higher priority, as His reply to them makes clear: "I have food to eat that you do not know about." Like the Samaritan woman (4:11), the disciples misunderstood Jesus' words and began saying doubt-fully to one another, "No one brought Him anything to eat, did he?"

Jesus took advantage of their confusion to teach them an important spiritual les-son. He said to them, "My food is to do the will of Him who sent Me and to accom-plish His work." Doing God's will by proclaiming the truth to a lost sinner gave the Lord satisfaction and sustenance far surpassing what food could give Him.

Jesus frequently referred to the Father as the One who sent Him. His goal dur-ing His earthly ministry was to accomplish His work of salvation. Throughout His ministry, Jesus walked in perfect intimacy with His Father, living in complete ac-cordance with the Father's will until His cry of triumph from the cross—"It is fin-ished!" (19:30)—marked the accomplishment of His mission on earth. Submitting to the Father was Jesus' constant devotion, consummate joy, and true sustenance.

Ask YOURSELF

How often does food come between you and sweet fellowship with your Fa-ther in heaven? In what ways does this legitimate appetite become a tyrannical force that overrules and overrides the greater necessity of daily dependence on God?

CHRIST'S CONCERN FOR SOULS

*Do you not say, "There are yet four months, and then comes the harvest"? Behold, I say to you, lift up
your eyes and look on the fields, that they are white for harvest. Already he who reaps is receiving
wages and is gathering fruit for life eternal; so that he who sows and he who reaps may rejoice
together. For in this case the saying is true, "One sows and another reaps." I sent you to reap that
for which you have not labored; others have labored and you have entered into their labor.*

JOHN 4:35–38

*U*SING THE GRAIN GROWING in the surrounding fields as an object lesson, Jesus impressed on the disciples the urgency of reaching the lost. There was no need to wait four months; the spiritual fields were already "white for harvest." He was likely referring to the Samaritans who at that moment were coming toward them (v. 30). Their white clothing formed a striking contrast with the brilliant green of the ripening grain and looked like the white heads on the stalks that indicated the time for harvest.

By telling the disciples that the one "who reaps is receiving wages and is gathering fruit for life eternal," the Lord highlighted their responsibility to participate in the harvest of souls. They would receive their "wages"—the rewarding joy of gathering "fruit" for all eternity.

You have the same responsibility as the disciples. Pray that the Lord will give you opportunities to experience the joy of gathering souls as you cooperate with His Spirit.

Ask YOURSELF

Part of the hindrance to our evangelistic fervor is that the Lord often uses us as one in a long line of invitation points. Though He may be drawing this very person to faith, our own encounter is subject to being met by rejection. How do you overcome the fatigue of knowing that faith can sometimes feel like failure?

FACING UNBELIEF

After the two days He went forth from there into Galilee. For Jesus Himself testified that a prophet has no honor in his own country. So when He came to Galilee, the Galileans received Him, having seen all the things that He did in Jerusalem at the feast; for they themselves also went to the feast. Therefore He came again to Cana of Galilee where He had made the water wine. And there was a royal official whose son was sick at Capernaum. When he heard that Jesus had come out of Judea into Galilee, he went to Him and was imploring Him to come down and heal his son; for he was at the point of death. So Jesus said to him, "Unless you people see signs and wonders, you simply will not believe." The royal official said to Him, "Sir, come down before my child dies."

JOHN 4:43–49

*T*HE PROVERBIAL STATEMENT "a prophet has no honor in his own country" contrasts Jesus' acceptance by the Samaritans with His general rejection by the Jewish people (1:11). Jesus returned to Galilee knowing that the saying would be proved true in His case.

John's statement, "so when He came to Galilee, the Galileans received Him," does not mean that they believed in Jesus as the Messiah; they welcomed Him merely as a miracle worker.

The Lord's encounter with the royal official in Cana is just one more example that the faith of many Galileans, like that of many Judeans, was only superficial, curious, non-saving interest. As a result, Jesus issued this stern rebuke: "Unless you people see signs and wonders, you simply will not believe."

Ask YOURSELF

Has familiarity with Jesus robbed you of recognizing the wonder of His ministry in and around you? How can a person guard against this natural tendency, living daily and actively in His presence while not growing ho-hum with the work He does and the blessings He provides?

CONQUERING UNBELIEF

Jesus said to him, "Go; your son lives." The man believed the word that Jesus spoke to him and started off. As he was now going down, his slaves met him, saying that his son was living. So he inquired of them the hour when he began to get better. Then they said to him, "Yesterday at the seventh hour the fever left him." So the father knew that it was at that hour in which Jesus said to him, "Your son lives"; and he himself believed and his whole household. This is again a second sign that Jesus performed when He had come out of Judea into Galilee.

JOHN 4:50–54

𝒯HE ROYAL OFFICIAL DID NOT dispute Jesus' assessment of him and his fellow Galileans. Instead, he poured out his heart, exclaiming, "Sir, come down before my child dies." Despite Christ's rebuke of the Galileans' faithless demand for miracles, the Lord graciously performed the miracle and drew the official's faith to a higher level.

Rather than agreeing to go back to Capernaum with him as the official had begged Him to do, Jesus said to him, "Go; your son lives." At that very instant (vv. 52–53), the boy was healed. Though he had no confirmation of it, "the man believed the word that Jesus spoke to him" and started off for home.

On the way, his slaves met him, and he received the good news he was hoping to get: "his son was living." When he discovered that the time of his son's recovery was at the very hour that Jesus spoke the proclamation of healing, not only did the royal official himself believe but also his whole household.

Ask YOURSELF

It is hard to be one faithful person among many others who are unfaithful. How are you being called to exercise the lonely, upstream walk of faith in your work or church or family environment? Pray that you would keep believing, even when all those around you discount your unflagging trust.

OCTOBER 13

MIRACLE AT BETHESDA

After these things there was a feast of the Jews, and Jesus went up to Jerusalem. Now there is in Jerusalem by the sheep gate a pool, which is called in Hebrew Bethesda, having five porticoes. In these lay a multitude of those who were sick, blind, lame, and withered, waiting for the moving of the waters; for an angel of the Lord went down at certain seasons into the pool and stirred up the water; whoever then first, after the stirring up of the water, stepped in was made well from whatever disease with which he was afflicted. A man was there who had been ill for thirty-eight years. When Jesus saw him lying there, and knew that he had already been a long time in that condition, He said to him, "Do you wish to get well?" The sick man answered Him, "Sir, I have no man to put me into the pool when the water is stirred up, but while I am coming, another steps down before me." Jesus said to him, "Get up, pick up your pallet and walk." Immediately the man became well, and picked up his pallet and began to walk.

JOHN 5:1–9A

THIS MIRACLE PERFECTLY ILLUSTRATES God's sovereign grace in action. Out of all the sick people at the pool, Jesus chose to heal this one man. There was nothing about him that made him more deserving than the others, nor did he seek out Jesus; Jesus approached him. The Lord did not choose him because He foresaw that he had the faith to believe; he never did express belief that Jesus could heal him.

It is the same way in salvation. Out of the spiritually dead multitude of Adam's fallen race, God chose and redeemed His elect—not because of anything they did to deserve it, or because of their foreseen faith, but because of His sovereign choice.

Ask YOURSELF

Be on the lookout for people in need—those you meet in very random encounters, as well as those you know well, people you see on a fairly routine basis. Wherever possible, be part of bringing hope and compassion to those who think no one really cares about them. Understand that you represent Jesus' love and mercy everywhere you go.

OCTOBER 14

LESSONS FROM BETHESDA, PART 1

Now it was the Sabbath on that day. So the Jews were saying to the man who was cured, "It is
the Sabbath, and it is not permissible for you to carry your pallet." But he answered them,
"He who made me well was the one who said to me, 'Pick up your pallet and walk.'" They asked him,
"Who is the man who said to you, 'Pick up your pallet and walk'?" But the man who was healed did
not know who it was, for Jesus had slipped away while there was a crowd in that place.

JOHN 5:9B–13

*J*OHN NOTES THAT THE HEALING took place on the Sabbath. Indeed, that was the key to this whole incident. It set the stage for the Jewish authorities' open hostility toward Christ. The fury of their opposition would only escalate through-out the remainder of His earthly ministry, finally culminating in His death.

Jesus' refusal to observe the legalistic and man-made Sabbath regulations was a major point of contention between Himself and Israel's religious establishment. In fact, the Lord deliberately chose to heal this man on the Sabbath to confront su-perficial and bankrupt Jewish legalism. The Lord wanted to show mercy to this man, but also to call the nation to repentance by confronting the self-righteous and un-biblical stipulations that led to their illusion of spiritual life.

Ask YOURSELF

Are there certain tastes, traditions, and preferences that cloud your view of God's activity in the world and in people's lives? How many could you name? What elevates these rigid absolutes beyond their biblical contexts, positioning them as bar-riers to grace rather than gateways to it?

LESSONS FROM BETHESDA, PART 2

Afterward Jesus found him in the temple and said to him, "Behold, you have become well;
do not sin anymore, so that nothing worse happens to you." The man went away,
and told the Jews that it was Jesus who had made him well. For this reason the
Jews were persecuting Jesus, because He was doing these things on the Sabbath.

JOHN 5:14–16

*I*N RESPONSE TO THIS MIRACLE, the Jewish authorities castigated the healed man for breaking their trivial rules (v. 10). They were more concerned with legalistic regulations than with the man's well-being—an attitude for which the Lord sharply rebuked them (Matt. 23:13ff.).

From this point on, the Jews were continually "persecuting Jesus, because He was doing these things on the Sabbath." So began their open opposition toward Jesus—persecution that would eventually result in His death.

The die was cast. Jesus confronted Jewish legalism by disregarding their Sabbath rules, challenging them with His true identity as the Son of God. The Jews' opposition to their own Messiah would harden and intensify until they crucified Him (1 Cor. 2:8).

Ask YOURSELF

Are there one or two individuals in your usual field of vision who are such sticklers for precision and protocol, they choke the life out of others' freedom in Christ? How do you deal with this kind of attitude? How might their predilection for order be of value to the Body if exercised properly?

OCTOBER 16

JESUS AND THE SABBATH

*He answered them, "My Father is working until now, and I Myself am working." For this reason
therefore the Jews were seeking all the more to kill Him, because He not only was breaking
the Sabbath, but also was calling God His own Father, making Himself equal with God.*

JOHN 5:17–18

*T*HE SABBATH OBSERVANCE was at the heart of Jewish worship in Jesus'
day. The Lord's reply to those who persecuted Him for violating it (5:16), "My Father
is working until now, and I Myself am working," implies that the Sabbath was not in-
stituted for God's benefit but for man's (Mark 2:27).

Jesus' statement that He worked on the Sabbath just like the Father was nothing less than a claim to full deity and equality with God—that "the Son of Man is
Lord of the Sabbath" (Matt. 12:8). His words also served as a subtle rebuke to the Jewish legalistic system, under which He had been indicted for doing good and showing mercy on the Sabbath. After all, God Himself does good and shows mercy on
the Sabbath. Jesus, therefore, maintained that it is right to do good on the Sabbath,
since God does.

The hostile Jews instantly grasped the import of Jesus' words and as a result
were continually seeking "all the more to kill Him." He was not just breaking the
Sabbath, but even worse, Jesus "also was calling God His own Father, making Himself equal with God." From this time forward they intensified their efforts to take
His life, not just for flouting their man-made Sabbath regulations, but even more
for asserting His deity.

Ask YOURSELF

Do you observe any Sabbath distinctions in your usual practice of the Lord's
Day? What are the benefits of these various habits or self-imposed restrictions?
Would you say that the church today has a healthy understanding of the Sabbath?
How could we lead each other to a better stance on it?

OCTOBER 17

Jesus' Deity in His Works

Jesus answered and was saying to them, "Truly, truly, I say to you, the Son can do nothing of
Himself, unless it is something He sees the Father doing; for whatever the Father does, these things
the Son also does in like manner. For the Father loves the Son, and shows Him all things that
He Himself is doing; and the Father will show Him greater works than these, so that you will marvel."

John 5:19–20

*F*OR A MERE MAN TO CLAIM to be God was, to the Jews, outrageous blasphemy. Therefore if they had misunderstood Him, Jesus surely would have immediately and vehemently denied making such a claim. But instead, He became even more forceful and emphatic. In the strongest possible terms, the Lord assured His hearers that what He said to them was true.

He further defended His healing on the Sabbath by tying His activities directly to those of the Father. "The Son can do nothing of Himself," Jesus declared, "unless it is something He sees the Father doing." He always acted in perfect harmony with and subordination to the Father's will. Thus His works paralleled those of the Father in both their nature and extent: "for whatever the Father does, these things the Son also does in like manner." Christ's statement is a clear declaration of His own divinity.

Jesus continued by declaring that the Father would show Him still greater works. His healing of the crippled man had amazed the crowds. But in obedience to the Father, Jesus predicted that He would perform even more spectacular deeds—deeds that would make His listeners marvel.

*Ask*YOURSELF

Is there any application of this principle for us—observing what the Father is doing, and then participating in those very things "in like manner"? How could this become more than a theory, shielded from human error? What would be some of the expected results from this kind of lifestyle and ministry approach?

JESUS' DEITY IN HIS POWER AND SOVEREIGNTY

For just as the Father raises the dead and gives them life,
even so the Son also gives life to whom He wishes.
JOHN 5:21

*B*Y ASSERTING HIS EQUALITY with God, Jesus claimed that He had the parallel power with God to raise the dead—"just as the Father raises the dead and gives them life." The Bible teaches that only God has the power to raise the dead (Deut. 32:39; Acts 26:8; Heb. 11:19), and the Old Testament records several instances in which He did so (1 Kings 17:17–24; 2 Kings 4:32–37; 13:20–21). Because His power is the same as the Father, Jesus Christ is able to raise the physically dead (John 11:25–44). Moreover, He has the power to give spiritual life to the spiritually dead. "Whoever drinks of the water that I will give him," Jesus promised, "shall never thirst; but the water that I will give him will become in him a well of water springing up to eternal life" (John 4:14).

Unlike Elijah and Elisha, Jesus did not merely act as God's representative when He raised the dead, but as God Himself. "The Son" Himself gives resurrection and spiritual "life to whom He wishes." As God is the source of life, so Jesus Christ is the source of life. As God chooses when He gives life, so does the Son choose, in perfect agreement with the Father—a truth illustrated by the salvation of sinners. All whom the Father chose before the foundation of the world to give to the Son will come to him, and He will not reject any of them (John 6:37).

*Ask*YOURSELF

Is there anything you've given up for dead in your own life, barely considering that God could raise it to life again? Even the possibility of victory over sin or the presence of Christian joy can be regarded as hopeless—lost relics from the past. Pray that Jesus would help you experience life anew.

OCTOBER 19

JESUS' DEITY IN HIS JUDGMENT

For not even the Father judges anyone, but He has given all judgment to the Son.

JOHN 5:22

*J*ESUS' AUTHORITY TO GRANT spiritual life to whomever He chooses is consistent with His authority to judge all men on the last day (cf. 3:18–19; 12:48). Since God is the "Judge of all the earth" (Gen. 18:25), the fact that the Father judges no one, but "has given all judgment to the Son," further attests to Christ's deity. Because their wills are in perfect harmony, all judgment can be given to Christ in the assurance that His judgment will be, in fact, the very same as the Father's judgment. Although judgment was not the primary purpose of Christ's first coming to earth (3:17; 12:47), it remains the inescapable final result of rejecting the salvation He offers (3:18).

In the future, "the Lord Jesus will be revealed from heaven with His mighty angels in flaming fire, dealing out retribution to those who do not know God and to those who do not obey the gospel of our Lord Jesus" (2 Thess. 1:7–8), because God "has fixed a day in which He will judge the world in righteousness through a Man whom He has appointed, having furnished proof to all men by raising Him from the dead" (Acts 17:31). On that final, terrible day of judgment, those who rejected Jesus will hear Him say, "I never knew you; depart from Me, you who practice lawlessness" (Matt. 7:23).

Take the time right now to examine your relationship to Christ. Make sure you are depending on His grace and mercy for salvation, not on your own sincere efforts.

*Ask*YOURSELF

Knowing ourselves and our tendency to sin, our view of God's power is perhaps most clearly seen, not in His ability and authority to judge but in His willingness to continually restrain it. That He doesn't begrudge His sacrifice but keeps applying it to our need is evidence of the highest form of mercy. Thank Him heartily for this today.

JESUS' DEITY IN HIS HONOR

... so that all will honor the Son even as they honor the Father. He who does not honor the Son does not honor the Father who sent Him. Truly, truly, I say to you, he who hears My word, and believes Him who sent Me, has eternal life, and does not come into judgment, but has passed out of death into life.

JOHN 5:23–24

*T*HE FATHER'S PURPOSE IN ENTRUSTING all judgment to Jesus is "so that all will honor the Son even as they honor the Father." It is only fitting that those equal in nature (vv. 17–18), works (vv. 19–20), power and sovereignty (v. 21), and judgment (v. 22) would be accorded equal honor. The Father's honor is not diminished by the honor paid to Christ; on the contrary, it is enhanced.

Although the unbelieving Jews thought they were truly worshiping God while rejecting His Son (cf. 16:2), instead the opposite was true: "he who does not honor the Son does not honor the Father who sent Him." "He who hates Me," Jesus warned, "hates My Father also" (John 15:23). Those who refuse to honor the Son while claiming to honor the Father are actually self-deceived.

That the Father and the Son are to be afforded equal honor forcefully asserts Christ's deity and equality with God, who declared through the prophet Isaiah, "I will not give My glory to another" (Isa. 42:8; cf. 48:11). Yet the Father has commanded that "all will honor the Son." Willingly or unwillingly, everyone will eventually obey the Father's command to honor Jesus Christ. The blessed promise to those who believe is that they "do not come into judgment, but [have] passed out of death into life."

Ask YOURSELF

Many in our culture today still don't have a lot of trouble believing in God, but Jesus is quite another matter. Are you sometimes convinced that a person is spiritually sound because he talks favorably of God and exhibits some good qualities? How do you speak to an individual like this about his or her need for Jesus?

WHO RECEIVES SPIRITUAL RESURRECTION?

Truly, truly, I say to you, an hour is coming and now is, when the dead
will hear the voice of the Son of God, and those who hear will live.

JOHN 5:25

JESUS BEGINS THIS EMPHATIC, unarguable declaration with the seemingly paradoxical statement "an hour is coming and now is." The hour of the believers' resurrection "now is" in the sense that when they "were dead in [their] trespasses and sins . . . [God] made [them] alive together with Christ, and raised [them] up with Him" (Eph. 2:1, 5–6). Yet the hour is still "coming" in the sense that the resurrection of their physical bodies is yet future (1 Cor. 15:35–54; Phil. 3:20–21).

This "already/not yet" sense of the phrase may be understood in another way. When Christ was present, He offered spiritual life to all who would heed His Word (6:37; Matt. 7:24–27). Yet the full expression of the new era He inaugurated would not come until the day of Pentecost (14:17). Both during Christ's earthly ministry and in the fullness of the Spirit's ministry after Pentecost, the spiritually dead who heard "the voice of the Son of God" would *live*.

Scripture frequently describes unbelievers as spiritually *dead*. To be spiritually dead is to be insensitive to the things of God and totally unable to respond to Him. Paul vividly described it as living "in the lusts of our flesh, indulging the desires of the flesh and of the mind, and [being] by nature children of wrath" (Eph. 2:3).

Rejoice in the amazing grace of God for making you alive together with Christ.

Ask YOURSELF

Try to define the ways you're experiencing the first rays of eternal life even while bound in this time and place. How would your life be different if you were still spiritually dead, removed from the grace of God?

SPIRITUAL RESURRECTION: PURPOSE AND POWER

Those who hear will live. For just as the Father has life in Himself,
even so He gave to the Son also to have life in Himself.
JOHN 5:25B–26

*T*HOSE, WHO EXPERIENCE SPIRITUAL resurrection will receive abundant (10:10), everlasting life. But the only ones who "will live" are "those who hear" in the sense of true faith and obedience to the gospel. "My sheep hear My voice," Jesus declared, "and I know them, and they follow Me" (10:27). Believers are those who have both the spiritual faculty and duty to respond to divine revelation. In contrast, the lost do not hear Christ's voice; they are not saved and thus do not understand or obey it (8:43, 47; 12:47; 14:24), and hence will not live spiritually.

The Son can give life (v. 21) because, like the Father, He "has life in Himself." No one can give to others what he himself lacks; thus no sinful human being can generate for himself eternal life. God alone possesses it, and He grants it through His Son to whomever He wills.

Those who deny His deity twist Jesus' statement about the Father giving life to the Son into a claim that He was created and thus inferior to the Father. Such is not the case, however. John has already stated in the prologue to his gospel that the Son possessed life in Himself from all eternity (1:4). When He became a man, our Lord voluntarily gave up the independent use of His divine attributes (Phil. 2:6–7). But the Father granted Him the authority to give life (both physical and spiritual) even during the self-limiting condescension of His earthly ministry.

Ask YOURSELF

What's the motivation behind those who try to downplay Jesus' divinity? What are they trying to avoid admitting or dealing with? What would you say to those who claim that doctrines like these are unimportant and nonessential?

PHYSICAL RESURRECTION

Do not marvel at this; for an hour is coming, in which all who are in the tombs will hear
His voice, and will come forth; those who did the good deeds to a resurrection of life,
those who committed the evil deeds to a resurrection of judgment.

JOHN 5:28–29

*T*HE UNBELIEVING JEWS WERE astonished and outraged at Jesus' bold claim to be the giver of spiritual life and the ultimate judge of all men. But then Jesus revealed another truth that astounded them: He would one day raise the dead from their graves. As He did with the spiritual resurrection (v. 25), Jesus said that the hour of physical resurrection is coming. The resurrection of "all who are in the tombs" is still future. At that time, the souls of the righteous dead, now in heaven with the Lord (2 Cor. 5:6–8), and of the wicked dead, now in torment in Hades (Luke 16:22–23), will be given resurrected bodies fit for eternity.

The final resurrection will usher believers into the glories of eternal life, and bring unbelievers to the endless suffering of eternal judgment. By characterizing believers as "those who did the good deeds" and unbelievers as "those who committed the evil deeds," Jesus was not teaching that salvation is by works. Throughout His ministry, Jesus clearly taught that salvation "is the work of God, that you believe in Him whom He has sent" (6:29). Good works are simply the evidence of salvation. Those who believe in the Son will as a result do "good deeds" (3:21; Eph. 2:10; James 2:14–20), while those who reject the Son will be characterized by "evil deeds."

Ask YOURSELF

How does the reality of a physical resurrection help deflect the disappointment you feel when you notice those telltale signs of aging and bodily decay? How do you balance the biblical stewardship of healthy living with the assurance that these temporary dwellings are destined for replacement?

JOHN THE BAPTIST'S TESTIMONY TO JESUS' DEITY

You have sent to John, and he has testified to the truth. But the testimony which I receive is not from man, but I say these things so that you may be saved. He was the lamp that was burning and was shining and you were willing to rejoice for a while in his light.

JOHN 5:33–35

*T*HE PURPOSE OF JOHN THE BAPTIST'S ministry was to prepare the nation for the Messiah (1:23), and to point Him out when He came (1:31).

John's testimony supported Jesus' claims to be the Messiah. Since he was generally regarded as a prophet (Matt. 21:26; Luke 20:6)—the first one in four centuries—his testimony carried considerable weight.

Jesus, of course, did not depend on human testimony to establish His claim to deity. He cited the testimony of John the Baptist to confirm by the mouth of one already recognized as God's true prophet that same truth concerning Himself. He did so for the sake of His hearers—that they might be saved on account of John's faithful witness.

Having mentioned John's testimony to Him, Jesus in turn gave both a tribute to the Baptist and a rebuke to the Jewish leaders for rejecting his witness. John was "the lamp that was burning and was shining." His "burning" inner zeal made him a "shining" light in the dark world. Unlike Jesus, who is the Light of the world (8:12), John was a lamp—he was a reflector of the Light. Just as a lamp lights the way for people, so John lit the way to Jesus (1:31).

Ask YOURSELF

We are never just standing still. We're either increasing our resemblance to Christ's character, or we're looking more like ourselves—more controlled by our own desires and appetites. What traits would make you a better reflection of the presence of Christ in your life?

FINISHED WORKS TESTIFY TO JESUS' DEITY

But the testimony which I have is greater than the testimony of John; for the works which the Father has given Me to accomplish—the very works that I do—testify about Me, that the Father has sent Me.

JOHN 5:36

*J*OHN THE BAPTIST'S TESTIMONY carried considerable weight; after all, he was the greatest man who had ever lived up to this time (Luke 7:28). But the testimony Jesus was about to introduce was far "greater than the testimony of John." More convincing than the greatest prophet's testimony to Christ were "the very works that" He did.

Throughout His ministry the Lord repeatedly pointed to His miraculous works as confirmation of His claim to be the Son of God and the Messiah (cf. 10:25, 37–38; 14:11; Matt. 11:3–5). The gospels record at least three dozen of His miracles, and Jesus performed countless others that Scripture does not record (20:30).

Throughout His earthly ministry, Jesus was conscious of carrying out the mission the Father had given Him in the energy of the Spirit (Luke 4:14). In John 4:34, Jesus told the disciples, "My food is to do the will of Him who sent Me and to accomplish His work." In His High Priestly Prayer to the Father, Jesus declared triumphantly, "I glorified You on the earth, having accomplished the work which You have given Me to do" (17:4).

Because Jesus' works were in perfect harmony with the will of His Father, they testified "that the Father sent" Him. His works were supernatural and in keeping with God's exact wishes.

Those very miracles, as recorded in Scripture, provide you with a powerful witnessing tool today.

Ask YOURSELF

What elements of God's nature are revealed when He performs a miracle in the lives of His people? What is revealed when He withholds the miracle we desire, choosing instead to work His will in another way?

OCTOBER 26

THE FATHER'S TESTIMONY TO JESUS' DEITY

There is another who testifies of Me, and I know that the testimony which He gives about Me is true. . . .
And the Father who sent Me, He has testified of Me. You have neither heard His voice at any time nor
seen His form. You do not have His word abiding in you, for you do not believe Him whom He sent.

JOHN 5:32, 37–38

*O*F INFINITELY GREATER IMPORTANCE than any human testimony is that the Father who sent Jesus has testified about Him. The gospels record two specific instances in which the Father gave verbal testimony to the Son: at His baptism and at His transfiguration, when "a voice out of the heavens said, 'This is My beloved Son, in whom I am well-pleased'" (Matt. 3:17; cf. Matt. 17:5).

Jesus' statement, "You have neither heard His voice at any time nor seen His form," was a further rebuke of the unbelieving Jews. No one can see God in the full glory of His infinitely holy essence (Ex. 33:20; John 1:18). However, there were times throughout Israel's history when God audibly or visibly interacted with His people. He spoke to Moses (Ex. 33:11) and the prophets (Heb. 1:1). He also appeared in some physical manifestation of His presence to Jacob (Gen. 32:30) and others.

Yet the unbelieving Jews of Jesus' day, who had both the Old Testament Scriptures and the full revelation of God in Jesus Christ, refused to listen to Jesus, God's final revelation to mankind (Heb. 1:2). On the other hand, those who love the Son have the internal witness from God in their hearts as to who Jesus is.

*Ask*YOURSELF

How has the presence of His Word in your thoughts and meditations spoken God's wisdom to you at a critical point in life? What have you noticed about the difference in your judgment and perspective when the Scriptures are a ready resource within your heart, when the Spirit has lots of biblical material inside you to work with?

SCRIPTURE TESTIFIES TO JESUS' DEITY

You search the Scriptures because you think that in them you have eternal life; it is these that testify about Me; and you are unwilling to come to Me so that you may have life. I do not receive glory from men; but I know you, that you do not have the love of God in yourselves. I have come in My Father's name, and you do not receive Me; if another comes in his own name, you will receive him.

JOHN 5:39–43

MERELY KNOWING THE FACTS of Scripture, without hiding them in your heart and acting on them, will not bring the blessings of salvation. That was the problem of Jewish unbelievers. Jesus understood their searching of the Scriptures in a desperate and futile attempt to find the key to eternal life. But ironically, they failed to grasp that it is those very Scriptures "that testify about" Jesus.

The Bible cannot be properly understood apart from the Holy Spirit's illumination or a transformed mind. The Jews' zeal for the Scripture was commendable, but because they were unwilling to come to Jesus—the sole source of eternal life—their knowledge did not result in salvation. Clinging in their stubborn unbelief to a superficial system of self-righteousness by works, they became ignorant of "God's righteousness and [sought] to establish their own" (Rom. 10:3). But self-righteousness cannot save anyone, since "all our righteous deeds are like a filthy garment" (Isa. 64:6).

Please be sure you are not trusting in your own righteous works for salvation. Be sure you are clinging in utter dependence on the grace of God in Christ.

Ask YOURSELF

Have you ever allowed your knowledge of the Scriptures to blind you to its more excellent meaning, whether through pride or tradition or a dogmatic overconfidence in your own interpretations? How do you guard against these kinds of snares and deceptions?

JEWISH LEADERS IGNORE TESTIMONIES

*How can you believe, when you receive glory from one another and you do not seek the glory that
is from the one and only God? Do not think that I will accuse you before the Father; the one who
accuses you is Moses, in whom you have set your hope. For if you believed Moses, you would believe
Me, for he wrote about Me. But if you do not believe his writings, how will you believe My words?*

JOHN 5:44–47

JESUS' PENSIVE QUESTION, "How can you believe, when you receive glory from one another and you do not seek the glory that is from the one and only God?" offers a crucial reason why the Jews rejected Him. Those engaged in seeking "glory from one another" do not humble themselves to believe in Jesus.

The Lord stunned them when He said the one who would accuse them of their rejection of Christ was Moses—the very one in whom they had set their hope. Can you imagine how profoundly shocked and outraged the Jewish leaders must have been? In their minds, it was incomprehensible to think that Moses—whom they proudly affirmed as their leader and teacher (9:28; cf. Matt 23:2)—would accuse them before God. But had they truly believed Moses, they would believe Jesus, since Moses wrote about Him.

It should come as no surprise that those who did not believe Moses' writings would not believe Christ's words either. If they rejected the truths taught by Moses, whom they revered, they could hardly be expected to accept the teaching of Jesus, whom they reviled. The sobering reality is that those who reject Moses' teaching about Jesus will face judgment.

Ask YOURSELF

Jesus was able to interact forcibly with His detractors because He knew them, understood their hearts, and was aware of what blinded them to the truth. If your witness is not as effective as it should be, have you considered that perhaps you're proclaiming the gospel without stopping to understand the people you're talking to?

JOHN THE BAPTIST AND HIS DOUBT, PART 1

Now when John, while imprisoned, heard of the works of Christ, he sent word by his
disciples and said to Him, "Are You the Expected One, or shall we look for someone else?"

MATT. 11:2–3

*C*OUNTLESS CHRISTIANS SINCE John the Baptist's time have dealt with doubt, which might better be called perplexity or confusion. Here John did not question the truthfulness of Old Testament Scripture or the veracity of Jesus' baptism, which he himself had seen. Rather, John was simply uncertain about his understanding of those truths. And the kind of question he asked could come only from a believer. In that transitional period between the Testaments, many things seemed unclear and called for further explanation.

Until this time, John the Baptist was the greatest man who had ever lived (Matt. 11:11); so when believers are confused, they can take comfort that even John was perplexed for a time. Also encouraging for us is that Jesus often said to His disciples, "You of little faith" and "How long will you doubt?" (e.g., Matt. 8:26; 14:31; Mark 11:23; Luke 12:28).

Although Christ understands His children's doubts, He is never pleased with such misgivings because they reflect against Him. When messengers from the Gentile Cornelius arrived where Peter was staying, the Holy Spirit told the apostle, "Get up, go downstairs and accompany them without misgivings, for I have sent them Myself" (Acts 10:20). James warns us that "the one who doubts is like the surf of the sea, driven and tossed by the wind" (James 1:6; cf. Eph. 4:14). But John's doubt derived from weakness, not sin, and the only remedy for similar doubt by us is sincere inquiry, prayerful confession, and reliance on Scripture for reassurance.

Ask YOURSELF

How do you respond to people in crisis, especially when the trauma of their situation has left them doubting God's goodness or shaken in their faith? How do you go about reassuring them of the Lord's faithfulness when they will hear none of it or aren't ready to listen?

JOHN THE BAPTIST AND HIS DOUBT, PART 2

Now when John, while imprisoned, heard of the works of Christ, he sent word by his
disciples and said to Him, "Are You the Expected One, or shall we look for someone else?"

MATT. 11:2–3

*T*HAT JOHN THE BAPTIST SENT some of his disciples to Jesus testifies to his genuine faith. John was not seeking more information about Christ but confirmation. In essence, he asked, "Even though I firmly believed You are the Messiah, could I have been wrong?" It was the same attitude as the father of the boy the Lord had cleansed of an evil spirit—"I do believe; help my unbelief" (Mark 9:24).

After being in prison for months, unable to minister and interact with the outside world except through periodic visits by his disciples, John had many doubts and uncertainties about Jesus. Those misgivings settled on his mind even though he had announced, baptized, and declared Jesus to be the Messiah.

This prompted John's disciples to ask Jesus directly, "Are You the Expected One?" This was a common title for the Messiah, along with Branch, Son of David, and King of kings. The name first appears in Psalms 40:7 and 118:26, and the gospel writers often use it (e.g., Matt. 3:11; Mark 1:7; Luke 3:16; John 1:27). There was no mistaking the fact that John wanted to know for sure if Jesus was indeed the promised Messiah.

Many Christians today wrestle with doubt from time to time, so it should reassure them that one with the spiritual stature of John the Baptist also doubted. And it ought to encourage us, as we'll see in the following days, that our doubts come for the same reasons as John's—and we, like he, can overcome them.

Ask YOURSELF

What (if anything) has caused you to doubt the reality of God's existence or the veracity of His promises? How did He bring you through the maze and mist of uncertainty into a surer place of confidence? What did you learn about Him and about yourself in the process?

OCTOBER 31

DIFFICULT CIRCUMSTANCES FOR JOHN

Now when John, while imprisoned, heard of the works of Christ, he sent word by his
disciples and said to Him, "Are You the Expected One, or shall we look for someone else?"

MATT. 11:2–3

*J*OHN THE BAPTIST WAS A TRUE saint and prophet of God, unreserved in His divine service. He had ministered precisely according to God's will, but now he couldn't help wondering why he was imprisoned and enduring other hardships.

He knew the Old Testament and maybe asked where the God of comfort (Ps. 119:50; Isa. 51:12) was at that time. Where was the promise that Messiah would "bind up the brokenhearted . . . proclaim liberty to captives and freedom to prisoners" (Isa. 61:1)?

Paul was also imprisoned, likely in Rome, when he wrote, "Rejoice in the Lord always; again I will say, rejoice! Let your gentle spirit be known to all men. The Lord is near. Be anxious for nothing, but in everything by prayer and supplication with thanksgiving let your requests be made known to God. And the peace of God, which surpasses all comprehension, will guard your hearts and your minds in Christ Jesus" (Phil. 4:4–7; cf. vv. 11–13, 19).

John knew where to find answers, even in the midst of doubt. That's why he sent his disciples to Jesus to plead, "Lord, please help me!" And Christ was glad to respond, performing miracles for John's sake and promising spiritual blessing if he remained steady.

Difficult circumstances can be stressful and painful, but our attitude and response should be like John's—and Paul's—trusting in the Lord to calm our doubts, anxieties, and fears (cf. James 1:2–12).

Ask YOURSELF

What causes some to be secure and steadfast no matter their circumstances, while others really struggle to keep their faith front and center? How are you preparing your heart to stay strong in the inevitable seasons of conflict to come?

INCOMPLETE INFORMATION FOR JOHN

Now when John, while imprisoned, heard of the works of Christ, he sent word by his disciples and said to Him, "Are You the Expected One, or shall we look for someone else?"

MATT. 11:2–3

*M*ANY OF US TODAY DOUBT CERTAIN truths about God, Christ, and God's Word due to lack of information. That's because we might have an inadequate understanding of Scripture. That's the kind of thing that contributed to John the Baptist's doubt—he had not experienced the full truth about Jesus Christ that God had sent him to proclaim. His position was similar to the Old Testament prophets: "As to this salvation, the prophets who prophesied of the grace that would come to you made careful searches and inquiries, seeking to know what person or time the Spirit of Christ within them was indicating as He predicted the sufferings of Christ and the glories to follow" (1 Peter 1:10–11).

Two disciples on the road to Emmaus were also confused and doubting. But the risen Christ first rebuked them for being "slow of heart to believe in all that the prophets have spoken" (Luke 24:25). After that, "beginning with Moses and with all the prophets, He explained to them the things concerning Himself in all the Scriptures" (v. 27). Even before they realized it was Jesus who had been teaching them, the truth of Scripture began removing the two men's doubts (vv. 31–32).

The truth of God's Word needs to continually inform our hearts and minds and protect us from doubt and dispel it when it does arise. If we are immersed in the Word, we have no reason to stumble (cf. Acts 17:11).

Ask YOURSELF

Have you noticed that when you stay regularly and intently in the Word, the Holy Spirit begins piecing the big picture of the Bible together, bringing to mind other Scriptures lodged in your memory bank? Why is this truth retrieval such a valuable blessing and benefit?

NOVEMBER 2

WORLDLY INFLUENCE ON JOHN

Now when John, while imprisoned, heard of the works of Christ, he sent word by his
disciples and said to Him, "Are You the Expected One, or shall we look for someone else?"

MATT. 11:2–3

*E*VEN THE RIGHTEOUS JOHN the Baptist was not totally freed from worldly influences that could cause him doubts about Jesus. The Lord's ministry did not completely square with what most Jews, including John, thought Messiah would do. The Christ could not set up His own kingdom without first freeing Israel from Roman bondage and injustice. But He had done nothing to oppose Rome. And Jesus' many miracles had still not yet banished all suffering from Israel or the world.

A common misunderstanding was that other prominent men would precede Him—perhaps Elijah, Jeremiah, and some other prophets. Thus when Jesus later asked the apostles who people thought He was, they replied, "Some say John the Baptist [who by then was dead]; and others, Elijah; but still others, Jeremiah, or one of the prophets" (Matt. 16:14).

The distorted and world-based ideas about Messiah—with Jesus not fitting their preconceived notions—almost inevitably rubbed off on John. Then some Jewish leaders challenged Jesus by asking, "How long will You keep us in suspense? If You are the Christ, tell us plainly." To this, Jesus responded, "I told you, and you do not believe; the works that I do in My Father's name, these testify of Me" (John 10:24–25).

The unbelieving world could affect even John's confidence in Jesus because it does not grasp God's plan, since such things "are foolishness to [them]; and [they] cannot understand them" (1 Cor. 2:14; cf. John 10:26). Worldly, unbelieving thinking will always try to sow doubts regarding the truth of Christ.

Ask YOURSELF

Can you identify a sliver of worldly thinking that has slipped into your way of looking at things? Why do we tend to embrace these kinds of perspectives at times? What do you do when you detect an unbiblical line of thought taking hold in your mind and attitude?

UNFULFILLED EXPECTATIONS FOR JOHN

Now when John, while imprisoned, heard of the works of Christ, he sent word by his
disciples and said to Him, "Are You the Expected One, or shall we look for someone else?"

MATT. 11:2–3

*I*T HAS OFTEN BEEN DIFFICULT for Christians to understand why the Lord allows them to wait for Him to fulfill certain promises. It was even harder for John the Baptist, given his expectations. John had a strong devotion to righteousness as a prophetic voice divinely called to preach repentance and judgment. God had also called him to herald the coming Messiah, who would render judgment. John expected this to happen immediately or at least soon after Messiah appeared.

The second part of John's question, "Shall we look for someone else?" would indicate he was dealing with unfulfilled expectations regarding Messiah. Under the Spirit's direction he had preached about Christ's ministry of judgment (see Matt. 3:11–12). John knew his preaching was true and that Jesus was that One about whom he preached, yet He had not yet done the stringent things John proclaimed.

As John sat in prison he must have recalled the psalmist's cry, "Surely there is a God who judges on earth!" (Ps. 58:11; cf. 9:3–4; 52:1–5; Rev. 6:10).

Believers today sometimes have high expectations about the soon return of Christ, but when that doesn't happen, their hope and dedication often fades. They don't stop believing in the second coming, but they don't think about that hope nearly as much as before. But, as Jesus reassured John, they can know that God's program remains on His schedule, as Peter assured his readers, "The Lord is not slow about His promise, as some count slowness, but is patient toward you" (2 Peter 3:9a; cf. vv. 3–8).

Ask YOURSELF

How have expectations affected your own outlook on God and the life of faith? Does this mean you should lower your expectations to make them less likely to go unmet? How do you make yourself less susceptible to being waylaid by disappointment?

JESUS REASSURES JOHN, PART 1

Jesus answered and said to them, "Go and report to John what you hear and see: the blind receive sight and the lame walk, the lepers are cleansed and the deaf hear, the dead are raised up, and the poor have the gospel preached to them. And blessed is he who does not take offense at Me."

MATT. 11:4–6

*T*HE LORD JESUS ALWAYS HAS the best answer for every distinct situation. Rather than a terse yes-or-no answer to John the Baptist, Jesus reported to his disciples a reminder of the healing miracles already so well-reported and witnessed. The signs had prompted many to follow Jesus (Matt. 4:23–25), and notable healings were well publicized: the cleansing of an unclean spirit (Mark 1:28), Jairus's daughter (Matt. 9:26), and the Galilean leper (Luke 5:15).

Jesus greatly loved John the Baptist, and because he was His faithful forerunner, our Lord purposed to give him a personal and direct report of miracle-working evidence about Himself. Concerning this time of John's doubting, Luke writes, "At that very time He cured many people of diseases and afflictions and evil spirits; and He gave sight to many who were blind" (Luke 7:21). What He did included nothing to improve John's difficult circumstances, but He did send him a special confirmation that He was indeed performing messianic works. Such miracles occurred in keeping with Isaiah's prophecy (Isa. 35:5; 61:1).

In essence, Jesus' initial reassurance to John said, "These things are just a preview of My coming kingdom. You can see by what I do now that I care, that I heal, and that I have control over all things."

Ask YOURSELF

Does anything please you more than seeing God's kingdom advanced and His name being honored? What other priorities threaten to dethrone this goal from being your top reason for satisfaction?

NOVEMBER 5

JESUS REASSURES JOHN, PART 2

Jesus answered and said to them, "Go and report to John what you hear and see: the blind receive sight and the lame walk, the lepers are cleansed and the deaf hear, the dead are raised up, and the poor have the gospel preached to them. And blessed is he who does not take offense at Me."

MATT. 11:4–6

*J*ESUS' DEITY AND HIS MESSAGE of salvation by grace through faith have been great stumbling blocks for many unbelieving sinners, but Christ did not want such doubt and unbelief to affect John. It is likely that the Lord's response was more than adequate to renew John's faith and confidence, even though his circumstances, humanly speaking, went from bad to worse and he was beheaded.

After burying John's body, his disciples reported the news to Jesus (Matt. 14:12), probably because the most important person in John's life was now their Savior as well. At death, John likely still wondered when Jesus would judge the wicked and establish His righteous kingdom. The forerunner probably also regretted not being able to see the great events he'd faithfully preached about. But his doubts about Jesus' identity were at an end, and he was content to leave in God's sovereign hands the things he never fully understood. This last trait is the secret for any saint who would be blessed and not cause offense.

The Baptist would have ultimately affirmed the apostle John's later declaration, "Beloved, now we are children of God . . . we know that when He appears, we will be like Him, because we will see Him just as He is. And everyone who has this hope fixed on Him purifies himself, just as He is pure" (1 John 3:2–3). Knowing this, we can always approach Jesus, even while in temporary doubt.

Ask YOURSELF

Have you ever thought about what your final words will be if the Lord enables you to utter some parting thoughts at your passing? How do you think you'd want to sum up your experience on earth with the Lord and your perspective on life, looking back?

JOHN'S GREATNESS: STRONG CONVICTIONS

As these men were going away, Jesus began to speak to the crowds about John,
"What did you go out into the wilderness to see? A reed shaken by the wind?"

MATT. 11:7

*T*HE WORLD USES MANY STANDARDS—intellectual achievement, public service, wealth, athletic skill, and others—to measure greatness. But here Jesus begins to portray real greatness in the character qualities of John the Baptist. Strength of conviction was one of those qualities, and it was even more remarkable given his doubts about Jesus that John's disciples had just presented. His foundational convictions were strong enough that raising some doubts was not a cause for embarrassment or shame for John.

But hearing of John's doubt caused perplexity among the onlookers. Was the Baptist, the model of boldness and certainty, no longer trustworthy in view of his public admission of misgivings about Jesus?

To reaffirm that John's convictions were strong, Jesus appealed to the listeners' own experiences, asking in effect, "Was the spokesman you saw preaching and baptizing uncertain and vacillating, like 'a reed shaken by the wind'?" The reed was common to the riverbanks of the Middle East, a light and flexible stalk that easily bent back and forth in the wind. But the people knew that if ever there had been a man of unswerving belief, it was John. In fact, his bold stand for righteousness had landed him in prison.

"A double-minded man [is] unstable in all his ways" (James 1:8; cf. Eph. 4:14). But that was not John the Baptist, who like William Penn believed that "right is right, even if everyone is against it, and wrong is wrong, even if everyone is for it."

Ask YOURSELF

In what ways has your life exhibited reed-like qualities, bending to challenges that required a sturdy backbone and a steady faith? How, on the other hand, has God enabled you to mirror the boldness of John in your obedience to Christ's call? Thank God for His provision and empowerment.

JOHN'S GREATNESS: HIS SELF-DENIAL

But what did you go out to see? A man dressed in soft clothing?
Those who wear soft clothing are in kings' palaces!
MATT. 11:8

*T*HE EASY WAY IS SELDOM IF EVER the way of success. Great generals risk their lives just as their troops do. Great athletes train relentlessly, forgoing the pleasure most people take for granted. And in order to help save other lives, medical researchers sometimes risk exposure to deadly disease to find cures.

The self-indulgent person is not willing to live as John the Baptist did. He wore camel's hair and a leather belt and ate locusts and honey (Matt. 3:4). His lifestyle was a down-to-earth protest against self-indulgence and self-centeredness. John lived completely apart from the hypocritical, corrupt political and religious systems of his day. His devotion to God's kingdom completely superseded any personal comforts or attractions to the world's standards.

Prior to John's birth, the angel predicted to Zacharias, John's father, that John would "be great in the sight of the Lord; and he will drink no wine or liquor, and he will be filled with the Holy Spirit" (Luke 1:15). That was part of the Nazirite vow, along with pledging not to cut one's hair or touch anything unclean, that many Jews took for a few months or years. But John, along with Samson (Judg. 13:7; 16:17) and Samuel (1 Sam. 1:11), took the vow for life. John the Baptist had a lifelong, voluntary commitment to self-denial as an act of devotion and service to God—one aspect of his greatness that Jesus praised.

Ask YOURSELF

What have you sacrificed in order to stay true to the will of God? What are some things—even good, sinless things—that others are allowed to enjoy, but which cannot be a part of your life for one reason or another?

John's Greatness: His Privileged Call

But what did you go out to see? A prophet? Yes, I tell you, and one who is more than a prophet. This is
the one about whom it is written, "Behold, I send My messenger ahead of You, who will prepare Your
way before You." Truly I say to you, among those born of women there has not arisen anyone greater
than John the Baptist! Yet the one who is least in the kingdom of heaven is greater than he.

MATT. 11:9–11

GOD ALWAYS CALLS THE RIGHT PERSON to the right position in the realm of greatness. In John, the greatest man and the greatest human assignment converged—God called him as the valedictory prophet, the most dynamic, articulate, confrontational, and powerful spokesman ever.

Jesus quotes Malachi 3:1 in declaring to the people that John's privileged call meant he was more than an ordinary prophet. We could expand the Lord's quotation this way: "Behold, I, Yahweh, send My messenger John the Baptist to be the forerunner of You, the Messiah, and to prepare the people for Your coming." After centuries of divine preparation and prophecy, God gave John the unequaled privilege of heralding Messiah's coming.

Jesus' point here in calling John the greatest is that, humanly speaking, he was the greatest person who had lived until that time. With his superior human qualities, John was unequaled until the God-Man Himself came to earth.

John the Baptist was a spiritual giant, but his privileged call mainly concerned his historic role. In spiritual inheritance, every believer is the equal of John: "The least in the kingdom of heaven [the spiritual realm] is greater than he." Average saints are greater than anyone in the human realm, including John the Baptist, the one called to be the messianic forerunner. That's a reality for which we should be ever thankful as Christians.

Ask YOURSELF

How would you define the specific calling God has placed on your life? What duties and responsibilities go into your faithful performance of it? How is God employing your natural abilities in serving Him, while also providing you spiritual gifts as vehicles of grace to others?

NOVEMBER 9

JOHN AND THE KINGDOM OF HEAVEN

From the days of John the Baptist until now the kingdom of
heaven suffers violence, and violent men take it by force.

MATT. 11:12

"THE KINGDOM OF HEAVEN" refers to God's general rule and represents His purpose, message, commands, and activities regarding humanity. This great concept was associated in some fashion with violence since John the Baptist began preaching. Wherever he went, his call for repentance and entrance into the kingdom generated strong and eventually violent opposition.

The verb translated "suffers violence" carries both negative and positive connotations. First is the idea of the kingdom being treated violently by its foes—by those outside it, like the Jewish leaders. They vociferously rejected its spiritual dimension, and so its earthly dimension could not begin for some time.

Second, there is a more proactive and primary meaning to the phrase "suffers violence"—which sees the kingdom as vigorously pressing forward and people forcefully entering it. The angel's prediction before John's birth illustrates this positive element (see Luke 1:16–17). Jesus was already teaching about the narrow gate and the narrow way (Matt. 7:13–14), declaring that kingdom citizenship requires self-denial and cross bearing (16:24; cf. 10:38).

To be a Christian today means swimming against the world's flow, going against its grain, because its satanic system is extremely powerful. Those who truly enter God's kingdom do so through faith and with great effort—effort that is not their own, but from the sovereign, converting power of the Holy Spirit.

Ask YOURSELF

You're certainly familiar with the kingdom of God arousing violent opposition from without. But have you ever thought of it flexing its strength to bring you into its borders? How has the kingdom met you in brute force, causing "violence" to your former manner of living?

JOHN LIKENED TO ELIJAH

For all the prophets and the Law prophesied until John. And if
you are willing to accept it, John himself is Elijah who was to come.

MATT. 11:13–14

*A*LL OF GOD'S OLD TESTAMENT revelation climaxed in John the Baptist. And the apostle John picked up the theme (which at times had been only implicit) that said, "The Messiah is coming!"

The Lord Jesus suggests a close likeness between John and the prophet Elijah, based on Malachi's prophecy, which are the final words of the Old Testament: "Behold, I am going to send you Elijah the prophet before the coming of the great and terrible day of the Lord. He will restore the hearts of the fathers to their children and the hearts of the children to their fathers, so that I will not come and smite the land with a curse" (Mal. 4:5–6).

That Malachi referred to the future John the Baptist and not a literally reincarnated Elijah is clear when we look at Luke 1:17—"It is he [John] who will go as a forerunner before Him in the spirit and power of Elijah." John himself clearly denied that he was actually Elijah come back (John 1:21). Rather he was *like* Elijah—inwardly in "spirit and power" and outwardly in independence and nonconformity.

John was uniquely great, in the mold of Elijah and more so than any man but Jesus; but God's highest bestowing of greatness is not John's. His greatness, Jesus declared, pales beside those like us who enter God's spiritual kingdom by trusting in the Son as Lord and Savior. Thus true greatness is to be like Jesus Christ, not like Elijah or John the Baptist.

Ask YOURSELF

"Spirit and power." How could these words more readily describe you and your ministry in the kingdom? Are these characteristics the sole possession of the overly demonstrably inclined? Or does "spirit and power" even have a gentle side in the cause of Christ?

CRITICISM OF JOHN AND JESUS

But to what shall I compare this generation? It is like children sitting in the market places, who call out to the other children, and say, "We played the flute for you, and you did not dance; we sang a dirge, and you did not mourn." For John came neither eating nor drinking, and they say, "He has a demon!" The Son of Man came eating and drinking, and they say, "Behold, a gluttonous man and a drunkard, a friend of tax collectors and sinners!" Yet wisdom is vindicated by her deeds.

MATT. 11:16–19

*C*ONTEMPORARY PEOPLE LOVE to criticize whatever the church does, which is really just a convenient excuse to reject the gospel. Such was also true in Jesus' day, and here He uses two illustrations of criticism to make that point.

First, He applies the children's game "Funeral" to the criticism of John the Baptist. John lived in the funeral mode, and people became so resentful of his constant stress on repentance and judgment that they claimed he had a demon. He would not let his audience be neutral—he called for commitment to truth and righteousness. But instead of accepting that call, they generally rebuked John's righteousness.

Second, Jesus applies the game of "Wedding" to Himself. In contrast to John's austere living, Jesus participated in society's usual activities. His ministry brought Him into contact with hundreds of ordinary people. This difference from John had not escaped his disciples (Matt. 9:14–15), but the critics exaggerated Jesus' activities and said His appetites were out of control. It was true that Jesus befriended tax collectors and sinners, but only to offer deliverance from their sins, not to be involved with them in sin (cf. 9:12–13).

Their opponents criticized John and Jesus differently, but the lesson is the same. Like today, the enemies of truth found it easy to criticize but difficult to explain how so many lives were transformed from despair to hope, from anger to love, from enmity to Christ to fellowship with Him.

Ask YOURSELF

What are some of the most common criticisms against Christianity? Which ones hold water, and which are just rebellious bluster?

UNBELIEVING INDIFFERENCE: CHORAZIN AND BETHSAIDA

Woe to you, Chorazin! Woe to you, Bethsaida! For if the miracles had occurred in Tyre and Sidon which occurred in you, they would have repented long ago in sackcloth and ashes. Nevertheless I say to you, it will be more tolerable for Tyre and Sidon in the day of judgment than for you.

MATT. 11:21–22

*I*NDIFFERENCE IS A TERRIBLE FORM of unbelief. It so totally ignores God that He is not even considered worth arguing about. As Josiah realized after God's people rediscovered His book, "great is the wrath of the Lord that burns against us, because our fathers have not listened to the words of this book" (2 Kings 22:13; cf. Matt. 22:5–6, 14).

Probably most citizens of Chorazin and Bethsaida had seen Christ's miracles, and others knew about them from reports of friends and relatives. But relatively few responded in saving faith (cf. Matt. 7:13–14). Hence the Lord's righteous wrath came down on them with exclamations of woe for their unrepentance. It is better to have never heard about Jesus than to hear and yet reject Him (cf. Heb. 10:26–27).

By contrast, Jesus tells us that pagan, corrupt cities such as Tyre and Sidon would have repented early on had they heard Jesus' message and seen His miracles. Few statements such as this from the Messiah would have shocked the Jews more than to be unfavorably compared to sinful Gentiles. At the great white throne, God will judge unbelievers from all eras, sentencing them to eternal punishment. At that time, many from places like Tyre and Sidon will fare better than unbelieving Jews. The greater the privilege God offers people, the greater the responsibility they have. The greater the light they see, the worse the consequences for not receiving it.

Ask YOURSELF

Does your church bear the marks of people who have grown lackadaisical in faith and protectively focused on side issues, or people who are active and animated in their love for the Lord? How can you be part of encouraging faithful zeal in those familiar with Christian faith?

NOVEMBER 13

UNBELIEVING INDIFFERENCE: CAPERNAUM

And you, Capernaum, will not be exalted to heaven, will you? You will descend to Hades; for if the
miracles had occurred in Sodom which occurred in you, it would have remained to this day.

MATT. 11:23

*O*FTEN THOSE WHO HAVE opportunity for the greatest spiritual privileges
take those most for granted and enjoy them least. Such could be said for the Galilean
city of Capernaum. It was the area where Christ made His headquarters and performed more miracles and preached more messages than in any other region during
His earthly ministry. Yet all of this marvelous activity apparently had little impact on
the indifferent citizens.

Had all of it happened in and around Sodom, Jesus says, that infamously wicked
city would have repented, turned in faith to God, and been spared destruction. Even
secular people know Sodom as a synonym for moral degradation and a place where
homosexuality and other perversions were rampant. On the other hand, Capernaum,
like many modern cities, probably had mostly law-abiding, decent residents.

Capernaum exceeded Chorazin and Bethsaida in advantage, and Sodom exceeded Tyre and Sidon in sinfulness. By such striking contrasts, our Lord shows that
people most blessed by God will be most punished if they spurn Him. Judgment
against the spiritual aloofness of Capernaum will far exceed judgment against the
egregious sins of Sodom. The sober truth is that the self-righteous, orthodox person
is more repugnant to the Father than the externally immoral, unbelieving person.

Johann Bengel once noted, "Every hearer of the New Testament truth is either
much happier or much more wretched than the men who lived before Christ's coming." Such people are either more secure or more condemned.

*Ask*YOURSELF

What is the basis for any feelings we have of superiority and supremacy? What
are some of the best cures for this type of sin? Which remedies would you prefer to
choose for yourself, rather than having some of the more extreme ones thrust upon
you?

Jesus Opens His Great Invitation

At that time Jesus said, "I praise You, Father, Lord of heaven and earth."

MATT. 11:25A

*W*HEN ALL LIFE'S RHETORIC, rationalizations, and routines are swept aside, a person is either for Jesus Christ or against Him (cf. Mark 9:40). After performing many miracles (Matt. 4:23–24) and preaching in detail the gospel and sanctification (chaps. 5–7), Jesus more specifically urged people either to accept Him or reject Him. Here begins a final appeal of grace and mercy during His first Galilean ministry.

This opening address to God calls our attention both to Christ's unique relationship to His Father and to the Father's sovereignty over all things, including salvation. Through the Holy Spirit, salvation is a divine provision and not a result of human wisdom, purposes, or ability, and Jesus is thankful for that.

Everyone who evangelizes is sometimes disappointed that so few people respond. We wonder how we can make the message clearer or more convincing, and what things we ought to change. But we also should remind ourselves that some will reject the gospel no matter how effectively we seem to present it. If people rebuffed the Lord when He was in their midst, we have to expect some will also refuse our imperfect witness to them.

We are sad and prayerful for those who don't want the gospel, but like Jesus we must praise our heavenly Father that He has sovereign control over the universe and that His plan for us and others—saved and unsaved—will not be thwarted. Men and women who reject Christ show their sinful disobedience, not any failure by God.

Ask YOURSELF

Seeing worship as such a natural reaction of Jesus—not in purely religious settings, but right in the middle of any moment—should spurn us on to make godly praise a frequent occupant in our heart and on our lips. How often does worship just well up inside you?

THOSE WHO MISS THE INVITATION

You have hidden these things from the wise and intelligent and have revealed
them to infants. Yes, Father, for this way was well-pleasing in Your sight.

MATT. 11:25B–26

*G*OD DOES NOT EXCLUDE INTELLIGENT people from His kingdom but
those who rely on their own intelligence for salvation. The apostle Paul was a scholar,
but he didn't abandon that brilliance to become a Christian. However, he did stop relying on that training to understand the things of God. Intellect is a gift from God,
but it becomes an impediment to authentic knowledge of Him when trust in it su-
persedes trust in the One who gave it.

The means God uses to hide things from certain people who relish their own
intelligence is the darkness of their proud hearts. God's truth is not knowable by
mere empirical means. Instead, it must be known and received through the faithful
heart, as God graciously reveals it. No amount of human insight can grasp God's saving truths since the unregenerate "cannot understand them, because they are spiritually appraised" (1 Cor. 2:14).

Of those who miss the divine invitation, the apostle John writes that, "though
He had performed so many signs before them, yet they were not believing in Him.
This was to fulfill the word of Isaiah the prophet which he spoke: 'Lord, who has believed our report? And to whom has the arm of the Lord been revealed?'. . . 'He has
blinded their eyes and He hardened their heart, so that they would not see with their
eyes and perceive with their heart, and be converted'" (John 12:37–38, 40). Those
who reject the gospel will one day have their unwise choice confirmed by God, the
all-wise Judge.

Ask YOURSELF

Yes, God's heart moves at the sight of simple trust, honest dependence, and
awareness of need. Does your heart likewise bend toward those who are the least deserving yet the most impoverished?

THOSE WHO ACCEPT THE INVITATION

You have hidden these things from the wise and intelligent and have revealed
them to infants. Yes, Father, for this way was well-pleasing in Your sight.

MATT. 11:25B–26

*A*N INFANT IS COMPLETELY DEPENDENT on others for everything he
or she needs. A baby has no resources of its own to draw upon for help. The same
Greek word (for "infants") is used of those who can't eat solid food (1 Cor. 3:1; Heb.
5:13). It is also used of those who can't speak (1 Cor. 13:11) and of those who are helpless (Eph. 4:14).

To such spiritual babes, those who realize they are utterly unable to save themselves, God wants to reveal the truths of His kingdom. As seen in the Sermon on the
Mount, the "poor in spirit" who humbly confess their dependency on the Father and
the Son receive a clear and irrevocable invitation to salvation.

Infants mentioned here are precisely the opposite kind of persons from the
proud Jewish leaders who opposed Jesus at every turn. They are also the antitheses
of supposed ideal practitioners of religion who glory in their own self-worth and
success.

God is totally satisfied to offer a gospel of grace because that glorifies Him. "For
thus says the high and exalted One who lives forever, whose name is Holy, 'I dwell
on a high and holy place, and also with the contrite and lowly of spirit in order to revive the spirit of the lowly and to revive the heart of the contrite'" (Isa. 57:15).

*Ask*YOURSELF

Would you say you've maintained this same spirit of contrition and trust since
you've entered into saving relationship with Jesus Christ? What tempts us to claim
more confidence in our own identity and our perceived deservedness?

JESUS IS GOD

All things have been handed over to Me by My Father; and no one knows the Son except the Father;
nor does anyone know the Father except the Son, and anyone to whom the Son wills to reveal Him.

MATT. 11:27

*A*NY GENUINE INVITATION to salvation such as Jesus gives here must include mention of God's revelation. Nobody, even the most sincerely religious or philosophically determined, has ever obtained real salvation unless God sovereignly revealed it—and such revelation has to include the truth that Jesus Christ is God.

Jesus without doubt or qualification equates Himself with God and calls Himself the Son of the Father. The Jews of His day would never have used the expression about divine fatherhood unless they were referring to God's fatherhood over their nation. Jesus' statement was and is one of His clearest declarations of deity, and it discloses an intimate, unique, and inseparable relationship with the Father.

Without question, Jesus' audience knew that His statements about a relationship with His heavenly Father meant He was claiming to be the Son of God. The unbelieving Jews did not at all accept this claim. On other similar occasions they would want to kill Him for such "blasphemous" assertions (see John 5:18; 10:30–38).

That Jesus is God is an essential component of the gospel, because apart from deity no savior could redeem a single soul. The heresy of making Christ just another human teacher or martyr devalues the gospel and robs it of its true saving power.

Ask YOURSELF

To trust God completely means also knowing that He is fully capable of revealing Himself to anyone He desires, any time He desires. Our task is merely to be faithful to reveal what we have heard and seen in Him, trusting the Lord to save His people. Are you being true to that calling?

REVELATION SOVEREIGNLY GIVEN

All things have been handed over to Me by My Father; and no one knows the Son except the Father;
nor does anyone know the Father except the Son, and anyone to whom the Son wills to reveal Him.

MATT. 11:27

*H*UMAN IDEAS AND CONCEPTS are temporal and completely incapable of producing spiritual truth or guidance. Only because God has sovereignly given all things to Christ and in turn revealed the Son to men and women can any of us be saved. God must break into the vacuum of the sinful human heart and reveal Himself before we can know Him.

Because the Father gave the Son all authority in the universe, Jesus had full right to send out His disciples to "make disciples of all the nations, baptizing them in the name of the Father and the Son and the Holy Spirit, teaching them to observe all that I commanded you" (Matt. 28:19–20a). When our Lord pronounced this Great Commission, His earthly ministry had already illustrated His sovereign authority and control over sin, disease, and death, as well as His supreme prerogative to forgive sins and redeem all who believe from the wrath to come. This was a divine preview of the complete authority Christ will have during His millennial reign over the earth.

Of God's sovereignty in revelation and salvation, we can apply the insight of the Reformer Martin Luther: "Here the bottom falls out of all merit, all powers and abilities of reason or the free will men dream of, and it all counts nothing before God. Christ must do and must give everything."

Ask YOURSELF

What did Christ reveal to you about Himself that led you to place your faith in Him? What has He revealed of Himself to you in recent days—fresh glimpses into His character, His nature, and His dealings with man?

JESUS CALLS FOR SAVING FAITH

Come to Me . . .
MATT. 11:28A

ALTHOUGH INFINITELY BEYOND HUMAN comprehension, God's sovereignty and human responsibility are inseparable in salvation. God sovereignly provides the grace that draws sinners, but they must humbly come in faith and commit to obey the Lord Jesus before salvation becomes complete. Christ makes this clear when He says, "All that the Father gives Me will come to Me, and the one who comes to Me I will certainly not cast out" (John 6:37).

Redemption comes not through human creed, denominational preferences, favorite rituals, certain pastors, priests, or theological gurus—but only through the atoning work of Jesus Christ. When He says "Come to Me," it means we must come to Him having trusted in His substitutionary death and having reached the point of willingness to submit to His lordship. The Lord teaches, "I am the bread of life; he who comes to Me will not hunger, and he who believes in Me will never thirst" (John 6:35). Coming to Jesus means believing in Him, and that results in no longer hungering or thirsting from a lack of salvation's blessings.

Jesus gave this summary of salvation, which includes the most well-known verse in Scripture: "Even so must the Son of Man be lifted up; so that whoever believes will in Him have eternal life. For God so loved the world, that He gave His only begotten Son, that whoever believes in Him shall not perish, but have eternal life" (John 3:14–16).

Ask YOURSELF

There are so many internal squabbles over the actual transaction of salvation. But can't we all agree that no one is saved unless Jesus does it—and that no one is given salvation unless the person receives it? May we be more concerned about men than we are about talks and meetings.

NOVEMBER 20

THE CONDITION OF THOSE CALLED

All who are weary and heavy-laden.

MATT. 11:28B

*E*VERYONE WHOM JESUS SPECIALLY invites for salvation already realizes their distress, that they are "weary and heavy-laden." The Lord mentions this after He refers to faith ("come to Me"), but chronologically it precedes faith—it is the repentance that prompts the person to trust in Jesus for salvation.

"Weary" refers symbolically to strenuous work in trying to find the divine path to salvation. Christ invites all to come to Him who have exhausted themselves in searching for salvation by their own resources. Whereas "weary" denotes internal exhaustion, "heavy-laden" implies that past heavy burdens dumped on the person caused him or her to engage in the futility of works righteousness to please God.

Any person in the condition Jesus describes despairs of his or her own ability to obtain salvation. They will realize the end of their own resources and want to turn to the Savior. The desperation implicit here is part of genuine salvation. Those not desperate will continue to rely on their own confidence, but those who are spiritually desperate will repent of the old burdensome life of sin and embrace the true redemption Christ offers. Such persons are the only ones God receives into His kingdom (cf. Matt. 3:2; 4:17; Acts 2:38; 2 Tim. 2:25).

Ask YOURSELF

What are the most common causes for that "weary and heavy-laden" feeling in our world today? Why are Jesus' ways of dealing with these problems infinitely superior to any other so-called solution?

THE NATURE OF TRUE REST

. . . and I will give you rest.

MATT. 11:28C

JESUS PROMISES GENUINE, unsurpassed spiritual rest to every person who turns to Him in repentance and humble faith. God's rest is a key scriptural theme, and the writer of Hebrews warns we must not take it for granted and miss it—especially if we think we're safe and yet do not believe, much as the Jews:

> Therefore, let us fear if, while a promise remains of entering His rest, any one of you may seem to have come short of it. For indeed we have had good news preached to us, just as they also; but the word they heard did not profit them, because it was not united by faith in those who heard. For we who have believed enter that rest, just as He has said, "As I swore in My wrath, they shall not enter My rest," although His works were finished from the foundation of the world. (Heb. 4:1–3)

The dictionary provides us several definitions of "rest" that remarkably parallel God's spiritual rest. *First*, rest is a cessation from activity and exertion. By analogy, divine rest means stopping all efforts at earning salvation. *Second*, rest means freedom from all that wearies or disturbs. And God's rest gives believers freedom from every worry.

Third, the dictionary calls rest a fixed, settled quality. Likewise spiritual rest means our eternal destiny is secure in Christ. And *finally*, rest means someone can be confident and trustful. The spiritual parallel is the assurance that "He who began a good work in you will perfect it until the day of Christ Jesus" (Phil. 1:6).

Ask YOURSELF

Are you suffering from a lack of rest and contentment in your life? What are the main culprits for this? Even if your current circumstances were to change very little, is it possible that God's brand of rest could still settle down among it all?

SUBMISSION TO JESUS CHRIST

*Take My yoke upon you and learn from Me, for I am gentle and humble in heart,
and you will find rest for your souls. For My yoke is easy and My burden is light.*

MATT. 11:29–30

*J*ESUS' GREAT INVITATION INCLUDES a call to submission, which inherently includes obedience and is symbolized by a yoke. The "yoke" was made of wood and designed to fit comfortably on the neck and shoulders of a work animal to prevent chafing. An ancient aphorism says, "Put your neck under the yoke and let your soul receive instruction."

By analogy, Christ wants His disciples to be submissive and learn from Him. They must submit for many reasons, but foremost is to be taught by Him through the Word.

But in the process of submission, Jesus is "gentle and humble in heart" and graciously gives rest, not weariness, to His obedient disciples. Our Lord will never give us burdens too heavy to carry, because His burdens have nothing to do with works of the law or the human tradition of good deeds.

If we are faithful and submissive, our work of obedience to Christ will be joyful and happy. The apostle John explains, "This is the love of God, that we keep His commandments; and His commandments are not burdensome" (1 John 5:3). Submission to Jesus Christ is the only true liberation anyone can experience, because only then can one become what God intended.

> Thy precious will, O conquering Saviour,
> Doth now embrace and compass me;
> All discords hushed, my peace a river,
> My soul a prisoned bird set free.
> Sweet will of God still fold me closer,
> Till I am wholly lost in Thee.

Ask YOURSELF

Jesus' purpose in calling you to submission is not to embitter you but to better you. Is anything keeping you from trusting that?

GRAINFIELDS AND THE SABBATH

At that time Jesus went through the grainfields on the Sabbath, and His disciples became
hungry and began to pick the heads of grain and eat. But when the Pharisees saw this,
they said to Him, "Look, Your disciples do what is not lawful to do on a Sabbath."

MATT. 12:1–2

*K*EEPING THE SABBATH was still a binding ceremonial duty for the Jews of Jesus' day, but most of them had little idea of God's original purpose for the day. Instead of being a day of rest, it had become a day of burden with thousands of manmade restrictions. Ironically it became harder to "rest" than to work the other six days.

The Sabbath had ceased being a delight for people but had become oppressive and frustrating. They were undoubtedly tired of the unscriptural system imposed on the day and welcomed any proper teaching about the Sabbath.

It's difficult to know what the Pharisees were doing in the fields this day, other than to be watchdogs over the human traditions of the Sabbath. Their accusation that Jesus' disciples had broken the Sabbath law was simply wrong because it elevated human tradition to the level of God's Word. Centuries of observing rabbinic ritual had given it the status of legitimate law in the legalistic minds of the Pharisees. They gave only lip service to Scripture and merely used it to justify their traditions, many of which "invalidated the word of God" (Matt. 15:6).

The Jewish leaders' indictment of Jesus and His disciples on this occasion illustrates a desire to merely protect their distorted, man-made conventions. In that way it perverted God's original purpose for the Sabbath, which was to give humanity a special day to rest and serve Him, not to deal with an exasperating list of regulations.

Ask YOURSELF

How do you deal with others' expectations, even when you know they're forcing unreasonable requirements on you? Do you fulfill them out of a need to be thought highly of? How does a person balance freedom with proper responsibility?

THE SABBATH AND DEEDS OF NECESSITY

But He said to them, "Have you not read what David did when he became hungry,
he and his companions, how he entered the house of God, and they ate the consecrated bread,
which was not lawful for him to eat nor for those with him, but for the priests alone?"

MATT. 12:3–4

*D*AVID THE GREAT KING, PSALMIST, and warrior was a true hero of the Jews, even more so than the prophets and patriarchs were. Jesus here reminds the Pharisees of what happened when David and his men sought to escape the vengeful and jealous King Saul south of Gibeah. They asked for food when they came to the town where the tabernacle was located.

Ahimelech the priest gave David and his men the bread of the Presence because there was "no ordinary bread on hand" (1 Sam. 21:4). That consecrated bread was baked weekly, and each Sabbath day twelve new loaves (representing the twelve tribes of Israel) replaced the previous ones. Only the priests could eat these loaves.

On that unusual occasion, however, God allowed an exception for the sake of David and his companions, who were weakened by hunger. This exceptional action did not offend the Lord, and consequently He did not discipline either David or Ahimelech. It was better for the men to violate a ceremonial regulation if it was necessary to meet their basic needs.

If God allowed His people to sometimes disregard His own law in order to benefit their welfare, how could He not allow the purposeless and silly traditions of men and women to be broken so a work of necessity could take place?

*Ask*YOURSELF

How does this picture of a practical God square with your perception of Him? Are we sometimes protective and provincial about the name of God for reasons all our own—or perhaps as excuses for not dirtying our hands with human need?

THE SABBATH AND SERVICE TO GOD

Or have you not read in the Law, that on the Sabbath the priests in the temple break the
Sabbath and are innocent? But I say to you that something greater than the temple is here.
MATT. 12:5–6

*S*ELDOM WOULD ANY CHRISTIAN today, even the most fastidious and rule-oriented among us, consider preaching, teaching Sunday school, leading youth ministry, or other similar work as profaning the Lord's Day. Yet these activities require much time and effort—on Sunday. Likewise, the most scrupulous of the Jewish leaders in Jesus' time viewed the priests as innocent of any Sabbath breaking, even though such men worked in the temple twice as hard as on other days. For instance, sacrifices offered on the Sabbath were actually double sacrifices, requiring double the work of offering the normal daily sacrifice (Num. 28:9–10; cf. Lev. 24:8–9).

In this encounter, Jesus embarrassed and upset the Pharisees by showing how inconsistent their legalistic logic was. But they were even more upset and angry when He told them that something far greater and more important than the temple was in their midst. This was somewhat of an oblique reference, but the Jews had no doubt that Jesus was referring to Himself and again claiming to be God (cf. Matt. 9:2–6; 11:3–5, 25–27).

Our Lord's main purpose, however, was not to prove His deity to the Jewish leaders. It was to argue that, in light of that deity, He had the right and authority to set aside Sabbath regulation as He saw fit—even more prerogative than did David or the temple priests. And above all, no human traditions or customary ways of doing things could or should ever hinder genuine service for God.

Ask YOURSELF

Some may view this as saying that Jesus was flippant about the commandments of God, as if they weren't actually that important and could be ignored if desired. How would you respond to a person who saw an inconsistency in the meaning of this passage?

THE SABBATH AND ACTS OF MERCY

But if you had known what this means, "I desire compassion, and not a sacrifice,"
you would not have condemned the innocent. For the Son of Man is Lord of the Sabbath.

MATT. 12:7–8

$\mathcal{G}$OD HAS NOT HESITATED to set aside His laws for the sake of mercy toward sinners. Otherwise none of them would be saved or even born, because He would have destroyed them right after they sinned. God's plan was not to condemn all sinners but to save from its penalty those who believe in His Son. And if a righteous and just God displays that kind of love and mercy, how much more ought His children reflect the same quality of mercy?

Because the Old Testament Sabbath was God's special day, faithful Jews would have wanted to show mercy on that day. But the leaders, due to their wrong-headed interpretation of the Sabbath and their basic unbelief, actually violated the spirit of the Sabbath. They refused acts of mercy on that day, not because of biblical devotion to the law, but because they lacked compassion.

Since the "Lord of the Sabbath" has come, the obligation of a Sabbath rest is no longer applicable to believers. Under the new covenant, they have the freedom as to whether or not they honor any day above others. Whatever position they take, they must glorify the Lord (Rom. 14:5–6), but not impose their thinking on fellow believers (Gal. 4:9–10; Col. 2:16).

Strict Sabbath observance was never to supplant sincere mercy and compassion by believers. God is merciful and commands us as Christians to be merciful.

Ask YOURSELF

Rather than looking at the Sabbath as a day for *not* doing certain things, what might be some deliberate actions you could undertake on the Sabbath, whether in hospitality or compassion or service?

THE SABBATH IN PERSPECTIVE: AN ILLUSTRATION

*He said to them, "What man is there among you who has a sheep, and if it falls into a pit on the
Sabbath, will he not take hold of it and lift it out? How much more valuable then is a man than
a sheep! So then, it is lawful to do good on the Sabbath." Then He said to the man, "Stretch
out your hand!" He stretched it out, and it was restored to normal, like the other.*

MATT. 12:11–13

ONE OF THE TRAGEDIES OF HINDUISM in India is its distorted disregard
for human welfare. You should not give food to a beggar because that might interfere
with his karma and keep him from suffering on a higher level of existence. You
should not kill a fly because it could be the reincarnation of a person. For the same
reason, you must allow rats to live and eat whatever they want. Hindus consider cows
sacred and feed them whatever food is available. At the same time, they let certain
people starve.

Similarly, the Jewish leaders in Jesus' time despised other people and showed
more compassion for their sheep than for the handicapped man here. Mark's account
says Jesus asked, "'Is it lawful to do good or to do harm on the Sabbath, to save a life
or to kill?' But they kept silent" (Mark 3:4). The Pharisees couldn't say anything because they would have been forced either to contradict their tradition or advocate
murder. Their only external response was to remain silent, but undoubtedly they
"were filled with rage" (Luke 6:11).

Our Lord answered His own question with the clear declaration, "So then, it is
lawful to do good on the Sabbath." He then healed the man's deformed hand as the
Pharisees' resentment no doubt rose to new heights. Christ not only *approved* of doing
good on the Sabbath, He went ahead and actually *performed* good on behalf of another. If anything, this set forth the Sabbath as *the* supreme day for doing good.

Ask YOURSELF

What teachings of Scripture do you still mainly follow out of dutiful habit, not
with an eye toward honoring God or being used as a blessing to others? What has
your legalistic adherence gained for you, and what has it cost you?

THE PERILS OF LEGALISM

But the Pharisees went out and conspired against Him, as to how they might destroy Him.

MATT. 12:14

*S*OMETIMES NEITHER THE MOST persuasive arguments nor the most convincing deeds will change someone's hard-hearted opposition. Such was the case for the Pharisees' challenge to Jesus in considering the proper significance and use of the Sabbath. He had irrefutably connected the divine virtues of benevolence, kindness, mercy, goodness, and compassion with scriptural Sabbath observance. But the Pharisees stubbornly rejected His exhortations and clung to their legalistic works and self-styled traditions. Not even God's Word or the powerful demonstration by His Son would change their hard hearts.

Such legalism has always been an implacable enemy of grace. Even the law of Moses, with all its demands, reflected a strong measure of God's grace in that it pointed men and women toward Christ as the only true hope of salvation. Paul says this about it: "Therefore the Law has become our tutor to lead us to Christ, so that we may be justified by faith" (Gal. 3:24). If the very law of God has this more secondary role, how much less place does human tradition have in pleasing God?

Legalism and man-centered customs are also barriers to faithful, biblical sanctification *after* we are saved. The apostle again asked the Galatians, "Are you so foolish? Having begun by the Spirit, are you now being perfected by the flesh?" (3:3). We must make sure that we, too, can answer this question rightly, bearing in mind Paul's later admonition to the Galatian believers: "It was for freedom that Christ set us free; therefore keep standing firm and do not be subject again to a yoke of slavery" (5:1).

Ask YOURSELF

What do you plan to do to any remaining vestiges of legalism in your heart? And how do you intend to encourage others to do the same purifying work?

JESUS COMMENDED BY HIS FATHER

Behold, My Servant whom I have chosen; My Beloved in whom My soul is well-pleased.
MATT. 12:18A

JESUS CHRIST IS GOD'S ULTIMATE Servant, the one and only Son chosen by the Father to die for fallen sinners. The divine commendation here is a modified quotation of Isaiah 42:1–4, one of the most beautiful descriptions of our Lord anywhere in the Bible. The Father's choice of Jesus to be His Servant was decisive and irrevocable—Christ was the one and only person perfectly qualified for the work of redemption.

As the perfect choice of God, Jesus is also completely pleasing in His Father's eyes. Although the world hated and rejected Him, Christ is God's Beloved—and in that role He brings us salvation by divine grace (Eph. 1:6–7).

This is not the only mention in the gospels of God's approval of His Son. The Father used similar words at Jesus' baptism (Matt. 3:17) and at His transfiguration (Matt. 17:5). Jesus Himself elaborates further: "If I alone testify about Myself, My testimony is not true. There is another who testifies of Me, and I know that the testimony which He gives about Me is true.... And the Father who sent Me, He has testified of Me" (John 5:31–32, 37).

If we want to be well-pleasing to God as Jesus is, we must come to the Father through His Son, drawn by the Holy Spirit. "Those who are in the flesh cannot please God. However, you are not in the flesh but in the Spirit, if indeed the Spirit of God dwells in you" (Rom. 8:8–9).

Ask YOURSELF

Have you grown "weary and heavy-laden" trying to please God with your best efforts? Will your heart ever find peace and satisfaction in knowing that your faith has been counted as righteousness, that the Father is already satisfied with the Son's sacrifice in your place?

NOVEMBER 30

Jesus Commissioned by the Holy Spirit

I will put My Spirit upon Him.

MATT. 12:18B

*T*HE PROPHET PROMISED that God would put His Holy Spirit upon Messiah in a special way, and the Spirit did descend on Jesus at His baptism (Matt. 3:16). But that was not when the Spirit first indwelt Him, because the Holy Spirit conceived Him (Matt. 1:20).

Yet, if Jesus was the preexistent Son, eternally a member of the Godhead, why would the Spirit need to come upon Him during His incarnation? *First*, the Spirit needed to empower Jesus' human nature. Our Lord was fully human, even to the extent of being tempted, yet He did not sin (Heb. 4:15). When He was a child, He grew and matured in favor with God and humanity (Luke 2:52). As an adult, He experienced the full range of human feelings and emotions. Therefore as a human being He needed the indwelling power of the Spirit (Acts 10:38) so He could function in concert with His deity.

Second, the Spirit commissioned Jesus in order to attest to His messianic service. Early in His ministry, Jesus applied Isaiah's prophecy to Himself: "The Spirit of the Lord is upon Me, because He anointed Me to preach the gospel to the poor. He has sent Me to proclaim release to the captives, and recovery of sight to the blind, to set free those who are oppressed, to proclaim the favorable year of the Lord" (Luke 4:18–19). This passage was not only fulfilled for Jesus' audience but for us as well—we can know He ministered fully empowered by the Holy Spirit.

Ask YOURSELF

When was the last time you saw love or wisdom or some other valuable trait come forth from your life, and you knew it had to be the Spirit of Christ at work in you? Respond to such instances with true praise, and with a desire for more and more of His nature to be implanted in you.

DECEMBER 1

JESUS' MESSAGE IS FOR EVERYONE

And He shall proclaim justice to the Gentiles.

MATT. 12:18C

*C*ONTRARY TO JEWISH THINKING and expectations, the Messiah would be the Redeemer for all nationalities, not just the Jews. In fact, the Jews were to be the ones to proclaim God's grace to the rest of the world. God told Abraham, "In you all the families of the earth will be blessed" (Gen. 12:3). It is therefore rather ironic that the Jews would resist the concept that God's good news was for all peoples.

The reality that Jesus' message would be for all mankind was readily apparent early in His ministry. The first woman He reached was a Samaritan (John 4:26). Concerning the Roman centurion whose servant He healed, the Lord said, "Truly I say to you, I have not found such great faith with anyone in Israel" (Matt. 8:10).

But the idea of Messiah coming to preach to and redeem some Gentiles was still anathema to the Jews. When Paul addressed a large number of Jews in Jerusalem and told them God had commanded him, "Go! For I will send you far away to the Gentiles," that sparked an intense reaction from them: "Away with such a fellow from the earth, for he should not be allowed to live!" (Acts 22:21, 22).

A real gospel stumbling block for the Jews was the truth that redemption and fellowship with God were for Gentiles as well as for them. But the saving message Jesus proclaimed has always been for people from every part of the world, without distinction—a fact over which we can all rejoice.

*Ask*YOURSELF

Increasingly each day, the makeup of America's population reflects the faces of numerous nationalities and people groups. How open is your heart to their need for Christ's salvation?

DECEMBER 2

MEEKNESS FROM JESUS, COMFORT FOR THE WEAK

He will not quarrel, nor cry out; nor will anyone hear His voice in the streets.
A battered reed He will not break off, and a smoldering wick He will not put out.

MATT. 12:19–20A

*T*HE LORD JESUS DID NOT CAJOLE or browbeat people with the gospel like some inflammatory demagogue who stirs up his listeners by pandering to their emotions and prejudices. Christ always spoke plainly, with dignity and control—His only persuasive technique was the truth. He never resorted to the lies and scheming of His enemies. As the Son of God and Messiah, He never attempted to gain a hearing or a following by appealing to political power or using physical force.

Christ's approach was the way of meekness, gentleness, and lowliness, because many of His hearers were like the battered reed or smoldering wick. They were people whose lives were broken or worn out, and the world wanted to discard them. An unbelieving society nearly always wants to cast off such people as useless or worthless.

The nature of sinful humanity is to destroy—people commit murder, arson, vandalism, and viciously slander one another in business, politics, the family—but God's nature is to restore. Jesus will not "break off" or "put out" the least of those who sincerely come to Him. He also issues a strong warning to any who would cause vulnerable people to fall: "Whoever causes one of these little ones who believe in Me to stumble, it would be better for him to have a heavy millstone hung around his neck, and to be drowned in the depth of the sea" (Matt. 18:6).

Our Lord will always restore the battered reed and rekindle the smoldering wick.

Ask YOURSELF

Is gentleness a trait that comes hard for you? In what way have you been aware of a hardness or coldness in your approach to other people—an insensitivity that dearly needs the restorative touch of Christ's nature in your heart and mind?

DECEMBER 3

TO SPEAK IN PARABLES

He spoke many things to them in parables.

MATT. 13:3A

*T*HE PARABLE WAS ONE of the staple teaching tools the Lord Jesus used to convey spiritual truth in an understandable way. The word *parable* contains the idea of placing something alongside something else to make a comparison. In this way, Jesus would place a moral truth alongside a physical example that people could more easily grasp. By this common form of Jewish teaching, He used a common object or practice to elucidate an intangible truth or principle.

From His earliest teaching sessions, Christ used graphic analogies to instruct on divine truth. He likened believers to salt and light in this world (Matt. 5:13–16), pointed to the example of the birds and flowers concerning life's essentials (6:26–30), and said Christians must build on the rock-solid foundation of Scripture rather than the loose sand of human philosophy (7:24–27). These and other illustrations contain clear meanings. They resonate with listeners. And they served the purpose of setting the stage for Jesus' use of full-fledged parables.

Parables and other symbolic and figurative communication methods, when correctly understood, are genuine friends of the student of God's Word. They make abstract truths more concrete, interesting, easier to remember, and easier to apply to life. Those were always the goals our Lord envisioned as He related any parables, such as the series of kingdom parables.

Ask YOURSELF

What can we learn from Jesus' teaching style to help us improve our own spiritual communication, whether in formal lessons and sermons or simply in the ordinary vehicles of conversation?

DECEMBER 4

THE KINGDOM OF HEAVEN

To you it has been granted to know the mysteries of the kingdom of heaven.

MATT. 13:11

*I*N THE LORD'S PRAYER (Matt. 6:10) we see two aspects of the kingdom of heaven. "On earth" refers to the present kingdom, mediated through God's servants, and "in heaven" refers to God's universal, direct reign.

Through the centuries the present kingdom has attracted both true and false citizens. Only God can infallibly distinguish true citizens (the redeemed) from false ones. Jesus shows that many branches that seem to belong to the vine actually do not. The spurious ones will be pruned away and thrown into the fire (John 15:2, 6). Such people only superficially identify with Christ but are never really citizens of the kingdom of heaven or part of the body of Christ. They appear to be true citizens only from an imperfect human perspective.

Paradoxically, Scripture uses terms such as *Israel, God's people,* and *disciples* that can include both nominal and genuine believers. Paul does make it clear, however, that "he is a Jew who is one inwardly; and circumcision is that which is of the heart" (Rom. 2:29; cf. 9:6–7). Only at the very end of the age, when the eternal kingdom begins, will those who are true citizens of God's kingdom be clear to everyone. (Even during the Millennium, when Christ directly rules on earth, there will be disloyal citizens; cf. Rev. 20:7–8.)

The only way now to ensure your kingdom citizenship is to repent, trust in Jesus Christ, and pursue the sanctification that new life in Him brings (cf. Mark 1:15).

Ask YOURSELF

What should churches do to discern and encourage those who are Christians in name only to put their faith in Christ wholeheartedly? Why do we tend to avoid dealing in touchy matters like these? And what is the result of our reticence?

DECEMBER 5

MEASURING PROGRESS: REVEALING AND CONCEALING

For whoever has, to him more shall be given, and he will have an abundance;
but whoever does not have, even what he has shall be taken away from him.

MATT. 13:12

*J*UST PRIOR TO THIS STATEMENT, Jesus told the disciples the twofold reason for His using parables: "To you it has been granted to know the mysteries of the kingdom of heaven, but to them it has not been granted" (Matt. 13:11). To believers, parables reveal kingdom truth; to unbelievers, they conceal it.

Those to whom God has sovereignly given eternal life through Christ are the true citizens of His kingdom. Of such persons Jesus says, "to him more shall be given." Believers receive additional light of truth as they grow in obedience and maturity in the Lord. As believers remain faithful, God reveals more and more light until they "have an abundance."

In contrast, false citizens of the kingdom, because of their unbelief, have whatever amount of divine truth that is nearby concealed from them. Thousands heard Jesus' teachings (including the parables) and saw His miracles, but most did not recognize Him as Messiah or receive Him as Lord and Savior. Because such unbelievers refuse God's light as it shines on them, He conceals it from them and they drift further into spiritual darkness.

All people are either progressing or regressing spiritually—there is no such thing as remaining static. The longer that believers serve Christ, the more He reveals His truth and power to them. And the longer unbelievers reject what little knowledge they may have of the gospel, the less of God's truth they will understand. It's vitally important to be on the right side of the revealing/concealing equation.

Ask YOURSELF

When have you experienced the exponential blessing of seeing your small amount of knowledge and insight transformed into increasing quantities? What does this tell you about the value of even small strides in study and learning?

DECEMBER 6

PARABLES CONCEAL

Therefore I speak to them in parables; because while seeing they do not see, and while hearing they do not hear, nor do they understand. In their case the prophecy of Isaiah is being fulfilled, which says, "You will keep on hearing, but will not understand; you will keep on seeing, but will not perceive; for the heart of this people has become dull, with their ears they scarcely hear, and they have closed their eyes, otherwise they would see with their eyes, hear with their ears, and understand with their heart and return, and I would heal them."

MATT. 13:13–15

*J*ESUS QUOTED THIS PASSAGE from Isaiah 6:9–10 to describe the unbelieving Jews of His day. Isaiah pronounced judgment on the people of Judah for their pervasive sin and rebellion. As part of the Lord's judgment, they were led away into captivity by Babylon, yet still they refused to repent and trust God's mercies. Because the people in the prophet's day intentionally closed their eyes and ears and refused any heartfelt understanding of truth, God judicially sealed them in their unbelief.

Christ's parables served as similar forms of judgment on unbelief. Those who refused His previous, straightforward teachings would not be able to grasp His deeper, parabolic instructions.

Paul also quotes from Isaiah in reference to another first-century judgment on unbelievers: "In the Law it is written, 'By men of strange tongues and by the lips of strangers I will speak to this people, and even so they will not listen to Me,' says the Lord. So then tongues are for a sign, not to those who believe but to unbelievers; but prophecy is for a sign, not to unbelievers but to those who believe" (1 Cor. 14:21–22). God allowed tongues (various human languages) to play a dramatic role on Pentecost and periodically thereafter as a testimony against those who refused to accept the gospel. Thus the Lord sometimes conceals His word to those predisposed to reject it.

Ask YOURSELF

Is there any pattern of rejection or disbelief in your mind as you deal with the holy Scriptures? Praise the Lord that He makes His Word plain to those called to be His children.

DECEMBER 7

PARABLES REVEAL

But blessed are your eyes, because they see; and your ears, because they hear. For truly I say to you that many prophets and righteous men desired to see what you see, and did not see it, and to hear what you hear, and did not hear it.

MATT. 13:16–17

*A*S BELIEVERS, WE CAN understand God's profoundest revelation, whether parables or other teachings, because biblical writers have recorded them and the Spirit has illumined them for us (cf. 1 Cor. 2:9–10). When Christ finished explaining some parables to the apostles and asked if they understood them, they could honestly answer "Yes" (Matt. 13:51). That's not because they were more intelligent than the educated yet unbelieving Jewish leaders, but because the apostles' eyes and ears were opened to God's truth by way of their belief.

In part, our Lord's ministry was to provide understanding of His Word to His followers (see Mark 4:34). Right to the end of His time on earth, Jesus "explained to them the things concerning Himself in all the Scriptures" (Luke 24:27; cf. v. 45).

Not even the most faithful Old Testament believers had the insights to revelation that the disciples and every believer since have had.

As to this salvation, the prophets who prophesied of the grace that would come to you made careful searches and inquiries, seeking to know what person or time the Spirit of Christ within them was indicating as He predicted the sufferings of Christ and the glories to follow. It was revealed to them that they were not serving themselves, but you, in these things which now have been announced to you through those who preached the gospel to you by the Holy Spirit sent from heaven. (1 Peter 1:10–12)

Ask YOURSELF

The psalmist prayed, "Open my eyes, that I may behold wonderful things from Your law" (Ps. 119:18). Make this your heartfelt prayer today, knowing that God will delight in answering you.

PARABLE OF THE SOWER: MAIN ELEMENTS

Hear then the parable of the sower . . .

MATT. 13:18

*T*HE BIBLE IS GOD'S WRITTEN Word, but His Son is the Living Word who gives Scripture life. Christ told the Jewish leaders, "You search the Scriptures because you think that in them you have eternal life; it is these that testify about Me" (John 5:39).

This parable centers on proclaiming the gospel and, perhaps more important, concerns the "heart soils" on which that truth, in seed form, falls as the sower preaches. Our Lord goes on to describe four such soils, representing four different hearts that hear the gospel.

Although every human heart is essentially hostile toward God (Rom. 8:7; Eph. 2:15–16), every one has the potential for redemption. If a heart does not respond savingly, it is because of its *own* sin and refusal to believe. Jesus declares, "All that the Father gives Me will come to Me, and the one who comes to Me I will certainly not cast out" (John 6:37).

In a general sense, any of us who preaches or testifies to the gospel is a sower of God's Word. This parable thus reminds us of the need to be faithful in truly presenting the gospel, given the wonderful results that can occur. As William Arnot wrote: "As every leaf of the forest and every ripple on the lake, which itself receives a sunbeam on its breast, may throw the sunbeam off again, and so spread the light around; in like manner, everyone, old or young, who receives Christ into his heart may and will publish with his life and lips that blessed name."

Ask YOURSELF

How have you experienced one or more of the various soils' responses to your sharing of gospel truth? What have you learned about the reasons why various people respond to Christ's message of salvation in different ways?

PARABLE OF THE SOWER: UNRESPONSIVE HEARERS

When anyone hears the word of the kingdom and does not understand it,
the evil one comes and snatches away what has been sown in his heart.
This is the one on whom seed was sown beside the road.

MATT. 13:19

*T*HE HARD-PACKED SOIL beside the road represents the unresponsive hearer who "does not understand" the gospel, solely because of his or her own hard-heartedness. The person has continually resisted the gospel or anything else related to true spirituality because of an insensitive, impervious heart.

The Word lies on the surface of the unresponsive heart, exposed to attack by Satan. Such a hearer's lack of repentance insulates him or her from Christ's help and leaves them victim to assault by the enemy of the soul.

Such people remind us of the fools who hate wisdom and instruction (Prov. 1:7) and say there is no God (Ps. 14:1). They are often self-satisfied and self-righteous, and the gospel is simply veiled to them because "the god of this world has blinded the minds of the unbelieving so that they might not see the light of the gospel" (2 Cor. 4:4).

Satan uses various means to snatch away the seed sown: false teachers who promote spiritual lies, fear of human opinion that opposes Christianity, pride that blinds people to their real needs, and all sorts of other sinful prejudices against the truth of God's Word. All of these realities ought to prompt us toward prayer for and reaching out to the lost so that God may save some.

Ask YOURSELF

If lack of repentance is the key ingredient in shielding people from their need for Christ, we must continually guard ourselves from this hardened condition, even after being saved. Would this be a good time to deal directly with any unconfessed sin, turning away from it and back to the mercies of God?

DECEMBER 10

PARABLE OF THE SOWER: SUPERFICIAL HEARERS, PART 1

The one on whom seed was sown on the rocky places, this is the man who hears the word
and immediately receives it with joy; yet he has no firm root in himself, but is only temporary,
and when affliction or persecution arises because of the word, immediately he falls away.

MATT. 13:20–21

SHALLOW ACCEPTANCE OF THE GOSPEL can be encouraged by shallow evangelism that promises blessings of salvation but ignores the costs of discipleship. If people just "make a decision" for Jesus Christ without accepting all His claims on their lives, they can become insulated from genuine salvation.

When superficial hearers first hear the gospel, they have a euphoric religious experience, believing that at last God has met their felt needs. They are often zealous and energetic in church activities and eager to tell others about their new happiness.

But sadly for such people, all the change is superficial rather than deep-down in the heart. Their feelings are changed, but not their souls. There is no repentance, mourning over sin, or humility, which is the first trait of real conversion (cf. Matt. 5:3). Such a person has placed his or her religious house on the sand, and when the storms of trials and persecution come, the house crumbles and washes away (Matt. 7:26–27).

For the superficial hearer, God's truth has penetrated only the edge of the mind, but not the heart. That is why, when the high cost of salvation does confront the person, the gospel can be as quickly renounced as it was once seemingly accepted. Spiritual reality has no root and thus can't produce true spiritual fruit, which as Jesus soon makes clear, is the only sure evidence of a transformed life.

Ask YOURSELF

How can you come closer to ensuring that those with whom you share your Christian faith are not given the impression that salvation is a quick, emotional, unthinking decision?

PARABLE OF THE SOWER: SUPERFICIAL HEARERS, PART 2

The one on whom seed was sown on the rocky places, this is the man who hears the word
and immediately receives it with joy; yet he has no firm root in himself, but is only temporary,
and when affliction or persecution arises because of the word, immediately he falls away.

MATT. 13:20–21

*T*HOSE WHO ONLY SUPERFICIALLY receive the gospel might be baptized, join a church, and seem for a long time to be Christians. But trials and testings will eventually expose such persons' spiritual lifelessness. Such difficulties are not the ordinary hardships of life but the problems encountered "because of the word." When the Christian life's demands get too severe, the person discontinues any pretense of following the Lord.

"Falls away" is the translation of *skandalizō*, the Greek verb that means to cause to stumble and can include the concept of offending someone. We get the English *scandalize* from it. All these ideas fit the superficial hearer because when something really tests his or her faith, they stumble, become offended, and abandon the gospel (cf. John 8:31; 1 John 2:19).

If a person's profession of salvation doesn't include real conviction of sin, a strong desire for the Lord, and a love for His Word, along with willingness to suffer for Him if need be, it's only a matter of time before that one renounces any previous profession of faith.

It is encouraging, however, that the same kind of tribulation that makes the false believer wither makes the true believer stronger. "All who desire to live godly in Christ Jesus will be persecuted" (2 Tim. 3:12); but "after you have suffered for a little while, the God of all grace, who called you to His eternal glory in Christ, will Himself perfect, confirm, strengthen and establish you" (1 Peter 5:10).

Ask YOURSELF

Everything of real value comes with a cost. Why should Christianity be any different? Where do we get the idea that following Christ should require little effort and be met with little resistance, both from within and without?

PARABLE OF THE SOWER: WORLDLY HEARERS

And the one on whom seed was sown among the thorns, this is the man who hears the word,
and the worry of the world and the deceitfulness of wealth choke the word, and it becomes unfruitful.

MATT. 13:22

*F*EW THINGS OBSTRUCT THE GOSPEL'S reception in someone's heart more than the general love of the world and wealth. Note these warnings:

> For the love of money is a root of all sorts of evil, and some by longing for it have wandered away from the faith and pierced themselves with many griefs. (1 Tim. 6:10)

> Do not love the world nor the things in the world. If anyone loves the world, the love of the Father is not in him. For all that is in the world, the lust of the flesh and the lust of the eyes and the boastful pride of life, is not from the Father, but is from the world. (1 John 2:15–16)

The worldly hearer in this parable is oblivious to the deception of money and its inability to give lasting satisfaction. He or she doesn't notice how worldliness—the worshipful priority of money, possessions, career, and other temporary affairs—can smother the Word. Such a reality shows that the individual has a heart full of sinful weeds that cannot coexist for long with the Word of God. If faith is genuine, it will forsake the world; otherwise, sin will choke out the Word.

Christ's cleansing is thorough in true conversion. Salvation removes sin's weeds from the heart and prepares it to receive the seed of the Word. Genuine believers will continually confess sin and allow the Lord to be "faithful and righteous to forgive" (1 John 1:9), freeing them from sin's domination.

Ask YOURSELF

Does this mean money is a bad thing? Should it be avoided by people who bear the name of Christ? How would you define a proper, biblical perspective on wealth and possessions?

DECEMBER 13

PARABLE OF THE SOWER: RECEPTIVE HEARERS

*And the one on whom seed was sown on the good soil, this is the man who hears the word and under-
stands it; who indeed bears fruit and brings forth, some a hundredfold, some sixty, and some thirty.*

MATT. 13:23

*T*HE ULTIMATE BARRIER TO SALVATION is unbelief, and anyone willing
to receive the gospel on Christ's terms proves he or she is "good soil." God honors the
humble faith of receptive hearers and opens their spiritual ears, minds, and hearts,
allowing them to understand the gospel.

The example of the receptive hearers ought to encourage everyone who has
ever witnessed in Christ's name. Despite the nature and prevalence of the other hearers, there are always some whose hearts have good soil in which the gospel can take
root and flourish—people prepared by the Spirit to receive the truth.

Spiritual fruit is the inevitable by-product of spiritual life. Receptive hearers
will demonstrate fruitfulness in both attitude—"love, joy, peace, patience, kindness,
goodness, faithfulness, gentleness, self-control" (Gal. 5:22–23)—and behavior, which
Paul calls "the fruit of righteousness which comes through Jesus Christ" (Phil. 1:11;
cf. Col. 1:6). We are not saved by bearing fruit or doing good works, but we are saved
to become fruitbearers (Eph. 2:10).

Jesus not only assures us here that believers will bear fruit, but that we will bear
it abundantly: "some a hundredfold, some sixty, and some thirty." These figures represent an extraordinarily abundant yield for the regions Jesus ministered in. They
do not guarantee that we all will produce that much; but they do show the produc-
tive results of sowing the Word and emphasize that true believers will indeed produce fruit. That's the point of Jesus' parable.

*Ask*YOURSELF

Besides the obvious blessings and service opportunities created by fruitbear-
ing, what other benefits pour into the lives of those who hear the Word and take it
to heart?

DECEMBER 14

THE WHEAT AND THE TARES

The kingdom of heaven may be compared to a man who sowed good seed in his field. But while his men were sleeping, his enemy came and sowed tares among the wheat, and went away. But when the wheat sprouted and bore grain, then the tares became evident also. The slaves of the landowner came and said to him, "Sir, did you not sow good seed in your field? How then does it have tares?" And he said to them, "An enemy has done this!" The slaves said to him, "Do you want us, then, to go and gather them up?" But he said, "No; for while you are gathering up the tares, you may uproot the wheat with them. Allow both to grow together until the harvest; and in the time of the harvest I will say to the reapers, 'First gather up the tares and bind them in bundles to burn them up; but gather the wheat into my barn.'"

MATT. 13:24–30; SEE VV. 36–43

*T*HROUGHOUT REDEMPTIVE HISTORY, our Lord has planted believers ("good seed") in the world as His witnesses, to be faithful to Him, become fruitful plants of righteousness, and reflect His will before a corrupt world. The tares, by contrast, are the children of Satan—unbelievers spread throughout the world until they thoroughly outnumber the wheat by a large margin.

"The harvest" represents the Father's judgment at the end of the age, when His angels will execute sentence on the many unbelievers, just as the human reapers separated the tares from the wheat and burned them.

The apostles likely were ready and eager to separate out the tares immediately, as seen by James' and John's attitudes toward the unbelieving Samaritans (Luke 9:54). But that was and is not God's plan, lest some of the good plants (believers) get inadvertently uprooted with the tares.

During His incarnation Jesus did nothing to destroy His enemies. He even appealed to Judas right to the end that he believe (John 13:26). On the cross He asked forgiveness for those who orchestrated His execution (Luke 23:34). Therefore we also should be instruments of truth and grace toward unbelievers.

Ask YOURSELF

This is not the age of God's judgment—certainly not by the church—but rather the age for evangelism. What does this mean concerning the way we are called to perform ministry in this generation?

DECEMBER 15

THE MUSTARD SEED, PART 1

*The kingdom of heaven is like a mustard seed, which a man took and sowed in his field;
and this is smaller than all other seeds, but when it is full grown, it is larger than the garden
plants and becomes a tree, so that the birds of the air come and nest in its branches.*

MATT. 13:31–32

*E*VEN THOUGH THE LORD JESUS in this parable speaks accurately about the size of the mustard seed and the size and use of its tree-like adult form, His purpose in the illustration is proverbial, not scientific. In context of His teachings about the kingdom of God, the parable's meaning is self-evident—the kingdom, though now seemingly small and insignificant, will one day grow into a large body of believers.

Even with Jesus ministering on earth, God's kingdom was almost imperceptible, both because its citizens were few and it was spiritual (invisible). Elsewhere the Lord explained it well: "The kingdom of God is not coming with signs to be observed; nor will they say, 'Look, here it is!' or, 'There it is!' For behold, the kingdom of God is in your midst" (Luke 17:20–21). When Christ ascended to heaven, the kingdom on earth was, figuratively and relatively speaking, very small (cf. Acts 1:15).

But the kingdom that began smaller than a mustard seed will grow larger and larger. The Old Testament writers knew that eventually the Lord would "rule from sea to sea and from the River to the ends of the earth" (Ps. 72:8). They rightly foresaw that all sorts of people, from all stations in life, would honor Messiah, bow down to Him, and serve Him (vv. 9–11). With the apostle, we will one day see the grand culmination: "The kingdom of the world has become the kingdom of our Lord and of His Christ; and He will reign forever and ever" (Rev. 11:15).

Ask YOURSELF

Are you currently involved in something for Christ that seems small in comparison with others' ministries or talent bases? Be sure that your Lord is the master at taking the seemingly insignificant and transforming it for mighty kingdom purposes.

DECEMBER 16

THE MUSTARD SEED, PART 2

*The kingdom of heaven is like a mustard seed, which a man took and sowed in his field;
and this is smaller than all other seeds, but when it is full grown, it is larger than the garden
plants and becomes a tree, so that the birds of the air come and nest in its branches.*

MATT. 13:31–32

A FURTHER LESSON FROM this parable is that God's kingdom will grow to become a blessing to the rest of the world. The tree that develops from the mustard seed symbolizes the kingdom, which in this age is Christ's true church. The metaphor of birds nesting suggests the positive idea of providing protection and safety for others.

Daniel interpreted a vision with parallels to this parable: Nebuchadnezzar's dream in which "there was a tree in the midst of the earth and its height was great. The tree grew large and became strong and its height reached to the sky, and it was visible to the end of the whole earth. Its foliage was beautiful and its fruit abundant, and in it was food for all. The beasts of the field found shade under it, and the birds of the sky dwelt in its branches, and all living creatures fed themselves from it" (Dan. 4:10–12). As Daniel explained to the king (vv. 20–22), his empire (the tree) brought unrivaled advancement and prosperity to many areas of world endeavor: architecture, the arts, economics, and others. The birds and animals in the vision that benefited from the tree's provisions were other world nations (cf. Ezek. 31:3–6).

For Jesus and His followers the parallel between the vision and the parable is obvious—God's kingdom will grow from small beginnings into a huge tree and will provide shelter, protection, and blessing for the whole world. When believers are obedient to God and when nations seek to pattern their ways after His Word, they can bless everyone around.

Ask YOURSELF

How are you seeing this nesting, sheltering function of the kingdom at work in your church? What kind of excitement could ensue if individual Christians saw more clearly the potential blessing their efforts could produce? What are some of the possibilities?

PARABLE OF THE LEAVEN, PART 1

He spoke another parable to them, "The kingdom of heaven is like leaven,
which a woman took and hid in three pecks of flour until it was all leavened."
MATT. 13:33

*S*MALL THINGS OFTEN HAVE a great influence, which is the first point of Jesus' parable here. The influence is analogous to the effect a small piece of leavened dough, as it permeates and rises, can have on a larger lump of unleavened dough. Here the influence represents the power of God's kingdom, which is much greater than its initial, small appearances. The smallest part of the kingdom will influence the world because it contains the Holy Spirit's power working through believers.

Secondly, the parable suggests that kingdom influence is positive, just as leavening is for bread. To symbolize their break with Egypt, God commanded His people to eat only unleavened bread (Ex. 12:15, 18–19). But apart from the Feast of Unleavened Bread, they were free to eat and enjoy leavened bread. The Jews always perceived leaven favorably, as when a bride-to-be received a small piece of leavened dough just before her wedding. From that she would bake bread the rest of her married life and consider the small gift among the most cherished she ever received.

As to how leaven represents the large and positive influence of God's kingdom against Satan's, William Arnot wrote,

> The evil spreads like leaven; you tremble . . . but be of good cheer, disciples of Jesus, greater is He that is for you than all that are against you; the word of life which has been hidden in the world, hidden in believing hearts, is a leaven too. The unction of the Holy One is more subtle and penetrating and subduing than sin and Satan. Where sin abounded, grace shall much more abound.

Ask YOURSELF

What small addition or adjustment could you make to your lifestyle priorities as a Christian that would result in a big change of usefulness and effectiveness?

PARABLE OF THE LEAVEN, PART 2

He spoke another parable to them, "The kingdom of heaven is like leaven,
which a woman took and hid in three pecks of flour until it was all leavened."

MATT. 13:33

*I*N ORDER FOR IT TO HAVE THE positive influence we referred to yesterday, the leaven of God's kingdom must be hid. And that does not mean hiding to be invisible but hiding to penetrate deeply, completely permeating the world as leaven thoroughly permeates bread dough. Believers are not to be of the world, but they must be in the world to reach and change it with the gospel (cf. Mark 16:15; John 17:14–16, 18).

When we faithfully serve as the moral and spiritual leaven of the kingdom, our influence in the world will be both positive and pervasive. And for this to happen, we don't have to be powerful national leaders, wealthy entrepreneurs, or popular sports figures—just obedient servants of Jesus Christ.

Evangelism and other aspects of kingdom ministry often seem to have little immediate effect. As the church grows bigger, the world's population grows at a much faster rate, and the church remains a remnant by comparison. But the Lord continues to add to His kingdom by reaching millions through radio, television, publications, and the Internet—means that were largely unavailable or untapped just a century ago.

The leavening work of the kingdom may seem invisible or ineffective to you—"a day of small things"—but that does not mean the Lord is not at work. Jesus' purpose in this parable and the previous one on the mustard seed was to assure the apostles as well as believers of every era that the kingdom would not fail but ultimately prosper and triumph (cf. Matt. 16:18).

Ask YOURSELF

Is God calling you or your church to infiltrate a certain segment of culture or an area of your community with the transforming agent of gospel influence? As He leads, begin dreaming about how you might do that—and what He might do as a result.

PARABLE OF THE HIDDEN TREASURE

*The kingdom of heaven is like a treasure hidden in the field, which a man found
and hid again; and from joy over it he goes and sells all that he has and buys that field.*

MATT. 13:44

*P*ALESTINE WAS A BATTLEGROUND for centuries; therefore families would commonly bury clothing, food, household valuables, money, and jewelry to protect them from plundering enemy soldiers. Josephus, the Jewish historian, wrote, "The gold and the silver and the rest of that most precious furniture which the Jews had and which the owners treasured underground was done to withstand the fortunes of war." When the owners of such treasures died or departed the country, the valuables would be forever lost unless someone accidentally discovered them.

Given that history, this parable's hidden treasure was probably long forgotten until the man found it as he passed through the field. The man was so joyful at his find that he was willing to sacrifice everything in order to possess it, the metaphor for God's kingdom. That is the point of Jesus' parable, not the ethics of what the man did, as some Christians wrongly suppose. Such observers think the man was *unethical* not to have told the field's owner about the treasure, since it rightfully belonged to him.

But the man was not unethical. *First*, he obviously knew the owner was not aware of the treasure or he would have first offered it to him. *Second*, rabbinic law said finders could keep what they found. *Third*, had the man been dishonest, he would have gone off with the treasure without any thought of buying the field. But he realized that a field with treasure—the kingdom—was so valuable that he sold all else to obtain it. Nothing is more important for us than possessing that treasure also.

Ask YOURSELF

What treasures of the kingdom have you stumbled upon recently? When you see them, what are you motivated to forsake in order to more fully and consistently experience the power, joy, and freedom of living in pure fellowship with God?

DECEMBER 20

PARABLE OF THE PEARL OF GREAT VALUE

Again, the kingdom of heaven is like a merchant seeking fine pearls, and upon finding one pearl of great value, he went and sold all that he had and bought it.

• MATT. 13:45–46

*P*EARLS WERE THE MOST HIGHLY valued gems in the ancient world, often purchased as investments, much like diamonds or precious metals are today. With pearls, a person could keep and conceal a great amount of wealth in a small space. The Jewish Talmud said the pearl was beyond the value of any set price, and that some ancients actually worshiped it.

Elsewhere the New Testament uses the pearl as a representation of something of immense value and worthy of protection. When the Lord warns believers not to throw pearls before swine (Matt. 7:6), He underscores the priceless value of the gospel and its corresponding truths, which unbelievers despise as worthless. The apostle John envisions the New Jerusalem as a glorious city with twelve gates of pearl, and more precisely "each one of the gates was a single pearl" (Rev. 21:21).

In this parable the merchant obviously considered the valuable pearl so precious and worth more than all his other pearls combined, because he no doubt included them in the sale of all his possessions, which he did to buy the one pearl. Jesus again illustrates the immense value of the kingdom of heaven and clearly implies that the merchant's transaction was one involving his salvation. Purchasing the great pearl—the kingdom—represents obtaining God's saving knowledge through trust in His Son, the Lord Jesus, and experiencing all the blessings which that relationship brings. It is another example of the greatest transaction any of us can make.

Ask YOURSELF

It's really all about one thing, isn't it—giving our hearts to Christ without limitation or restriction. Consider today how the rest of your life is lining up under the one priority of walking boldly with Jesus.

GOD'S KINGDOM MUST BE PERSONALLY APPROPRIATED

The kingdom of heaven is like a treasure hidden in the field, which a man found and hid again.

MATT. 13:44A

*J*ESUS' CONCISE BUT PROFOUND parables of the hidden treasure and the pearl of great value show us that, above all, we must personally appropriate God's kingdom. People automatically at birth become members of their parents' family and country, but such natural inheritance doesn't apply regarding the kingdom.

Everyone is under God's dominion because they live on the earth, which is under His sovereign control. And if unbelievers associate with believers, they can potentially enjoy many kingdom benefits. But if an unbeliever attends a biblical church, enjoys sound preaching, and gets baptized, he or she is not necessarily a kingdom citizen. More often than not, such are "sons of the kingdom [who] will be cast out into the outer darkness" where "there will be weeping and gnashing of teeth" (Matt. 8:12)—in other words, they are not really children of God.

Paul reminds his readers, Jews in particular, "They are not all Israel who are descended from Israel; nor are they all children because they are Abraham's descendants" (Rom. 9:6–7). Even during the Old Testament era one could be Jewish—fully identified with God's people racially, nationally, and religiously—and still not be a member of the true spiritual Israel.

Similarly, you can be a member of a family that has had membership in a good church for many generations and yet not be part of Christ's true church. Being born into a godly family does not make you a believer. Under the Spirit's guidance, you must personally decide to trust Jesus as Lord and Savior.

Ask YOURSELF

Here toward the end of the year, settle this issue in your heart once and for all. You can live with the full assurance of your salvation by surrendering your life to Christ—repenting of your sins and believing in His sacrifice on your behalf. Don't live another day unsure.

DECEMBER 22

GOD'S KINGDOM IS PRICELESS

. . . finding one pearl of great value.

MATT. 13:46A

*J*OB'S ANCIENT DESCRIPTION of humanity's relentless quest for wealth sounds amazingly up-to-date:

> Man puts an end to darkness, and to the farthest limit he searches out the rock in gloom and deep shadow. He sinks a shaft far from habitation, forgotten by the foot; they hang and swing to and fro far from men . . . Its rocks are the source of sapphires, and its dust contains gold. . . . He hews out channels through the rocks, and his eye sees anything precious. (Job 28:3–4, 6, 10)

For all the efforts to mine and process precious metals and gems, none of those riches offers anything of lasting value (cf. Job 28:12–15, 21, 23, 28).

The blessing of being a kingdom citizen—a child of God through faith in Jesus Christ—is truly priceless and more valuable than all the world's greatest riches combined. That citizenship is so incomparable because it is "an inheritance which is imperishable and undefiled and will not fade away" (1 Peter 1:4). This heavenly inheritance includes the unsurpassed, divine spiritual blessings of forgiveness, love, peace, purity, righteousness, eternal life, and more.

Even with its priceless nature and ultimate value, God offers His kingdom to any person who surrenders all, repents, and trusts in Christ as Lord and Savior. Whatever values a man or woman has clung to in the past, God will happily exchange for the priceless kingdom treasure.

Ask YOURSELF

Are you in one of those phases of life in which Christianity feels like all cost and little return? Reflect today on the treasures of faith. Ask God to bring them to mind whenever you get discouraged or weary of the battle. They are worth much, much more than the price of admission.

GOD'S KINGDOM IS NOT SUPERFICIALLY VISIBLE

The kingdom of heaven is like a treasure hidden in the field.

MATT. 13:44A

*T*HE TREASURE OF SALVATION is not evident to unregenerate people, which is why they don't naturally seek it. They don't understand why believers prize God's saving kingdom so much and why they willingly give up so much—their self-sufficiency, sinful pleasures, and expensive worldly goods and social status—to gain what appears to be so insignificant and barely visible. Kingdom living is too narrow and unattractive to the unsaved, and that's why so few find this life or desire to walk it (Matt. 7:14)—in reality, most of the lost cannot even see God's truth and spiritual riches (1 Cor. 2:14; 2 Cor. 4:4).

When Christ answered the Pharisees' question about the kingdom, He said, "The kingdom of God is not coming with signs to be observed; nor will they say, 'Look, here it is!' or, 'There it is!'" (Luke 17:20–21). The kingdom of God will not be fully seen until our Lord returns and establishes His millennial rule over the world. At that time He "is going to come in the glory of His Father with His angels," and people will "see the Son of Man coming in His kingdom" (Matt. 16:27, 28b). However, right now that kingdom "is not of this realm" (John 18:36).

People can have passing respect for Christ and the gospel but can be completely oblivious to the invaluable blessing that could be theirs by belonging to His kingdom (cf. John 1:9–11). The pearl or treasure may be in sight, but worldly eyes will not see its worth.

Ask YOURSELF

Be in specific prayer today for that number of unbelievers who populate your extended family, your work environment, or your usual circle of contact. Will you recommit to remaining sensitive to opportunities in which God can use you to represent His treasure?

GOD'S KINGDOM IS THE SOURCE OF TRUE JOY

. . . and from joy over it he goes and sells all that he has and buys that field.

MATT. 13:44B

*E*VERY MAN OR WOMAN DESIRES basic joy in his or her life—a desire that all others directly or indirectly serve. We like to eat because tasty food brings joy and usually a feeling of good health to our bodies. We enjoy money because of the prospect of good and necessary things it can buy. Many of us also seek prestige, power, knowledge, and other advantages for the supposed joy they will bring.

But all such joys are fleeting and disappointing. The only genuine and lasting joy is that found in the kingdom of God, because God Himself created mankind and wants to provide them with complete satisfaction. After Christ exhorted the apostles to abide in Him and let His words abide in them, to verify their discipleship by bearing much fruit, and to obey His commandments and thus abide in His love (John 15:1–10), the Lord told them, "These things I have spoken to you so that My joy may be in you, and that your joy may be made full" (v. 11; cf. 16:24; 1 John 1:4).

The apostle Paul tells us that "the kingdom of God is . . . peace and joy in the Holy Spirit" (Rom. 14:17). Then he prays for the Romans, "Now may the God of hope fill you with all joy and peace in believing, so that you will abound in hope by the power of the Holy Spirit" (15:13). Authentic joy comes only when we find and accept Jesus Christ and His kingdom by faith in Him.

*Ask*YOURSELF

Have you noticed that the feeling you sense after watching a sporting event, attending a movie, coming home with a major purchase—or even enjoying Christmas—is never quite as robust as the anticipation was? How is it different from the experience of engaging in Christian worship and service?

DECEMBER 25

ENTERING THE KINGDOM
FROM DIFFERENT CIRCUMSTANCES

He goes and sells all that he has and buys that field . . . and upon finding
one pearl of great value, he went and sold all that he had and bought it.

MATT. 13:44B, 46

*T*HERE IS NO PRESET FORMULA for turning from sin and by faith embracing Christ's kingdom. A person does not have to perform certain rituals to become a Christian, and he or she can come from a variety of circumstances. In each parable referred to here, a man finds something of huge value and sacrifices all to possess it. But in the first parable the man was not even looking for anything, certainly not a valuable treasure. He came upon it quite by accident. In tending to his normal business, the man was working in a field or perhaps passing through on a trip. Finding the treasure was the furthest thing from his plans.

Similarly, people often encounter the gospel while pursuing their daily activities. As they are busily occupied with their job, family, or schooling, they hear a sermon, read a book, listen to a CD, or have a believer witness to them. Through the Spirit's gracious power they realize the gospel's infinite value and are drawn into God's kingdom.

In contrast, the second parable portrays a man whose career was searching for a valuable commodity, which he eventually found. He's the seeker who looks many places for life's meaning. When not finding that which satisfies, he nevertheless perseveres, believing the truth can be found. He is like the Ethiopian whom Philip directed to Christ (Acts 8:26–39), or the God-fearing Cornelius who found salvation (Acts 10).

Whether "by accident" or deliberately, all who are in the right place can and do find God's priceless kingdom.

Ask YOURSELF

On this Christmas Day, celebrate the gift of salvation that has brought ultimate worth and value—and energy and excitement—into your life experience. Thank Him enthusiastically for seeking you with purpose and precision, even while you weren't particularly looking for Him.

A Transaction Makes the Kingdom Personal

And from joy over it he goes and sells all that he has and buys that field.

MATT. 13:44B

*S*OME BELIEVERS FEEL UNCOMFORTABLE about the parables we have been considering, thinking they teach salvation can be bought. But Scripture always teaches that salvation is completely free. Salvation is "bought" only in the sense that one trusts Jesus as Lord and Savior and surrenders all to Him. The treasure and the pearl illustrate the spiritual transaction of surrender. In salvation, we exchange the old for the new.

Isaiah 55:1 describes salvation as God's gift, yet refers to buying: "Every one who thirsts, come to the waters; and you who have no money come, buy and eat. Come, buy wine and milk without money and without cost." As in the two parables, the sinner gives up all the worthless things he or she has while receiving all the invaluable kingdom wealth. Therefore this does *not* depict a buying of salvation, because with God that is totally unacceptable (cf. Isa. 64:6).

Without surrendering everything, people's professions of faith are meaningless (cf. Matt. 19:16–22). Jesus declared, "He who has found his life will lose it, and he who has lost his life for My sake will find it" (Matt. 10:39). Our Lord also said, "If anyone wishes to come after Me, he must deny himself, and take up his cross and follow Me" (Matt. 16:24).

When confronted with the true gospel, most people don't inventory all their possessions to see if Jesus is worth following (cf. Luke 14:28–33). When they see the infinite value of His kingdom riches, they simply yield to Him, surrender all, and faithfully follow.

Ask YOURSELF

Are you holding anything back from God in your service to Him, hoping He won't ask to touch or remove it? If the Spirit has made you aware of a habit, activity, or possession that restricts the free flow of your worship, seek your security blanket in Him alone. He will be more than enough—a blessed replacement.

PRINCIPLES OF THE DRAGNET, PART 1

Again, the kingdom of heaven is like a dragnet cast into the sea, and gathering fish of every kind;
and when it was filled, they drew it up on the beach; and they sat down and gathered the good
fish into containers, but the bad they threw away. So it will be at the end of the age;
the angels will come forth and take out the wicked from among the righteous.

MATT. 13:47–49

$\mathcal{D}$URING THE PRESENT CHURCH era, God allows unbelief and unright-eousness to exist in His kingdom. Therefore believers and unbelievers coexist, as Jesus already illustrated in His parable of the wheat and tares. This parable of the dragnet, however, depicts the separation of believers and unbelievers as the kingdom's form changes at the end of the age. The dragnet of the Father's judgment quietly moves through the sea of humanity drawing all people to the shores of eternity for separation to their final destinies—believers to heaven and unbelievers to hell.

The invisible net of God's judgment affects every person just as the dragnet impinges on every sea creature. Most people don't perceive God's sovereign plan or His eternal kingdom. They don't realize He is working in this world. At times they can be moved by hearing of the gospel's grace, or scared by the threat of judgment. But usually they quickly return to their worldly lifestyles and disregard matters of eternity.

However, we can be certain that when this era ends and the Lord Jesus returns to establish His glorious kingdom, final judgment will be at hand. Here Christ does not fully describe the end times, but He focuses on judgment of unbelievers. He pictures a general judgment with particular reference to the final, great white throne judgment (Rev. 20:11–15). There "the dead, the great and the small" will be "judged, every one of them" (vv. 12, 13). But thank the Lord we do not have to fear that fate if we are trusting Him for salvation.

$\mathcal{A}sk$ YOURSELF

How does your heart react when you contemplate the vastness and grandeur of God's plan—His knowledge and oversight throughout history and forward into eternity?

PRINCIPLES OF THE DRAGNET, PART 2

*So it will be at the end of the age; the angels will come forth
and take out the wicked from among the righteous.*

MATT. 13:49

ONE WAY THAT GOD'S ANGELS SERVE Him in the judgment is as instruments of separation and execution of final sentence (cf. Matt. 24:31; 25:31–32; Rev. 14:19; 15:5–16:21). This separation will be from among all the living and the dead of humanity from all time—"those who did the good deeds to a resurrection of life, those who committed the evil deeds to a resurrection of judgment" (John 5:29).

During His earthly ministry, Jesus repeatedly warned about the horrors of hell (Matt. 10:28; 25:41; Luke 16:23) and pled with people to avoid such a terrible fate by fleeing to Him for salvation. Even though life will seem normal, our Lord predicts that one day the righteous and unrighteous will part ways:

> For the coming of the Son of Man will be just like the days of Noah. For as in those days before the flood they were eating and drinking, marrying and giving in marriage, until the day that Noah entered the ark, and they did not understand until the flood came and took them all away; so will the coming of the Son of Man be. Then there will be two men in the field; one will be taken and one will be left. Two women will be grinding at the mill; one will be taken and one will be left. (Matt. 24:37–41)

God does not want any sinner to perish (Ezek. 18:23; 2 Peter 3:9). Jesus wept over Jerusalem because its people would not turn to Him (Luke 19:41)—He does not desire anyone to experience hell.

*Ask*YOURSELF

One way you see the distinction between the world and the church is how quickly the serene atmosphere of Christmas devolves into the bawdy recklessness of New Year's Eve plans. Why are so many people content to treat Christianity like a part-time occupation?

PERILS OF THE DRAGNET, PART 1

... and will throw them into the furnace of fire; in that
place there will be weeping and gnashing of teeth.

MATT. 13:50

*T*HE DOCTRINE OF HELL IS undoubtedly the most difficult one for Christians to accept emotionally. Yet Scripture mentions it too often for us to deny or ignore it. Jesus gives several warnings of it in the Sermon on the Mount. "It is better for you to lose one of the parts of your body, than for your whole body to be thrown into hell" (Matt. 5:29; cf. 5:22; see also Matt. 11:23; 23:33; Mark 3:29; Luke 12:9–10; John 15:6).

God's Word teaches us some basic truths about hell—what this parable calls "the furnace of fire"—that aid us in partially grasping its terror. *First,* it is a place of constant torment and pain. Jesus called its torment darkness (Matt. 22:13), which means no light penetrates and nothing is visible. Our Lord also called the torment a fire that never goes out (Mark 9:43), from which the damned find no relief.

Second, hell includes the torment of both body and soul. Contrary to some teachings, neither is annihilated at death and never will be. Just as believers' souls will receive resurrected bodies to enjoy heaven forever, unbelievers' souls will receive resurrected bodies to experience hell forever (cf. Matt. 10:28; John 5:29; Acts 24:15). Jesus further called hell a place "where their worm does not die" (Mark 9:44). Once the bodies of deceased believers are consumed by worms, no more harm can be done to them. But the resurrected bodies of unbelievers will never be consumed. Such sobering reminders ought to prompt us to pray for the lost with greater urgency.

Ask YOURSELF

We do try to avoid thinking of things so gruesome and unending. Even though we don't treat it as a myth or analogy, we still bristle at the thought of it. But how does a proper understanding of the truth of hell benefit you in your own worship and in your interactions with others?

PERILS OF THE DRAGNET, PART 2

... and will throw them into the furnace of fire; in that
place there will be weeping and gnashing of teeth.

MATT. 13:50

*C*ONTINUING FROM YESTERDAY, we can learn several more biblical truths
about hell, the dragnet's ultimate peril. For example, the lost will suffer hell's tor-
ments in varying degrees. Those who willfully reject Jesus Christ and blatantly scorn
His sacrifice will receive far greater punishment than people who had only the light
of the Old Testament. The author of Hebrews writes, "Anyone who has set aside the
Law of Moses dies without mercy on the testimony of two or three witnesses. How
much severer punishment do you think he will deserve who has trampled under
foot the Son of God, and has regarded as unclean the blood of the covenant by which
he was sanctified, and has insulted the Spirit of grace?" (Heb. 10:28–29; cf. Matt.
11:22–23).

Concerning the slaves who waited for their master's return, Christ's parable
states that "that slave who knew his master's will and did not get ready or act in accord with his will, will receive many lashes, but the one who did not know it, and
committed deeds worthy of a flogging, will receive but few" (Luke 12:47–48).

Finally, nothing will be as horrible about hell's torment as its endlessness. The
Lord uses "eternal" to describe both heaven's and hell's duration: "These will go away
into eternal punishment, but the righteous into eternal life" (Matt. 25:46). Sadly, people who experience hell will realize a complete absence of hope for all eternity. But
rejoice if you are a believer—you have a hope of heaven that will be validated for all
eternity.

*Ask*YOURSELF

The sensitive person asks, "How can a loving God doom a person to hell?" What
is your answer to this common question and complaint? How is justice involved?
Why would some be spared? Know how to respond to this type of opinion ahead of
time.

THE PARABLE OF THE HOUSEHOLDER

"Have you understood all these things?" They said to Him, "Yes." And Jesus said to them,
"Therefore every scribe who has become a disciple of the kingdom of heaven is like
a head of a household, who brings out of his treasure things new and old."
MATT. 13:51–52

*J*ESUS' TWELVE DISCIPLES would eventually become His twelve apostles (Matthias replacing Judas, Acts 1:23). Through these men, and later Paul, our Lord entrusted the continued revelation of His Word and the extension of His church. Like "head[s] of a household," which was analogous to being disciples in Christ's kingdom, they drew from the old treasures of previous revelation and received additional, new truths. And these faithful men would proclaim both.

"Brings out" conveys the concept of scattering or distributing widely. Here it also connotes generosity—giving out God's truth of the gospel wisely and liberally. Second only to their Lord, the apostles would be supreme scholars of Scripture, preachers, and teachers—scribes and disciples without equal (cf. Matt. 11:11) and superb evangelists.

With a slightly lesser degree of authority, the Lord's charge to His apostles applies to every Christian (Matt. 28:16–20), and especially to those pastors, teachers, and missionaries He has called to spread His Word. It is a tremendous responsibility to warn the lost about hell and to offer them salvation through the blood of Jesus Christ. Paul stated it this way, "Knowing the fear [terror] of the Lord, we persuade men" (2 Cor. 5:11). The believer's heart is cold indeed that is not profoundly concerned about those all around who are without Christ and headed for hell. Pray that you would genuinely warm to the task of reaching the lost in your community and beyond with saving gospel treasure.

Ask YOURSELF

The end of a year and the dawn of a new is always a time of reflection and renewed hope. What have you gleaned from walking with Jesus through these past months and seasons? What are your priorities for the coming year? May the Lord bless you as you follow Him there.

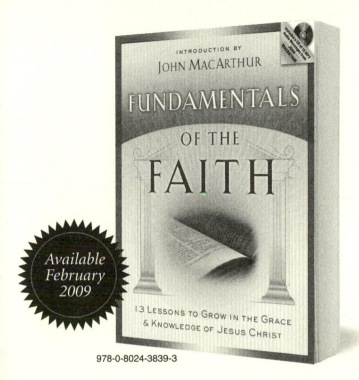

978-0-8024-7845-0

It is absolutely essential that a church perceive itself as an institution for the glory of God, and to do that, claims John MacArthur, the local church must adhere unfalteringly to biblical leadership principles. Christ never intended church leadership to be earned by seniority, purchased with money, or inherited through family ties. He never compared church leaders to governing monarchs, but rather to humble shepherds; not to slick celebrities, but to laboring servants. Drawing from some of the best-received material on church leadership, this updated edition guides the church with crucial, effective lessons in leadership. This book is valuable not only for pastors and elders, but for anyone else who wants the church to be what God intended it to be.